MODERN RELIGIOUS
VERSE AND PROSE

MODERN RELIGIOUS VERSE AND PROSE

AN ANTHOLOGY

BY

FRED MERRIFIELD

ASSISTANT PROFESSOR OF NEW TESTAMENT HISTORY AND
INTERPRETATION IN THE UNIVERSITY OF CHICAGO

NEW YORK
CHARLES SCRIBNER'S SONS
1925

ACKNOWLEDGMENTS

Acknowledgment is gratefully made to the following authors and publishers for permission to use selections from their publications: To George Allen & Unwin, for selection from "Towards Democracy," by Edward Carpenter. For "The Debt," and "America the Beautiful," by Katharine Lee Bates, published by T. Y. Crowell & Company. To The Pacific Short Story Club for "Multiple Stars," "Sierran Pan," "A Song of Joy," "The Watchers," and "Divine Rhythm," from *Sierran Pan and Other Poems*, by Henry Meade Bland. For "Hearken to the Hammers," by Laurence Binyon. To The Bobbs-Merrill Company, for "Central Calm," "The Legend Glorified," and "Faith," by James Whitcomb Riley. To Boni & Liveright, Inc., for "I Track Upstream the Spirit's Call," by Horace Traubel. For "There Is No Age," by Eva Gore Booth, published by Longmans, Green & Company, London. For "Life," by Clondesley Brereton, published by the Quarterly Review, London. For "Each in His Own Tongue," by William Herbert Carruth, published by G. P. Putnam's Sons. To The Century Company, for "The Great Hunger," by Johan Bojer; for "Caliban in the Coal Mines," and "Daybreak," by Louis Untermeyer. To Chatto & Windus, London, for "Ode" and "Song of Palms," by Arthur O'Shaughnessy. For "The Great Minimum," by Gilbert Keith Chesterton, published by Dodd, Mead & Company, and for "A Word," by Gilbert Keith Chesterton, published by John Lane Company. For "Rejected," "Thanksgiving," "Song," "Song," "Death," "The Ideal," and "A Narrow Window," by Florence Earle Coates, published by Houghton Mifflin Company. For "After Sunset," by Grace Hazard Conkling, published by Henry Holt & Company. For "The Hounds of God," by Frank Crane. To T. Y. Crowell & Company, for "Blind," by John Kendrick Bangs; for "Under the Leaves," from *The Cambridge Book of Poetry*, by Albert Laighton; for "Abide With Me," by Henry Francis Lyte. For "Sympathy," "Praise," "The Little Words," and "Immortality," by Edith Daley. For "Higher Towers," by Mary Carolyn Davies. For "Human Nature and Conduct," by John Dewey, published by Henry Holt & Company. To Dodd, Mead & Company, for "The Spell of the Yukon" and "Rhymes of a Rolling Stone," by Robert W. Service; for "What is Nature's Self?" by William Watson. For "A Religion for the New Day," by Charles F. Dole. For "The Vision of Peace," from *The Building of the Organ*, by Nathan Haskell Dole. To George H. Doran Company, for "The Voice of the Unborn" and "What Can Be Worth This Cost of Gold and Tears?" by Amelia Josephine Burr; for "God Is at the Organ" and "Thanksgiving," by Joyce Kilmer; for "O Love That Wilt Not Let Me Go," by George Matheson. To Double-day, Page & Company, for "The Master's Touch," by Horatius Bonar; for "The Mystic Trumpeter," "Song of the Universal," "Passage to India," "Joy, Shipmate, Joy!" "Starting from Paumanok," "Grand is the Seen," "Unseen Buds," "Death's Valley," "Night on the Prairies," "Farther Sail," and "Memories of President Lincoln: When Lilacs Last in the Dooryard Bloom'd," by Walt Whitman. For "The New Miracle," "The Fires of God," "Travel Talk: Ladywood, 1912," "Last Confessional," "Epilogue for a Masque," and "A Prayer," by John Drinkwater, published by Houghton Mifflin Company. To E. P. Dutton & Company, for "The Common Street," by Helen Gray Cone; for "A New Song," by Richard Rolle. For "Caliban and I," "Faith," "If Winter Comes," and "Resurgence," by Laura Bell Everett; and for "The Sabbath of the Soul," by Laura Bell Everett, published by Houghton, Mifflin Company. For "The Ballad of the Cross," by Theodosia Garrison Faulks, published by Harper & Brothers. To Forbes & Company, for "As I Go On My Way," by Strickland Gillilan. For "The House by the Side of the Road," "The Creedless Love," "The Higher Catechism," and "The Turn of the Road: A New Year's Song," by Sam Walter Foss, published by Lothrop, Lee & Shepard Company. For "The Last Enigma," by Henry Frank, published by Erskine MacDonald, Ltd., London. For "Wanting So the Face Divine," "The Hungry," and "Overnight, a Rose," by Caroline Giltinan. For "The March of Men," by Charles Buxton Going, published by Harper & Brothers. For "Ultimate Conceptions of Faith," by George A. Gordon, published by Houghton Mifflin Company. For "Christmas, 1919," "The Path to Home," and "Visions," by Edgar A. Guest. For "The Greater Birth" and "Broadway," from *Poems and Ballads*, by Hermann Hagedorn. To Harcourt, Brace & Company, for "Summons" and "Prayer," by Louis Untermeyer. To Harper & Brothers, for "Vestigia," by Bliss Carman; for "The Superman," by Albert Bigelow Paine. To Harr Wagner & Company, for "The Greatest Battle That Ever Was Fought," by Joaquin Miller. For "The Meaning of God in Human Experience," by William Ernest Hocking, published by the Yale University Press. For "Song of Honor," by Ralph Hodgson, published by The Macmillan Company. To Houghton Mifflin Company, for "The Heritage," by Abbie Farwell Brown; for "Accepting the Universe," by John Burroughs; for "O Love, that Dost with Goodness Crown," by John W. Chadwick; for "There Is a Soul Above the Soul," by R. W. Dixon; for "Christ of Judea" and "If the Christ You Mean," by Richard Watson Gilder; for "O Master, Let Me Walk with Thee" and "Ultima Veritas," by Washington

Gladden; for "The Wild Ride," by Louise Imogen Guiney; for "The Nameless Saints," by Edward Everett Hale; for "Hymn of Trust" and "The Lord is My Light," by Oliver Wendell Holmes; for "Doubt," by William D. Howells; for "God of the Earth, the Sky, the Sea," and "Thought for the Day," by Samuel Longfellow; for "The Thing We Long For," "The Vision of Sir Launfal," "God Is Not Dumb," "A Parable," "Sub Pondere Crescit," "To M. O. S.," and "The Present Crisis," by James Russell Lowell; for "Road-Hymn for the Start," and "The Fire-Bringer," by William Vaughn Moody; for "Kinship," "God Prays," and "Work: A Song of Triumph," by Angela Morgan; for "The Butterfly" and "On a Gloomy Easter," by Alice Freeman Palmer; for "Confession," by Frank Dempster Sherman; for "Exaltation," by Paul Shivell; for "A Prayer," "The First Cause," and "The Invisible," by Edward Rowland Sill; for "The Riddle of the World," "Within Our Lives," "The Brother of Mercy," "The Eternal Goodness," "Wherever Through the Ages," "Sometimes Comes to Soul and Sense," "Our Master," "Laborers Together With God," "Harvest Thanksgiving," "Brotherhood," "Dear Lord and Father of Mankind," "Forgive," and "Requirement," by John G. Whittier. To The Incorporated Society of Authors, Playwrights, and Composers, London, for "The Central I" and "The Unexplored, Unconquered," by John Masefield. To the University of Chicago Press, for "Summer: In June," "The Singer of the Stillness," "Night and Day," and "Follow the Gleam," by Bertha Ten Eyck James. For "Altruism," by David Starr Jordan. For "The Servant in the House," by Charles Rann Kennedy, published by Harper & Brothers. To Mitchell Kennerley, for "Where is Heaven?" by Bliss Carman, and for "The Dreamer," by Shaemus O'Sheel. To The J. Knight Company, for "Another Year," by John W. Chadwick. For "The Eternal Spirit," "L'Envoi," "Golgotha," and "To Jesus the Nazarene," by Frederic L. Knowles. To John Lane Company, for "The Dead," "O Thou, God of All," and "Second Best," by Rupert Brooke. For "Gaudeamus," by Richard Le Gallienne, published by Harper & Brothers. To Lindsay & Blakiston, for "Come Unto Me," by Catherine H. Watterman Esling. To Little, Brown & Company, for "If Winter Comes," by Arthur Stuart Mentell Hutchinson; for "The Immigrant," by Edward Everett Hale; and for "Is This the End?" by John White Chadwick. To Longmans, Green & Company, London, for "The Everlasting God," by Edward Henry Bickersteth. To Lothrop, Lee & Shepard Company, for "At First I Prayed for Light," by Mrs. E. D. Cheney; and for "The Wordless Voice," by Sam Walter Foss. For "The Lamp of Life," by Amy Lowell; and for "Autumn and Death," by Amy Lowell, published by Houghton Mifflin & Company. For "The Unknown Dead," by Percy

MacKaye. To The Macmillan Company, for "Penetralia," by Madison Cawein; for "The Everlasting Mercy," by John Masefield; and for "Gitanjali," by Rabindranath Tagore. For "A Comrade Rides Ahead: To the Memory of Emerson Hough," and "'Tis But the Night," by Douglas Malloch. For "Wind and Lyre," "Love's Vigil," "The Climb of Life," and "World-Purpose," by Edwin Markham, published by Doubleday, Page & Company. For "The God-Maker, Man," and "Unrest," by Don Marquis, published by Harper & Brothers. To A. C. Mc-Clurg & Company, for "Thou Must be True," by Horatius Bonar; for "The Heart of the Eternal," from *Golden Gleams of Thought*, by Frederick W. Faber; for "All Souls Are Thine" and "Easter Gladness," by F. L. Hosmer; for "A Deed and a Word," by Charles MacKay; and for "My Creed," by David Swing. For "In My Flesh Shall I See God," "Closing the Doors," and "The Road-Song of the Race," by Irene Pettit McKeehan. For "The Immortality in Our Hands," by Gerald Mygatt. For "Night," "We Dead! Awake!" and "We Unborn," by James Oppenheim. For "Beauty's Birth," "It Is Enough," "The Better Fate," "And Yet I Know," "Disillusionment," and "So Were We Born to Dread," by Robert Hugh Orr. For "Chaos—and the Way Out," by John Oxenham, published by George H. Doran Company. To L. C. Page & Company, for "Lord of My Heart's Elation," from *The Green Book of the Bards*, by Bliss Carman; and for "Oh! The Earth and the Air!" by James T. McKay. To The Penn Publishing Company, for "An Eastern Legend," by Wallace Bruce. For "Present Philosophical Tendencies," by Ralph Barton Perry, published by Longmans, Green & Company, London. To The Pilgrim Press, for "Martyrs of Humanity," "The Innocent Ones Who Come After," "Thy Higher Contentment," "Fellowship With All," "The Eternal Passion," "A Cooperative Commonwealth," and "A Paraphrase of I Corinthians, XIII," by Walter Rauschenbusch; and for "We Forget the Goal," by Alice Hegan Rice. For "I Accept" and "The Harvest of Time," by Harold Trowbridge Pulsifer; and for "In the Mantle of God," by Harold Trowbridge Pulsifer, published by Houghton Mifflin Company. To G. P. Putnam's Sons, for "The Saint," by Fogazzaro. For "An Invocation—Christmas, 1923," "Stretch Out Your Hand," "The Forgotten Countersign," "After," "The Call of Brotherhood," "Pain the Interpreter," "Life, A Question?" and "Grief," by Corinne Roosevelt Robinson, published by Charles Scribner's Sons. For "The Altar," "The Children of the Night," "Sonnet," "Two Sonnets," "L'Envoi," "Octaves," and "Credo," by Edwin Arlington Robinson, published by Charles Scribner's Sons. To Mitchell Kennerley, for "Psalm," by Jessie E. Sampter. To Maxwell S. Savage, for "Earth's Common Things," by Rev. Minot Judson Savage. To Charles Scribner's Sons, for "Creation," by Mary

Raymond Shipman Andrews; for "Be Strong," by Maltbie D. Babcock; for "Empty," by Berton Braley; for "Codicil," by H. G. Dwight; for "The Marshes of Glynn" and "A Ballad of Trees and the Master," by Sidney Lanier; for "A New Birth of Freedom," by Abraham Lincoln; for "I Have a Rendezvous with Death" and "Makatoob," by Alan Seeger. For "Jesus the Carpenter," by Charles M. Sheldon, published by George H. Doran Company. To Small, Maynard & Company, for "Unmanifest Destiny" and "At the End of the Day," by Richard Hovey. For "Invocation," by Wendell Phillips Stafford. To Frederick A. Stokes Company, for "The Trumpet of the Law," "The Paradox," and "The Loom of Years," by Alfred Noyes. For "Thou Art the Sky" and "Sādhāna," by Rabindranath Tagore, published by The Macmillan Company. For "The Lamp," "Leaves," "Songs Out of Sorrow," "Longing," and "Immortal," by Sara Teasdale, published by The Macmillan Company. For "The System of Animate Nature," by J. Arthur Thomson, published by Henry Holt & Company. For "God With Us," by Nancy Byrd Turner. For "Immanence," by Evelyn Underhill, published by E. P. Dutton & Company. For "How Much of Godhead," and "Challenge," by Louis Untermeyer, published by The Century Company. For "The Blessing of Work," "This is the Gospel of Labour," "They Who Tread the Path of Labour," "Work," "My Own," "These Are the Gifts I Ask," "Beyond Our Power of Vision," and "The Other Wise Man," by Henry van Dyke, published by Charles Scribner's Sons. For "The Ultimate Harvest," by Mrs. Schuyler Van Rensselaer, published by Harper & Brothers. For "Rhapsody of the Waves," "A. M. D. G.: The Christian Hero," "Cynthia," and "Who Can Tell?" by John G. Walshe, S. J. For "Purpose," "Borne of Four," "A Song of Faith," and "Above the Heavens," by Amos R. Wells. For "The Outline of History" and "The Undying Fire," by H. G. Wells, published by The Macmillan Company. For "With the Tide," by Edith Wharton. For "Earth," "Be Born Again," "Sea-Horizons," "Thy Kingdom Come," "The Human Phantasy," "Exile from God," "Song of the Moth," "Zenith," "The Far Land," and "Midnight," by John Hall Wheelock, published by Charles Scribner's Sons. To J. T. White & Company, for "Utopia" and "God's Dreams," by Thomas Curtis Clark. For "To the Factories," by Margaret Widdemer, published by Henry Holt & Company. For "Fugitives," by Florence Wilkinson, published by Doubleday, Page & Company. To John C. Winston Company, for "Peace on Earth," by Edmund H. Sears. To The Woodberry Society, for "The Flight," by George Edward Woodberry. To Yale University Press, for "What Have I Laid Upon the Altar?" by T. R. Lounsbury.

FOREWORD

HUMANITY has been slow to express, and still more tardy to preserve, its deepest thoughts and experiences in all the ages past. Only as it has come to realize the significance of its long and tortuous journey down the trail of the years, only as it has risen to the inspiring faith that Time has just begun to unfold the wonderful possibilities of the human race, has it perceived the educational value of its greatest literary treasures.

To-day, with a perspective born of fateful dreams and tragic losses, we are beginning to garner in every virile and ennobling thought—from whatever race or time it may come —which shall furnish the successive generations of youth with an immortal power that shall guarantee even the frailest of them against the ravages of a none too kindly fate.

This book of verse and prose, gathered through many years and from many lands, is an offering laid upon the altar of our dreams. Running through its pages one may feel the heart-throbs of millions of desperate, longing souls seeking light. Here are voiced millions of happy hopes as youth breaks forth into its soul's awakening; or as clear-eyed age pierces the veils of the once dread future and dares to build even there its future home as a challenge to death and oblivion. This is our better selves thinking God's timeless thoughts after Him. The language is varied, but the heart is one. Many are the experiences here unfolded, but all are the outreach of the restless Soul of the Race as it utters eternal yearnings, and rises to undimmed visions of its vaster destiny.

Because this is sacred ground, because it deals with our most cherished experiences, because it represents the highest and purest within the human breast, we call it all by that age-old term Religion; sincere, deep-down, open-eyed, and universal religion.

It is refreshing to discover that the inspired voices of the sacred past are continued and supplemented in the best literature of our own time. Indeed, a careful survey of modern poetry, drama, essay, story, and other high forms of literature should easily convince the unprejudiced reader that never in all human history have there been so many pens at work in the interest of man's highest moral achievements. And it is equally true that never before has the religion of the deepest inner life of the race found such rich and varied expression. The fine tolerance and the scientific understanding of our day also help us to enter with new and very real sympathy into appreciation of all this inspiring thought, thus helping to unify the race experience and hasten the longed-for day of universal peace and friendliness. To this great end these earnest experiences have been gathered.

FRED MERRIFIELD.

CONTENTS

CONTENTS

VI

VII

VIII

IX

I

THE IRREPRESSIBLE YEARNING AFTER GOD

I

O THOU, GOD OF ALL

O Thou,
God of all long desirous roaming,
Our hearts are sick of fruitless homing,
And crying after lost desire.
Hearten us onward! as with fire
Consuming dreams of other bliss.
The best Thou givest, giving this
Sufficient thing—to travel still
Over the plain, beyond the hill,
Unhesitating through the shade,
Amid the silence unafraid,
Till, at some sudden turn, one sees
Against the black and muttering trees
Thine altar, wonderfully white,
Among the Forests of the Night.

RUPERT BROOKE

WIND AND LYRE

Thou art the wind and I the lyre:
    Strike, O Wind, on the sleeping strings—
    Strike till the dead heart stirs and sings!
I am the altar and thou the fire:
    Burn, O Fire, to a snowy flame—
    Burn me clean of the mortal blame!

I am the night and thou the dream:
    Touch me softly and thrill me deep,
    When all is white on the hills of sleep.

3

Thou art the moon and I the stream:
Shine to the trembling heart of me,
Light my soul to the mother-sea.

EDWIN MARKHAM

O LOVE THAT WILT NOT LET ME GO

O Love that wilt not let me go,
I rest my weary soul in Thee;
I give Thee back the life I owe,
That in Thine ocean depths its flow
May richer, fuller be.

O Light that followest all my way,
I yield my flickering torch to Thee;
My heart restores its borrowed ray
That in Thy sunshine's blaze its day
May brighter, fairer be.

O Joy that seekest me through pain,
I cannot close my heart to Thee;
I trace the rainbow through the rain,
And feel the promise is not vain
That morn shall tearless be.

O Cross that liftest up my head,
I dare not ask to fly from Thee;
I lay in dust life's glory dead
And from the ground there blossoms red
Life that shall endless be.

GEORGE MATHESON

WANTING SO THE FACE DIVINE

Wanting so the Face divine,
I searched within this soul of mine,

But there the Image is so dim:
Unlike, unlike, it seems to Him.

Weary of heart, with faith grown weak,
Again, the vanished Face I seek.
Lo! In my need, God sends me thee:
And from thy soul, He smiles on me!

CAROLINE GILTINAN

THE HUNGRY

WHOM does He love the most—
    The poor, the sick, the blind,
The rich, the maimed, the host
    Unknowingly unkind?

The ones who strive, and fail;
    The ones who have, and lose;
The ones who will not quail
    Nor martyrdom refuse?

The wind went sobbing low
    To His great Heart and cried;
"Dear God, they need you so,—
    Who die unsatisfied."

CAROLINE GILTINAN

PAULINE

.   .   .   .

A MIND like this must dissipate itself,
But I have always had one lode-star; now,
As I look back, I see that I have halted
Or hastened as I looked towards that star—
A need, a trust, a yearning after God:

A feeling I have analyzed but late,
But it existed, and was reconciled
With a neglect of all I deemed his laws,
Which yet, when seen in others, I abhorred.
I felt as one beloved, and so shut in
From fear: and thence I date my trust in signs
And omens, for I saw God everywhere;
And I can only lay it to the fruit
Of a sad after-time that I could doubt
Even his being—e'en the while I felt
His presence, never acted from myself,
Still trusted in a hand to lead me through
All danger;

.   .   .   .

O God, where do they tend—these struggling aims?
What would I have? What is this "sleep" which seems
To bound all? can there be a "waking" point
Of crowning life? The soul would never rule;
It would be first in all things, it would have
Its utmost pleasure filled, but, that complete,
Commanding, for commanding, sickens it.
The last point I can trace is—rest beneath
Some better essence than itself, in weakness;
This is "myself," not what I think should be:
And what is that I hunger for but God?

My God, my God, let me for once look on thee
As though naught else existed, we alone!
And as creation crumbles, my soul's spark
Expands till I can say,—Even from myself
I need thee and I feel thee and I love thee.

ROBERT BROWNING

NOTE I

THIS first group of six brief poems points to the universal fact that human nature reaches out instinctively, persistently, passionately, for self-fulfilment. The resulting growth, the expanding experience, which accompany this attitude of moral earnestness are commonly attributed to the influence of God, the unseen but most real Power which impels one to seek the noblest and be satisfied with nothing but the best. All of these writers seem to feel that the divine response to human need is as certain as the longing of man is intense.

1. *Rupert Brooke* ("O Thou, God of All"), expresses the common race-experience that desperate homesickness for inner satisfaction tends to spur one to such courageous and patient search for God that the latter is inevitably discovered, oftentimes in most unexpected ways and places. The hunger and lonesomeness of the World War battlefields are here given voice, and tribute is paid to the Power that nerves the soul for its heroic tasks.

2. *Edwin Markham* ("Wind and Lyre"), beloved Californian and poet of the common people, seems to see the whole human life reaching upward, conscious of its incompleteness but unquestioning in its faith that God can and will transform its silent yearnings into the loftiest spiritual realities: joyful consciousness of a divine Presence, purest worship, a sense of new power, light all the way through life.

3. *George Matheson* ("O Love That Wilt Not Let Me Go"), blind poet and minister at large to human need, finds in God a power which more than compensates for the bitter, soul-racking loss which has stunned all his senses. The very intensity of his suffering, the very shame of his defeat, enable him to rise to heights of faith seldom attained in human experience.

4. In "Wanting So the Face Divine" and "The Hungry" is reflected the sad experience with lives whose dreams have

7

never come true. Sometimes God is found in friendships; many times longings remain unsatisfied—but surely are understood by the universal Heart.

5. *Robert Browning*, in his early study of soul-struggles ("Pauline"), finds that all the doubts and uncertainties which tend to puzzle the intellect are dissipated by a steady faith that the very yearning for oneness with God, and the growing consciousness that God is to be seen everywhere in experience, are, after all, the most real and fruitful portions of his life. Human need, struggle and longing, satisfaction, and grateful love—these are the psychological steps which man ascends to find his moral destiny.

II

WHAT CAN IT MEAN?

WHAT can it mean? is it aught to Him
That the nights are long and the days are dim?
Can He be touched by the griefs I bear—
Which sadden the heart and whiten the hair?
Around His throne are eternal calms,
And strong glad music of happy psalms,
And bliss unruffled by any strife;
How can He care for my poor life?

And yet I want Him to care for me,
While I live in this world where the sorrows be,
When the light dies down on the path I take,
When strength is feeble and friends forsake;
When love and music that once did bless
Have left me to silence and loneliness;
And life's song changes to sobbing prayers—
Then my heart cries out for a God who cares.

When shadows hang o'er me the whole day long;
And my spirit is bowed with shame and wrong;
When I am not good, and the deeper shade
Of conscious sin makes my heart afraid;
And the busy world has too much to do
To stay its course to help me through,
And I long for a Saviour, can it be
That the God of the universe cares for me?

Let all who are sad take heart again;
We are not alone in our hours of pain,
Our Father stoops from His throne above
To soothe and quiet us with His love.

He leaves us not when the storm is high,
And we have safety for He is nigh;
Can it be trouble which He doth share?
Oh, rest in peace for the Lord does care.

ANON.

EMPTY

OH Little House of Pleasant Dreams,
　The dreams are fled;
And you are but four empty walls
　Whose soul is dead.
The garden that was magic soil
　Is common loam,
And there is nothing but a house
　Which was a Home.

Still through your windows shines the sun
　And breathes the air,
The quaint old rugs and furniture,
　Unchanged, are there;
Yet they seem bathed in ghostly light
　Chill, pale and wan,
For there's no warmth in any house
　Whose dreams are gone.

Love touched you with its rosy glow
　By night and day,
But love, with clipped and wounded wings,
　Has limped away,
And leaves a shelter—nothing more—
　Of wood and stone,
A Little House of Pleasant Dreams
　Whose dreams are flown!

BERTON BRALEY

CALIBAN—AND I

. . . .

Saith He is terrible: watch His feats in proof!
One hurricane will spoil six good months' hope.
—Browning's "Caliban upon Setebos."

DEAR God, dear God, the soul that knows not Thee,
But wills to know, and seeks Thee in the dark,
Oh, Thou wilt hearken to his crying. Hark
  To me.
He knows Thee only in the thunder roll,
The fire from heaven that strikes a sheltering tree,
The fear of Nature's force. Divinity
  His soul
Spells out as Will besotted into whim.
He sees Thee tyrant, gay with brutal joy,
Thy creatures here to hinder, plague, annoy.
  To him
Thy ways past finding out are ways of hate,
Thy depth of wisdom is but depth of woe
For all his fellow-creatures. Could he know,
  Elate,
Thee in Thy mercy, wisdom, Fatherhood—
Dear God, dear God, I veil mine eyes with shame:
Humbly and prayerfully we call Thy name
  As Good,
Yet cavil like poor Caliban, and fail
To see Thee as Thou art. We still ascribe
To Thee our pettiness, our hate beside;
  We hail
Thee as Omnipotent, yet bound Thy power.
We paint Thee, while we call Thee Lord and King,
In likeness of our poor selves groveling
  And cower
Like Caliban, when our recoiling deeds
Strike us, and loud we cry, "The chastening rod!

Who can escape from an avenging God?"
  Our needs
We press importunate, for we must live.
Dear God, dear God, our spirits are but weak;
Help us to seek Thee, find Thee as we seek.
  Forgive.
  Forgive us, help us to be like to Thee,
Since we can see Thee but in humanwise,
And our dull senses, holden ears and eyes,
  Make free.

LAURA BELL EVERETT

UMNOS ÂUMNOS

O THOU whose image in the shrine
Of human spirits dwells divine;
Which from that precinct once conveyed,
To be to outer day displayed,
Doth vanish, part, and leave behind
Mere blank and void of empty mind,
Which wilful fancy seeks in vain
With casual shapes to fill again!

O Thou that in our bosom's shrine
Dost dwell, unknown because divine!
I thought to speak, I thought to say,
"The light is here," "behold the way,"
"The voice was thus," and "thus the words,"
And "thus I saw," and "that I heard"—
But from the lips that half essayed
The imperfect utterance fell unmade.

O Thou, in that mysterious shrine
Enthroned, as I must say, divine!
I will not frame one thought of what
Thou mayest either be or not.
I will not prate of "thus" and "so,"

And be profane with "yes" and "no,"
Enough that in our soul and heart
Thou, whatsoe'er Thou may'st be, art.

Unseen, secure in that high shrine
Acknowledged present and divine,
I will not ask some upper air,
Some future day to place Thee there;
Nor say, nor yet deny, such men
And women saw Thee thus and then:
Thy name was such, and there or here
To him or her Thou didst appear.

Do only Thou in that dim shrine,
Unknown or known, remain, divine;
There, or if not, at least in eyes
That scan the fact that round them lies,
The hand to sway, the judgment guide,
In sight and sense Thyself divide:
Be Thou but there,—in soul and heart,
I will not ask to feel Thou art.

ARTHUR HUGH CLOUGH

STAGIRIUS

THOU, who dost dwell alone;
Thou, who dost know thine own;
Thou, to whom all are known
From the cradle to the grave,—
　　Save, oh! save.
From the world's temptations,
From tribulations,
From that fierce anguish
Wherein we languish,
From that torpor deep

Wherein we lie asleep,
Heavy as death, cold as the grave,
Save, oh! save.

When the soul, growing clearer,
Sees God no nearer;
When the soul, mounting higher,
To God comes no nigher;
But the arch-fiend Pride
Mounts at her side,
Foiling her high emprise,
Sealing her eagle eyes,
And, when she fain would soar,
Makes idols to adore,
Changing the pure emotion
Of her high devotion,
To a skin-deep sense
Of her own eloquence;
Strong to deceive, strong to enslave,—
Save, oh! save.

From the ingrained fashion
Of this earthly nature
That mars thy creature;
From grief that is but passion,
From mirth that is but feigning,
From tears that bring no healing,
From wild and weak complaining,
Thine old strength revealing,
Save, oh! save.
From doubt, where all is double;
Where wise men are not strong,
Where comfort turns to trouble,
Where just men suffer wrong;
Where sorrow treads on joy,
Where sweet things soonest cloy,

Where faiths are built on dust,
Where love is half mistrust,
Hungry, and barren, and sharp as the sea,—
Oh! set us free.
Oh, let the false dream fly,
Where our sick souls do lie,
Tossing continually!
Oh, where thy voice doth come,
Let all doubts be dumb,
Let all words be mild,
All strifes be reconciled,
All pains beguiled!
Light bring no blindness,
Love no unkindness,
Knowledge no ruin,
Fear no undoing!
From the cradle to the grave,
Save, oh! save.

MATTHEW ARNOLD

[From "Matthew Arnold's Poems," The Macmillan Co.]

NOTE II

In this group of poems, the notes of greater desperation and uncertainty prevail. Man must win his great battle with Life or perish in the attempt. The authors here describe five very common moods of the workaday world: (1) childlike and reassuring confidence under the successive burdens of the average life; (2) tragic loneliness in the hour of unmitigated grief, when all of the joyous meaning has gone, seemingly forever beyond recall; (3) a splendid Job-like certainty that finds God on the side of weakness and ignorance, patient with man's petty fears and superstitions, and as fatherly as he is powerful in the interests of his uncomprehending children of earth; (4) appreciation of the fact that human words are altogether too limited to describe that Ultimate of life called God, who is yet known as most real of all realities through experience; and, (5) last of all, that age-long yearning for a Champion who shall turn man's repeated defeats to certain victory and transform all life into one brilliant, triumphant advance into the Perfect.

III

THE CREEDLESS LOVE

A CREEDLESS love, that knows no clan,
  No caste, no cult, no church but Man;
That deems to-day and now and here,
  Are voice and vision of the seer;
That through this lifted human clod
  The inflow of the breath of God
Still sheds its apostolic powers,—
  Such love, such trust, such faith be ours.

We deem man climbs an endless slope
  Tow'rd far-seen tablelands of hope;
That he, through filth and shame of sin,
  Still seeks the God that speaks within;
That all the years since time began
  Work the eternal Rise of Man;
And all the days that time shall see
  Tend tow'rd the Eden yet to be.

Too long our music-hungering needs
  Have heard the iron clash of creeds.
The creedless love that knows no clan,
  No caste, no cult, no church but Man,
Shall drown with mellow music all,
  The dying jangle of their brawl;—
Such love with all its quickening powers,
  Such love to God and Man be ours.

SAM WALTER FOSS

17

FROM "THE HIGHER CATECHISM"

. . . .

WHERE shall we get religion? Beneath the open sky,
The sphere of crystal silence surcharged with deity.
The winds blow from a thousand ways and waft their balms
    abroad,
The winds blow toward a million goals—but all winds blow
    from God.
The stars the old Chaldæans saw still weave their maze on
    high
And write a thousand thousand years their Bible in the sky.
The midnight earth sends incense up sweet with the breath
    of prayer—
Go out beneath the naked night and get religion there.

Where shall we get religion? Beneath the blooming tree,
Beside the hill-encircling brooks that loiter to the sea,
Beside all twilight waters, beneath all noonday shades,
Beneath the dark cathedral pines and through the tangled
    glades;
Wherever the old urge of life provokes the dumb, dead sod
To tell its thought in violets, the soul takes hold on God.
Go smell the growing clover, and scent the blooming pear,
Go forth to seek religion—and find it anywhere.

. . . .

And what is faith? The anchored trust that at the core of
    things
Health, goodness, animating strength flow from exhaustless
    springs;
That no star rolls unguided down the rings of endless maze,
That no feet tread an aimless path through wastes of empty
    days;
That trusts the everlasting voice, the glad, calm voice that
    saith

That Order grows from Chaos, and that life is born from
    death;
That from the wreck of rending stars behind the storm and
    scathe,
There dwells a heart of central calm;—and this, and this is
    faith.
                                        SAM WALTER FOSS

FROM "ACCEPTING THE UNIVERSE"

THE term "religion" is an equivocal and much-abused
word, but I am convinced that no man's life is complete without some kind of an emotional experience that may be called
religious. Not necessarily so much a definite creed or belief
as an attraction and aspiration toward the Infinite, or a
feeling of awe and reverence inspired by the contemplation
of this wonderful and mysterious universe, something to
lift a man above purely selfish and material ends, and open
his soul to influences from the highest heavens of thought.

Religion in some form is as natural to man as are eating
and sleeping.

.   .   .   .

Do your work, deal justly, love rightness, make the most
of yourself, cherish the good, the beautiful, the true, practice
the Christian and the heathen virtues of soberness, meekness,
reverence, charity, unselfishness, justice, mercy, singleness
of purpose; obey the commandments, the Golden Rule, imbue
your spirit with the wisdom of all ages, for thus is the moral
order of the world upheld.

.   .   .   .

Nature . . . is too big for us to grasp . . . in these seas
we can find no soundings. But we are here, the world is
beautiful, life is worth living, love always pays.
                                        JOHN BURROUGHS

THE GOD–MAKER, MAN

As the mind of man grows broader, so do his creeds;
And his gods they are shaped in his image and mirror his
    needs;
And he clothes them with thunders and beauty, he clothes
    them with music and fire;
Seeing not as he bows by their altars that he worships his
    own desires.
And mixed with his trust there is terror, and mixed with his
    madness is ruth,
And every man grovels in error, and every man glimpses a
    truth.
For all of the creeds are false, and all of the creeds are true;
And low at the shrines where my brothers bow, there will I
    bow, too;
For no form of a god, and no fashion
Man has made in his desperate passion,
But is worthy some worship of mine;—
Neither hot with a gross belief,
Nor yet too cold with pride,
I will bow me down where my brothers bow,
Humble—but open-eyed!   DON MARQUIS

NOTE III

A NEW and higher type of religious yearning is presented in "Creedless Love," "The Higher Catechism," "Accepting the Universe," and "The God-Maker, Man." Science, nature study, historical perspective and brotherly interest have entered here, showing the limited uses and the endless abuses of the creeds which have divided rather than united men in the pursuit of truth. Worldwide love, the heavenly music of a world at one, the peace of God actually unifying a whole race of men, and a religion drawn as naturally as the breath of our nostrils from invigorating contact with all life (without and within),—these, with strong emphasis upon the everyday, homely, and practical nature of religion and upon the ideal nature of divinely human love, are the strong notes sounded by this sterling trio of writers.

IV

MULTIPLE STARS

To my friend, and schoolfellow, Doctor Robert G. Aitken

WHEN twilight comes and with it my fair star
Flashes her variant scarlet blue and gold,
Assured am I the half has not been told,
And seems my soul to pass the utmost bar
That holds us ever from the things that are.
Here are my mystic lights and I am bold;
For know I not the truth as known of old?
And is not this the Truth no time can mar?

Is not this radiance the sign of Him
Whose power holds sway in the most ancient skies,
Whose whisper reaches to the outmost rim
Of starry dream, and infinitely flies
Into the timeless dark? Never grows dim
This wonder-light from skyey Paradise!

HENRY MEADE BLAND

SEA–HORIZONS

THE sorrowful expanse from heaven to heaven,
From zone to zone, from deep to height above,
The mute arch of the everlasting heaven
Bends over me with Your unwearied love.

Immeasurable, unutterable, and soundless—
Wide as the east from the west Your love is wide;
The unfathomable distances are boundless
Infinite tenderness on every side.

Against the dark strength of Your huge endurance
My little being beats her baffled wings,

22

Lifts her shrill voice, and wounds the calm assurance
  And tenderness of Your large evenings.

In the vast robes of Your serene compassion
  She hides her soiled and burning face of shame—
Your solemn and inexorable passion
  Lifts her blurred eyes to meet Your glance of flame.

As bread that for my daily fare is broken,
  The eternal loveliness before me spread—
Unutterable gesture—word unspoken,
  In the proud silences forever said!

The sun puts forth his strength, the reaches shimmer
  With inarticulate rapture, and the proud
Waters are thrilled; the fields of ocean glimmer
  With shifting light and overshadowing cloud.

Noon upon noon in heaven takes up his station,
  Day follows night, and night succeeds to day:
Your infinite and lonely meditation
  Sinks with the sunset down the starry way.

Veiled is the Vast: the heaven of evening burning,
  Reveals on the large waters of the sea
Hopelessness—hopelessness—the patient yearning
  And dumb caress of the Immensity.

What message have You left for me, what token
  Of Your lone love, whose laboring Will has wrought
The firmament over my head, and spoken
  Unto my nothingness Your starry Thought!

Sorrowful is the mighty Heart that reaches
  Around this brief and scornful heart of mine—
The dim curve of the melancholy beaches,
  And vacancies along the lone sea-line.

In the huge longing of the far sea-spaces,
    The tremulous rim about the waters curled,
Waits the eternal Gentleness, and traces
    His sad horizons 'round the fading world.

Cloud beyond cloud, the arch of heaven goes over—
    Steep beyond steep, the patient skies descend:
The illimitable wastes and waves discover
    Loneliness—loneliness—without an end.

Inexorable Compassion, may I never
    Reach the last verge and limits of Your love!
Beyond me, still beyond me melt forever
    The eternal margins, fading as I move.

                                    JOHN HALL WHEELOCK

THE NEW MIRACLE

OF old men wrought strange gods for mystery,
    Implored miraculous tokens in the skies,
And lips that most were strange in prophecy
    Were most accounted wise.

The hearthstone's commerce between mate and mate,
    Barren of wonder, prospered in content,
And still the hunger of their thought was great
    For sweet astonishment.

And so they built them altars of retreat
    Where life's familiar use was overthrown,
And left the shining world about their feet,
    To travel worlds unknown.

We hunger still. But wonder has come down
    From alien skies upon the midst of us;
The sparkling hedgerow and the clamorous town
    Have grown miraculous.

And man from his far travelling returns
 To find yet stranger wisdom than he sought,
Where in the habit of his threshold burns
 Unfathomable thought. JOHN DRINKWATER

EARTH'S COMMON THINGS

SEEK not afar for beauty. Lo! it glows
 In dew-wet grasses all about thy feet;
 In birds, in sunshine, childish faces sweet,
In stars and mountain summits topped with snows.

Go not abroad for happiness. For see,
 It is a flower that blooms at thy door!
 Bring love and justice home, and then no more
Thou'lt wonder in what dwelling joy may be.

Dream not of noble service elsewhere wrought;
 The simple duty that awaits thy hand
 Is God's voice uttering a divine command,
Life's common deeds build all that saints have thought.

In wonder-workings, or some bush aflame,
 Men look for God and fancy him concealed;
 But in earth's common things he stands revealed
While grass and flowers and stars spell out his name.

MINOT J. SAVAGE

NOTE IV

IN these great days of Science, when physics and astronomy, more particularly, are making such tremendous advances across the vast stretches of space, men of intense religious imagination are fairly on tiptoe with eagerness, as if expecting that the next flash of starlight, or the removal of one more veil of mist, would surely reveal the God of Universes himself in all his tremendous power and majesty. Or, at times, they feel hopelessly lost in the very vastness of space—were it not that all of this immensity, this secrecy, this exacting sternness, this everlasting patience and tenderness, are felt to be the intimate qualities of a Power that cared, that understood, and that somehow shared (or perhaps even created) humanity's longings to be equal to its boundless dreams.

Or, worn out with fruitless journeyings, shall man let his yearnings lead him back home to the commonplace things which time and distance have now clothed with new and divine meanings? So the whole universal round is seen to thrill with the voice of God. He is both afar and near, if men will train their eyes for the great realities. Thus runs the argument in "Multiple Stars," "Sea-Horizons," "The New Miracle," and "Earth's Common Things."

V

THE THING WE LONG FOR

THE thing we long for, that we are
  For one transcendent moment,
Before the Present, poor and bare,
  Can make its sneering comment.
Still, through our paltry stir and strife,
  Glows down the wished Ideal,
And longing molds in clay what Life
  Carves in the marble Real.

To let the new life in, we know
  Desire must ope the portal;
Perhaps the longing to be so
  Helps make the soul immortal.

. . . .

Longing is God's fresh, heavenward will
  With our poor earthward striving;
We quench it, that we may be still
  Content with merely living;
But, would we learn that heart's full scope
  Which we are hourly wronging,
Our lives must climb from hope to hope
  And realize our longing.

JAMES RUSSELL LOWELL

THE SOUL'S EXPRESSION

WITH stammering lips and insufficient sound
I strive and struggle to deliver right
That music of my nature, day and night
With dream and thought and feeling interwound,

And inly answering all the senses round
With octaves of a mystic depth and height
Which step out grandly to the infinite
From the dark edges of the sensual ground.
This song of soul I struggle to outbear
Through portals of the sense, sublime and whole,
And utter all myself into the air:
But if I did it,—as the thunder-roll
Breaks its own cloud, my flesh would perish there,
Before that dread apocalypse of soul.

ELIZABETH BARRETT BROWNING

THE TRUE MEASURE OF LIFE

WE live in deeds, not years; in thoughts, not breath;
In feelings, not in figures on the dial.
We should count time by heart-throbs when they beat
For God, for man, for duty. He most lives,
Who thinks most, feels noblest, acts the best.
Life is but a means unto an end—that end,
Beginning, mean, and end to all things, God.

P. J. BAILEY

A CHILD'S THOUGHT OF GOD

I

THEY say that God lives very high;
But if you look above the pines
You cannot see our God; and why?

II

And if you dig down in the mines
You never see Him in the gold;
Though from Him all that's glory shines.

III

God is so good, He wears a fold
  Of heaven and earth across his face—
Like secrets kept, for love, untold.

IV

But still I feel that His embrace
  Slides down by thrills, through all things made,
Through sight and sound of every place:

V

As if my tender mother laid
  On my shut lips her kisses' pressure,
Half-waking me at night, and said
  'Who kissed you through the dark, dear guesser?'

ELIZABETH BARRETT BROWNING

WE CANNOT KINDLE

WE cannot kindle when we will
The fire which in the heart resides,
The spirit bloweth and is still,
In mystery our soul abides:
But tasks, in hours of insight will'd,
May be through hours of gloom fulfilled.

MATTHEW ARNOLD

'From " Matthew Arnold's Poems," The Macmillan Co.]

FAITH

THERE is no unbelief;
Whoever plants a seed beneath the sod
And waits to see it push away the clod,
  He trusts in God.

Whoever says when clouds are in the sky,
"Be patient, heart, light breaketh by and by,"
Trusts the Most High.

Whoever sees, 'neath fields of winter snow,
The silent harvest of the future grow,
God's power must know.

Whoever lies down on his couch to sleep,
Content to lock each sense in slumber deep,
Knows God will keep.

Whoever says, "To-morrow," "The Unknown,"
"The Future," trusts that power alone
He dares disown.

There is no unbelief;
And day by day and night, unconsciously,
The heart lives by that faith the lips deny,
God knoweth why.

EDWARD BULWER LYTTON

THE RIDDLE OF THE WORLD

THE riddle of the world is understood
Only by him who feels that God is good;
As only he can feel who makes his love
The ladder of his faith, and climbs above
On the rounds of his best instincts; draws no line
Between mere human goodness and divine.
But judging God by what in him is best,
With a child's trust leans on a Father's breast.

WHITTIER

THE BROTHER OF MERCY

"My son," the monk said soothingly, "thy work is done;
And no more as a servant, but the guest
Of God thou enterest thy eternal rest.
No toil, no tears, no sorrow for the lost,
Shall mar thy perfect bliss. Thou shalt sit down
Clad in white robes, and wear a golden crown
Forever and forever." Piero tossed
On his sick pillow: "Miserable me!
I am too poor for such grand company;
The crown would be too heavy for this gray
Old head; and God forgive me if I say
It would be hard to sit there night and day,
Like an image in the Tribune, doing naught
With these hard hands, that all my life have wrought,
Not for bread only, but for pity's sake.
I'm dull at prayers, I could not keep awake."

Angry at these words the confessor rises and leaves him alone.

Then was he made aware by soul or ear,
Of something pure and holy bending over him,
And of a voice like that of her who bore him,
Tender and most compassionate: "Never fear!
For heaven is love, as God himself is love:
Thy work below shall be thy work above."
And when he looked, lo! in the stern monk's place
He saw the shining of an angel's face!

WHITTIER

THE THREAD OF TRUTH

TRUTH is a golden thread, seen here and there
In small bright specks upon the visible side
Of our strange being's party-colored web.

How rich the converse! 'Tis a vein of ore
Emerging now and then on earth's rude breast,
But flowing full below. Like islands set
At distant intervals on Ocean's face,
We see it on our course; but in the depths
The mystic colonnade unbroken keeps
Its fateful way, invisible but sure.
Oh, if it be so, wherefore do we men
Pass by so many works, so little heeding?

ARTHUR HUGH CLOUGH

[Copyright by The Macmillan Co.]

STARTING FROM PAUMANOK

I SAY the whole earth and all the stars in the sky are for
religion's sake.
I say no man has ever yet been half devout enough,
None has ever yet adored or worship'd half enough,
None has begun to think how divine he himself is, and how
certain the future is.
I say that the real and permanent grandeur of these States
must be their religion,
Otherwise there is no real and permanent grandeur;
(Nor character nor life worthy the name without religion,
Nor land nor man or woman without religion.)

WHITMAN

GRAND IS THE SEEN

GRAND is the seen, the light, to me—grand are the sky and
stars,
Grand is the earth, and grand are lasting time and space,
And grand their laws, so multiform, puzzling, evolutionary;
But grander far the unseen soul of me, comprehending, endow-
ing all those,

Lighting the light, the sky and stars, delving the earth,
  sailing the sea,
(What were all those, indeed, without thee, unseen soul? of
  what amount without thee?)
More evolutionary, vast, puzzling, O my soul!
More multiform far—more lasting thou than they.

WHITMAN

FROM "EVOLUTION AND ETHICS"

THE student of nature, who starts from the axiom of the universality of the law of causation, cannot refuse to admit an eternal existence; if he admits the conservation of energy, he cannot deny the possibility of an eternal energy; if he admits the existence of immaterial phenomena in the form of consciousness, he must admit the possibility, at any rate, of an eternal series of such phenomena; and, if his studies have not been barren of the best fruit of the investigation of nature, he will have enough sense to see that—the God so conceived is one that only a very great fool would deny, even in his heart. Physical science is as little Atheistic as it is Materialistic.

THOMAS HENRY HUXLEY

FROM "NIGHT"

A Priest, A Poet, A Scientist.
Hilltop, in October: the stars shining.
  (The Priest kneels; the Scientist looks at the heavens
  through a telescope; the Poet writes in a little note-book.)

THE PRIEST

WHEN I consider Thy heavens, the work of Thy fingers, the
  moon and the stars, which Thou hast ordained;
What is man, that Thou art mindful of him,
And the son of man, that Thou visitest him?

THE SCIENTIST

Algol which is dim, becomes again a star of the second magnitude.

THE POET

My beloved is far from this hilltop, where the firs breathe
heavily, and the needles fall;
But from the middle of the sea
She, too, gazes on the lustrous stars of calm October, and
in her heart
She stands with me beneath these heavens—daintily blows
Breath of the sighing pines, and from the loaded and bowed-
down orchards and from the fields
With smokes of the valley, peace steps up on this hill.

THE PRIEST

Thou art the Shepherd that strides down the Milky Way;
Thou art the Lord, our God; glorified be Thy name and Thy
works.
I see Thee with Thy staff driving the star-sheep to the fold
of dawn.

THE SCIENTIST

The Spiral Nebula in Ursa Major, that forever turns
Slowly like a flaming pinwheel . . . thus are worlds born;
Thus was the sun and all the planets a handful of million
years ago.

THE POET

She is far from me . . . but in the cradle of the sea
Sleepless she rocks, calling her beloved: he heeds her call:
On this hilltop he picks the North Star for his beacon . . .
For by that star the sailors steer, and beneath that star
She and I are one in the gaze of the heavens.

THE PRIEST

(Slowly rising and turning to the others)

Let us glorify the Creator of this magnificence of infinite
    Night,
His footstool is the Earth, and we are but the sheep of this
    Shepherd.

THE SCIENTIST

Thus shall we only glorify ourselves,
That of this energy that rolls and drives in suns and planets
Are but the split-off forces with cunning brains,
And questioning consciousness . . . Pray if you must—
Only your own ears hear you, and only the heart in your
    breast
Responds to the grandiose emotion . . . See yonder star?
That is the great Aldebaran, great in the night,
Needing a whole sky, as a vat and a reservoir, which he fills
    with his flame . . .
But no astronomer with his eye to his lenses
Has seen ears on the monster.

THE PRIEST

Thou that hast never seen an atom, nor the ether thou
    pratest of,
Thou that hast never seen the consciousness of man,
What knowest thou of the invisible arms about this sky,
And the Father that leans above us?

THE POET

We need know nothing of any Father
When the grasses themselves, withering in October, stand up
    and sing their own dirges in the great west wind,
And every pine is like a winter lodging house where the
    needles may remember the greenness of the world,
And the great shadow is jagged at its top with stars,

And the heart of man is as a wanderer looking for the light
    in a window,
And the kiss and warm joy of his beloved.

THE PRIEST

Man of Song and Man of Science,
Truly you are as people on the outside of a house,
And one of you only sees that it is made of stone, and its
    windows of glass, and that fire burns in the hearth,
And the other of you sees that the house is beautiful and
    very human,
But I have gone inside the house,
And I live with the host in that house
And have broken bread with him, and drunk his wine,
And seen the transfiguration that love and awe make in the
    brain . . .
For that house is the world, and the Lord is my host and
    my Father:
It is my Father's house.

THE SCIENTIST

He that has gone mad and insane may call himself a king,
And behold himself in a king's palace, with feasting, and
    dancing women, and with captains,
And none can convince him that he is mad,
Slave of hallucination . . .
We that weigh the atom and weigh a world in the night, and
    we
Who probe down into the brain, and see how desire discolors
    reality,
And we that see how chemical energy changes and trans-
    forms the molecule,
So that one thing and another changes and so man arises—
With neither microscope, nor telescope, nor spectroscope, nor
    finest violet ray

Have we found any Father lurking in the intricate unreason-
able drive of things
And the strange chances of nature.

THE POET

O Priest, is it not enough that the world and a Woman are
very beautiful,
And that the works and tragic lives of men are terribly glorious?
There is a dance of miracles, of miracles holding hands in a
chain around the Earth and out through space to the
moon, and to the stars, and beyond the stars,
And to behold this dance is enough;
So much laughter, and secret looking, and glimpses of wonder, and dreams of terror . . .
It is enough! it is enough!

THE PRIEST

Enough? I see what is enough!
Machinery is enough for a Scientist,
And Beauty is enough for a Poet;
But in the hearts of men and women, and in the thirsty
hearts of little children
There is a hunger, and there is an unappeasable longing,
For a Father and for the love of a Father . . .
For the root of a soul is mystery,
And the Night is mystery,
And in that mystery men would open inward into Eternity,
And know love, the Lord.
Blessed be his works, and his angels, and his sons crowned
with his glory!
(*A pause. The Woman with a burden in her arms comes
in slowly.*)

JAMES OPPENHEIM

FROM "PRESENT PHILOSOPHICAL TENDENCIES"

ALL religion of the positive and hopeful type is based on the belief that the good will prevail. . . . Religious belief is a confidence that what is indifferent will acquire value, and that what is bad will be made good—through the operation of moral agents on a preëxisting and independent environment. . . .

There is promise and not discouragement in the fact that nature has yielded life; and in the fact that life, once established, has imposed its interests upon the environment . . . life triumphs in and through mechanical law. The systems of nature enter intact into the systems of life. The temporal antecedence of mechanism is in no way prejudicial to the subsequent ascendency of life. If life can have established itself at all, it can by the same means enlarge its domain. And . . . interests . . . can by a further and like progression still further reduce the tribute which they pay to the once omnipotent environment.

There is in fact such a forward movement of life. It becomes freer and more powerful with time. . . . "The earth is the abode of the strong, but it is also the home of the loving." And that which is true of the development of animal life at large, is true in greater measure of the development of human life. The liberalization and betterment of life through the agencies of civilization—the diversification and refinement of interests, the organization and solidification of society, and above all the growth of reason—is at the same time the guarantee of its stability and further expansion. . . .

It is true that the claims of religious optimism cannot be proved. But neither can it be proved "that all the labours of the age, all the devotion, all the inspiration, all the noon-day brightness of human genius, are destined to extinction in the vast death of the solar system, and that the whole temple of Man's achievement must inevitably be buried beneath the débris of a universe of ruins." . . .

And if it be granted that in either case it is a question of over-belief, of the hazard of faith, no devoted soul can hesitate. Justified by the victories already won, he will with good heart invite his will to the completion of the conquest.

RALPH BARTON PERRY

NOTE V

In this group of writers we have, perhaps, a somewhat more positive and reassuring statement of faith in man's ability to reach out and find God. Poet, scientist, and philosopher all agree in viewing life and human destiny with superb optimism.

There is a noticeable tendency among the younger writers of the more sympathetic type, to find in their broadening study of the universe and of Nature's laws of progress a new and vastly more transcendent conception of Power upon the throne of life. Some of them, with Huxley and Darwin, frankly offer this as the real God of *Law* whom men have been forever seeking. Others find Something akin to the highest human qualities, developed to the nth degree, enthusiastically at work—but, not least of all, for the good of all humanity.

The more cautious of these moderns content themselves with an ardent optimism in view of the beneficent trend of human life. A determined and thrifty humanity, plus a Universe of reasonable law and order, are, in their judgment, an undefeatable majority. Man, with his will to conquer, *finds himself* simply the junior partner in a tremendous task which requires (and possesses) the eternal years for its accomplishment. He cannot lose faith in the goodness and the successful issue of Life, once having had this experience.

VI

THE ETERNAL GOODNESS

O FRIENDS! with whom my feet have trod
 The quiet aisles of prayer,
Glad witness to your zeal for God
 And love of man I bear.

I trace your lines of argument;
 Your logic linked and strong
I weigh as one who dreads dissent,
 And fears a doubt as wrong.

But still my human hands are weak
 To hold your iron creeds;
Against the words ye bid me speak
 My heart within me pleads.

Who fathoms the Eternal Thought?
 Who talks of scheme and plan?
The Lord is God! He needeth not
 The poor device of man.

I walk with bare, hushed feet the ground
 Ye tread with boldness shod;
I dare not fix with mete and bound
 The love and power of God.

Ye praise His justice; even such
 His pitying love I deem:
Ye seek a king; I fain would touch
 The robe that hath no seam.

Ye see the curse which overbroods
 A world of pain and loss;
I hear our Lord's beatitudes
 And prayer upon the cross.

More than your schoolmen teach, within
   Myself, alas! I know:
Too dark ye cannot paint the sin,
   Too small the merit show.

I bow my forehead to the dust,
   I veil mine eyes for shame,
And urge, in trembling self-distrust,
   A prayer without a claim.

I see the wrong that round me lies,
   I feel the guilt within;
I hear, with groan and travail-cries,
   The world confess its sin.

Yet, in the maddening maze of things,
   And tossed by storm and flood,
To one fixed trust my spirit clings;
   I know that God is good!

Not mine to look where cherubim
   And seraphs may not see,
But nothing can be good in Him
   Which evil is in me.

The wrong that pains my soul below
   I dare not throne above,
I know not of His hate,—I know
   His goodness and His love.

I dimly guess from blessings known
   Of greater out of sight,
And, with the chastened Psalmist, own
   His judgments too are right.

I long for household voices gone,
   For vanished smiles I long,
But God hath led my dear ones on,
   And He can do no wrong.

I know not what the future hath
  Of marvel or surprise,
Assured alone that life and death
  His mercy underlies.

And if my heart and flesh are weak
  To bear an untried pain,
The bruised reed He will not break
  But strengthen and sustain.

No offering of my own I have,
  Nor works my faith to prove;
I can but give the gifts He gave,
  And plead His love for love.

And so beside the Silent Sea
  I wait the muffled oar;
No harm from Him can come to me
  On ocean or on shore.

I know not where His islands lift
  Their fronded palms in air;
I only know I cannot drift
  Beyond His love and care.

O brothers! if my faith is vain,
  If hopes like these betray,
Pray for me that my feet may gain
  The sure and safer way.

And Thou, O Lord! by whom are seen
  Thy creatures as they be,
Forgive me if too close I lean
  My human heart on Thee!

WHITTIER

NOTE VI

WHITTIER'S own experience, and that of many of his Quaker brethren, are here made so real that this beautiful poem seems like a leaf out of the experience of many a struggling and very sincere and thoughtful soul of our own day. He seems to say: When one finds himself tossed between new-born convictions and the friendships which have ripened through many years and have, up to this time, been the source of supreme joy; when one finds himself misunderstood by his closest friends because of his broadening vision of truth, there wells up in his life a strange and very insistent kind of yearning for God. As a follower of Truth at any cost, he must now throw himself upon the God who is Truth, who called him to obey his behest at so great a price. A new desperation seizes him, a renewed dedication to all Truth possesses him, an increasing antipathy toward the *divisive* creeds and petty quibbles of sectarian groups haunts him, a divine patience and tender love for all mankind—including his lost friends—enters into his experience. He knows God henceforth as his Friend in grief—and asks not that he himself be spared the pain of so deep an experience, so satisfying is this nobler friendship.

II

THE UPWARD URGE OF LIFE

VII

THE LAMP OF LIFE

ALWAYS we are following a light,
Always the light recedes; with groping hands
We stretch toward this glory, while the lands
We journey through are hidden from our sight
Dim and mysterious, folded deep in night,
We care not, all our utmost need demands
Is but the light, the light! So still it stands
Surely our own if we exert our might.
Fool! Never can'st thou grasp this fleeting gleam,
Its glowing flame would die if it were caught,
Its value is that it doth always seem
But just a little farther on. Distraught,
But lighted ever onward, we are brought
Upon our way unknowing, in a dream.

AMY LOWELL

I TRACK UPSTREAM THE SPIRIT'S CALL

I TRACK upstream the spirit's call.
Far, far I go, past all the seasoned ways,
Challenging the cautious calendars and towns.
I track upstream the spirit's call:
Where it will take me I do not know,
But my soul sees that it is all right and that we are not being
deluded,
And my feet follow my soul, often tardily, but the soul
keeps on.
I linger with a last apology, I play with toys,

I make light of what is off there for what I can have put
    into my palm,
I delay all farewells until the farewell of departure,
And finally when leaving shed tears of genuine regret.
I track upstream the spirit's call,
Not daring now to disobey my dream.
I am swept with the living current on and on:
Into whatever storm I contentedly go, into whatever peace.

HORACE TRAUBEL

EACH IN HIS OWN TONGUE

A FIRE-MIST and a planet,
    A crystal and a cell,
A jelly-fish and a saurian,
    And caves where the cave-men dwell;
Then a sense of law and beauty
    And a face turned from the clod—
Some call it Evolution,
    And others call it God.

A haze on the far horizon,
    The infinite, tender sky,
The ripe rich tint of the cornfields,
    And the wild geese sailing high—
And over all upland and lowland
    The charm of the golden-rod—
Some of us call it Autumn
    And others call it God.

Like tides on a crescent sea-beach,
    When the moon is new and thin,
Into our hearts high yearnings
    Come welling and surging in—
Come from the mystic ocean,
    Whose rim no foot has trod,—

Some of us call it Longing,
  And others call it God.

A picket frozen on duty,
  A mother starved for her brood,
Socrates drinking the hemlock,
  And Jesus on the rood;
And millions who, humble and nameless,
  The straight, hard pathway plod,—
Some call it Consecration,
  And others call it God.

WILLIAM HERBERT CARRUTH

THE FORGOTTEN COUNTERSIGN

LIFE met me on the threshold—young, divine,
And promised me unutterable things;
And Love, with fragrant greeting on his wings,
Looked in my eyes and laid his lips on mine,
And bade me quaff the magic of his wine
That deep delight, or disillusion brings.
Ah! had I kept my fair imaginings,
I had not lost the heavenly countersign;
The Shibboleth of soul supremacy;
The dower from my birth in higher spheres.
Then might I know the purer ecstasy
Of conquering Earth's test of alien tears,—
And Life, perchance, her promise might redeem,
And Love be more than a delusive dream!

CORINNE ROOSEVELT ROBINSON

BE BORN AGAIN!

WHO shall lay bare love's inmost meaning, who
  Reveal the sovereign splendor on its throne,

Or utter forth in language the unknown!—
Old is all language, but all love is new.
How may I tell you of this love that to
   Your bosom draws me from my very own,
   And wakes me to one need, and one alone,—
O love, the need to be reborn from you!

There is no word whereby love may declare
   His holy will; but in the breathless deed
Of adoration, in the primal prayer
   At the belovèd breast, he tells his need
     To the one kind and conquering heart, and she
     In the great silence answers silently.

.   .   .   .

Listen, dear love, now in this solemn light
   The Eternal Silence speaks. What tremulous,
Sweet, radiant word troubles the moonlit night—
   What is it God is trying to say to us?

JOHN HALL WHEELOCK

THE CLIMB OF LIFE

There's a feel of all things flowing,
And no power of Earth can bind them;
There's a sense of all things growing,
And through all their forms a glowing
Of the shaping souls behind them.

And the break of beauty heightens
With the swiftening of the motion,
And the soul behind it lightens,
As a gleam of splendor whitens
From a running wave of ocean.

See the still hand of the Shaper,
Moving in the dusk of being:

Burns at first a misty taper,
Like the moon in veil of vapor,
When the rack of night is fleeing.

In the stone a dream is sleeping,
Just a tinge of life, a tremor;
In the tree a soul is creeping—
Last, a rush of angels sweeping
With the skies beyond the dreamer.

So the Lord of Life is flinging
Out a splendor that conceals Him;
And the God is softly singing
And on secret ways is winging,
Till the rush of song reveals Him.

EDWIN MARKHAM

ROAD-HYMN FOR THE START

. . . .
WE have felt the ancient swaying
Of the earth before the sun,
On the darkened marge of midnight heard
sidereal rivers playing;
Rash it was to bathe our souls there, but
we plunged and all was done.
That is lives and lives behind us—lo,
our journey is begun!

Careless where our face is set,
Let us take the open way.
What we are no tongue has told us:
Errand-goers who forget?
Soldiers heedless of their hurry? Pilgrim
people gone astray?
We have heard a voice cry "Wander!" That
was all we heard it say.

Ask no more: 'tis much, 'tis much!
Down the road the day-star calls;
Touched with change in the wide heavens, like
    a leaf the frost winds touch,
Flames the failing moon a moment, ere it
    shrivels white and falls;
Hid aloft, a wild throat holdeth sweet and
    sweeter intervals.

Leave him still to ease in song
Half his little heart's unrest:
Speech is his, but we may journey toward the
    life for which we long.
God, who gives the bird its anguish, maketh
    nothing manifest,
But upon our lifted foreheads pours the boon
    of endless conquest.

WILLIAM VAUGHN MOODY

THE ALTAR

ALONE, remote, nor witting where I went,
I found an altar builded in a dream—
A fiery place, whereof there was a gleam
So swift, so searching, and so eloquent
Of upward promise, that love's murmur, blent
With sorrow's warning, gave but a supreme
Unending impulse to that human stream
Whose flood was all for the flame's fury bent.

Alas! I said,—the world is in the wrong.
But the same quenchless fever of unrest
That thrilled the foremost of that martyred throng
Thrilled me, and I awoke . . . and was the same
Bewildered insect plunging for the flame
That burns, and must burn somehow for the best.

EDWIN ARLINGTON ROBINSON

UNSEEN BUDS

UNSEEN buds, infinite, hidden well,
Under the snow and ice, under the darkness, in every square
    or cubic inch,
Germinal, exquisite, in delicate lace, microscopic, unborn,
Like babes in wombs, latent, folded, compact, sleeping;
Billions of billions, and trillions of trillions of them waiting,
(On earth and in the sea—the universe—the stars there in
    the heavens),
Urging slowly, surely forward, forming endless,
And waiting ever more, forever more behind.

WHITMAN

THE IDEAL

*"Not the treasures is it that have awakened in me so-unspeakable
a desire, but the 'Blue Flower' is what I long to behold."*—Novalis.

SOMETHING I may not win attracts me ever,—
    Something elusive, yet supremely fair,
Thrills me with gladness, but contents me never,
    Fills me with sadness, yet forbids despair.

It blossoms just beyond the paths I follow,
    It shines beyond the farthest stars I see,
It echoes faint from ocean caverns hollow,
    And from the land of dreams it beckons me.

It calls, and all my best, with joyful feeling,
    Essays to reach it as I make reply;
I feel its sweetness o'er my spirit stealing,
    Yet know ere I attain it I must die!

FLORENCE EARLE COATES

NOTE VII

THE writers of this group of poems, in trying to describe the nature of Life in the physical world and in human experience, seem to be fully conscious of the fact that the theme is too vast for their pens. Man's loftiest imaginings simply touch the fringe of so great a subject. And yet, they feel that the alluring reality, the persistent nature, and the increasingly natural qualities of this Life render the pursuit of such knowledge imperative in spite of the mystery and elusiveness which inevitably surround this greatest of all questions.

1. "The Lamp of Life" pictures the upward trend of humanity as the groping progress of one who, in a dream, urges his way through the darkness, through lands unknown, in pursuit of a mysterious lamp which lights the way dimly but can never be fully reached. Shall one despair? Rather should he be glad for the progress attained, knowing the light leads steadily homeward.

2. In "I Track Upstream the Spirit's Call," one hears Life as a spirit of progress calling one beyond the conventional bounds of custom to a greater sphere of freedom and self-realization. To tarry, to disobey, to follow lower ideals however tempting, means untold loss. In following one's highest vision, even through hardship, in yielding to the rushing stream of Life, lie the only safety and peace which Destiny offers.

3. *Carruth* ("Each in His Own Tongue"), finds the whole evolutionary sweep of both inanimate and animate life surging forward toward its worthy consummation in the loftiest instincts and experiences of the human soul. He finds God, the universal Power, at work in all the mighty and orderly processes of Nature, in the beauty and wonder of seasonal changes, in the longings of the human heart, and in the all too common sacrifices of the struggling world. He thinks each person should feel free to describe his view of this cosmic power in accordance with his own experience.

4. The remaining seven poems of this group, written by Mrs. Robinson, Wheelock, Markham, Moody, Edwin Arlington Robinson, Whitman, and Florence Earle Coates, continue to accentuate the supreme importance and significance of this mysterious and indescribable Power which urges all life, and humanity in particular, along the road of progress toward increasing perfection.

Now it is Life, now Love, now an alluring Ideal, now the instinct to worship, or to sacrifice for others, through which the sovereign voice is heard, but always calling people to the highest realization of their powers. All Nature is alive and pressing steadily toward the goal of being. Vast objectives are being wrought out both in the physical and in the moral realm. Yet how little mankind seems to appreciate the tremendous issues at stake, or the honor of sharing in the age-long advance with the Universal God!

VIII

EARTH

GRASSHOPPER, your fairy song
And my poem alike belong
To the dark and silent earth
From which all poetry has birth;
All we say and all we sing
Is but as the murmuring
Of that drowsy heart of hers
When from her deep dream she stirs:
If we sorrow, or rejoice,
You and I are but her voice.

Deftly does the dust express
In mind her hidden loveliness,
And from her cool silence stream
The cricket's cry and Dante's dream;
For the earth that breeds the trees
Breeds cities too, and symphonies,
Equally her beauty flows
Into a savior, or a rose—
Looks down in dream, and from above
Smiles at herself in Jesus' love.
Christ's love and Homer's art
Are but the workings of her heart;
Through Leonardo's hand she seeks
Herself, and through Beethoven speaks
In holy thunderings around
The awful message of the ground.

The serene and humble mold
Does in herself all selves enfold—
Kingdoms, destinies, and creeds,

Great dreams, and dauntless deeds,
Science that metes the firmament,
The high, inflexible intent
Of one for many sacrificed—
Plato's brain, the heart of Christ;
All love, all legend, and all lore
Are in the dust forevermore.

Even as the growing grass
Up from the soil religions pass,
And the field that bears the rye
Bears parables and prophecy.
Out of the earth the poem grows
Like the lily, or the rose;
And all man is, or yet may be,
Is but herself in agony
Toiling up the steep ascent
Toward the complete accomplishment
When all dust shall be, the whole
Universe, one conscious soul.

Yea, the quiet and cool sod
Bears in her breast the dream of God.

If you would know what earth is, scan
The intricate, proud heart of man,
Which is the earth articulate,
And learn how holy and how great,
How limitless and how profound
Is the nature of the ground—
How without terror or demur
We may entrust ourselves to her
When we are wearied out, and lay
Our faces in the common clay.

For she is pity, she is love,
All wisdom, she, all thoughts that move

About her everlasting breast
Till she gathers them to rest:
All tenderness of all the ages,
Seraphic secrets of the sages,
Vision and hope of all the seers,
All prayer, all anguish, and all tears
Are but the dust, that from her dream
Awakes, and knows herself supreme—
Are but earth, when she reveals
All that her secret heart conceals
Down in the dark and silent loam,
Which is ourselves, asleep, at home.

Yea, and this, my poem, too,
Is part of her as dust and dew,
Wherein herself she doth declare
Through my lips, and say her prayer.

JOHN HALL WHEELOCK

THREADS

THROUGH the fantastic tapestry called Existence
Each human being is drawn like a thread
By the invisible hand of the Master Weaver.

Threads, threads, threads! No two colors alike—
Some scarlet, some yellow, some green, some ultra-violet.

Modulated in myriad degrees of shading,
But for the most part interblended
Of black and white in varying tones of gray,

As they leave the spool to be swept through the loom
The threads are white. Then the mechanism whirls them
Into other hues till, at the end, a slight tracery of black
Marks where clumsy shears have snipped them short.

Threads, threads, threads! Threads of textures as innu-
    merable as themselves—
Some soft as silk, some linty and frayed, some steely hard,
Some limp and slack, others taut and true as bowstrings:
The majority wavering and irresolute, like marks made on
    paper by a child.

Schools, race-tracks, churches, brothels.
Passions that surge to war, the lovely quiet of homes,
Glamour of gold, clamor of crowds in frenzy,
Ocean liners that ride the waves, airplanes that outspeed the
    swallows,
Railways that spin on glistening steel bands—
All, all are shuttles in the loom of Life.

The shuttles snatch up the threads, flick them forward,
Intertwine them one with another in weird abandon,
Twist and snarl them inextricably, send them forward
On lonely ways, or blend them harmoniously with the major
    pattern.

Drawn through the tapestry in its making on the loom
The frail protoplasmic threads fail to see
The iridescent glory of the complete design;
Each thinks his own tiny stipple of color dominates the
    scheme.

MARTIN H. WEYRAUCH

FROM "THE GREATER BIRTH"

I FELT the heart-throbs of the world
    Beating in me the greater birth;
And I sang, I laughed, I cried in my glee
    That I was part of earth!

Yet though the sunshine glistened fair,
    And clear springs sparkled in the sod,

I trembled as I raised my eyes,
For I was part of God.

HERMAN HAGEDORN

KINSHIP

I AM aware,
As I go commonly sweeping the stair,
Doing my part of the everyday care—
Human and simple my lot and my share—
  I am aware of a marvelous thing:
  Voices that murmur and ethers that ring
  In the far stellar spaces where cherubim sing
I am aware of the passion that pours
Down the channels of fire through Infinity's doors;
  Forces terrific, with melody shod,
  Music that mates with the pulses of God.
I am aware of the glory that runs
From the core of myself to the core of the suns.
  Bound to the stars by invisible chains,
  Blaze of eternity now in my veins,
  Seeing the rush of ethereal rains
Here in the midst of the everyday air—
      I am aware.

I am aware,
As I sit quietly here in my chair,
Sewing or reading or braiding my hair—
Human and simple my lot and my share—
  I am aware of the systems that swing
Through the aisles of creation on heavenly wing,
  I am aware of a marvelous thing.
Trail of the comets in furious flight,
Thunders of beauty that shatter the night,
  Terrible triumph of pageants that march
  To the trumpets of time through Eternity's arch.

I am aware of the splendor that ties
All the things of the earth with the things of the skies,
  Here in my body the heavenly heat,
  Here in my flesh the melodious beat
  Of the planets that circle Divinity's feet.
As I sit silently here in my chair,
        I am aware.

                                    ANGELA MORGAN

LIFE

LIFE is Eternal Becoming that down the cascade of the ages
Streams with tumultuous force, to which the glittering rapids
Of the broad-flowing Milky Way seem an insignificant
    runnel
That gleams for a moment beneath the ageless sun of eter-
    nity.
Life is a torrent outpoured from an inexhaustible chalice,
A cornucopia held in the hand of an unseen Divinity,
A supreme thank-offering made to Himself, a mystic liba-
    tion,
Whose myriad drops when united prefigure the Oneness of
    Spirit.
It carries the galleon of Time on its flood like a lordly Ama-
    zon.
It worms its way through the tiniest crevice of Space, re-
    turning
To the chalice from which it has issued, as water returns to
    the fountains,
Pulsing through every vein of an universe otherwise lifeless,
Till it recurs at long last to the mighty Heart of All Things.
Yet every moment 'tis real, as real as the Mind that controls
    it,
That sits enthroned in the midst of all, unmoved and un-
    altered.

For consider the Ocean, the symbol alike of Time and
    Eternity,
Whose restless bosom heaves with the rhythmical throb of
    the billow,
While the fathomless depths below the turmoil and toil of
    its fluxes
Abide unchanged in their watery fortress forever and ever.
Yet real is the transient course, as real as the changeless
    abysses.

CLONDESLEY BRERETON

CREATION

ONE must say it; it presses against the brain;
It pours through the pulse like a deluge of mad, sweet spring
    rain;
How may one say it—the aching thing that is wordless,
    evanescent, concrete—
Jubilant, sorrowful, trumpet-toned, whispering; sometimes
    terrible, sometimes sweet?
How may one trap the flash of the wing of a passing bird?
How fold the rustle—and then the stillness—of the forest
    into a word?
It is life. Pushing, singing, dragging, winging, always rush-
    ing to be spoken;
Life, big in the hop of a sparrow, in adoring eyes of a dog—
    life, tender, fierce, joyful, heart-broken;
How, when it floods being, may we, going down under the
    rolling wave, many-splendored, unswerving,
Stand again, dripping wet with life, and catch the glory of it
    in a cupped palm curving?
How may one say it? For it urges, it aches in the nerves to
    be said;
Are they fools then, they who eagerly shoulder that pressure,
    and stammer pale words—so few—and are dead?

On sweeps the beautiful-universal ocean through racked,
    inadequate finite souls,
On and on; and one paints, and one writes; such a little—
    the fringe of creating; and the day is done; and on and
    on life rolls.
Against a copper-pink sunset sky
Black laces of tree-tops peacefully lie;
A robin, with antique art untold,
Both light feet together, is tearing the mould;
The sea roars with storms—is dimpled with calms;
A child runs, shouting, to its father's arms;
Lord, who are we to catalogue living?
Yet, Lord of life, 'tis to us you are giving
To suffer the joy, to exult in the pain of the glory of every
    day;
To see the thing, and to feel the thing, and forever be trying,
Till the day we are dying,
To say the thing some other way.

MARY RAYMOND SHIPMAN ANDREWS

THE WILD RIDE

I hear in my heart, I hear in its ominous pulses,
All day, on the road, the hoofs of invisible horses,
All night, from their stalls, the importunate pawing and neigh-
    ing.

Let cowards and laggards fall back! But alert to the saddle
Weatherworn and abreast, go men of our galloping legion,
With a stirrup-cup each to the lily of women that loves him.

The trail is through dolor and dread, over crags and morasses;
There are shapes by the way, there are things that appal or
    entice us:
What odds? We are Knights of the Grail, we are vowed to
    the riding.

Thought's self is a vanishing wing, and joy is a cobweb,
And friendship a flower in the dust, and glory a sunbeam:
Not here is our prize, nor, alas! after these our pursuing.

A dipping of plumes, a tear, a shake of the bridle,
A passing salute to this world and her pitiful beauty;
We hurry with never a word in the track of our fathers.

I hear in my heart, I hear in its ominous pulses,
All day, on the road, the hoofs of invisible horses,
All night, from their stalls, the importunate pawing and neigh-
ing.

We spur to a land of no name, outracing the storm-wind;
We leap to the infinite dark like sparks from the anvil.
Thou leadest, O God! All's well with Thy troopers that
follow.

LOUISE IMOGEN GUINEY

UNREST

A FIERCE unrest seethes at the core
  Of all existing things:
It was the eager wish to soar
  That gave the gods their wings.

From what flat wastes of cosmic slime,
  And stung by what quick fire,
Sunward the restless races climb!—
  Men risen out of mire!

There throbs through all the worlds that are
  This heart-beat hot and strong,
And shaken systems, star by star,
  Awake and glow in song.

But for the urge of this unrest
  These joyous spheres are mute;

But for the rebel in his breast
  Had man remained a brute.

When baffled lips demanded speech,
  Speech trembled into birth—
(One day the lyric word shall reach
  From earth to laughing earth.)—

When man's dim eyes demanded light,
  The light he sought was born—
His wish, a Titan, scaled the height
  And flung him back the morn!

From deed to dream, from dream to deed,
  From daring hope to hope,
The restless wish, the instant need,
  Still lashed him up the slope!

. . . .

I sing no governed firmament,
  Cold, ordered, regular—
I sing the stinging discontent
  That leaps from star to star!

DON MARQUIS

THE LAST ENIGMA

I was and have been and shall be,
Without end or beginning in time,
The Source whence eternally
Flows Nature's unending rhyme.

I am the soul of all things,
And ever their spirit inspire,
With hope that forever springs
From yearnings that Godward aspire.

On, on, I urge them ahead,
Yet whither, I know not myself;
My feet with tentative tread,
Climb each dang'rous, rocky shelf.

I must go, I must go, I must go,
On the Stream of Eternity,
Whose waters forever flow
To a shoreless and mystical sea.

'Tis I that's the pain in th' heart;
The throb and the pressure of Will;
I smite with the Lover's dart;
'T is I give Life's first thrill.

I gather the atoms as one,
And congregate worlds in space,
From first scintilla to sun,
I am the Urge in the race.

I chisel and crystal the grains
Of sand that lie on the shore:
I build with infinite pains,
The structure of cell and spore.

I push the seed forward to soul,
That moves from mammal to Man;
O'er brains I rumble and roll,
Till thoughts in the mind expand.

Whither, oh, whither away?
I know not, and care not, nor why!
'T is my fate to wander and stray,
Wheresoe'er the winds may ply.

I am the good and the bad:
I am love and hardship and hate:
The soul of the glad and the sad:
I am Destiny and Fate.

For of Motion, all things consist:
Without Me the world were naught;
Thou canst not my spirit resist:
I shall determine thy lot.

HENRY FRANK

SIERRAN PAN

I AM fire and dew and sunshine,
  I am mist on the foamy wave,
I'm the rippling note from the field-lark's throat,
  I'm the jewel hid in the cave.

I'm the lightning flash on the mountain,
  And the cold rose-red of the dawn,
I'm the odor of pine and purple vine,
  And the willowy leap of the fawn.

I'm the sigh of the south wind of autumn,
  I'm the scent of the earth at first rain,
I'm the wild honker call of the earliest fall,
  I'm the yellow of ripening grain.

I'm the music no singer has dreamed of,
  I'm joy in the heart of man;
I'm the lyric time of no poet's rhyme,
  I'm the glad, the immortal Pan.

HENRY MEADE BLAND

FROM "THE MEANING OF GOD IN HUMAN EXPERIENCE"

TRUTH must be transformed; but the transformation of truth must be marked by a conservation of power. . . . No religion, then, is a true religion which is not able to make men tingle, yes, even to their physical nerve tips, with the sense of an infinite hazard, a wrath to come, a heavenly city to be gained or lost in the process of time and by the use of our freedom. The flesh and blood of historical contingencies cannot be sapped up in the timeless issues of a certain type of idealism without loss of power, hence loss of truth. . . .

Here is an energy of huge potency but of ambiguous character. From such a survey but one uncontradicted impression emerges: the thing has been radical; it has had some grip upon the original instincts of human nature; it has known how to rule and to swirl into its own vortex all the currents of love, of hunger, and of self-defense; and it has been able to put these severally and together under its feet. It is this dynamic aspect of religion, an infinite resource, which has appealed to capable political intelligence since the days of Roman, perhaps of Persian, imperial policy; and it is this same aspect which appeals now to the scientist of society, whose eye is quick for usable elements of public power.

But religion, though a social force of unknown magnitude, has never been tamed to harness by statesman, diplomat, or sociologue. . . .

And in fact, from the side of its deeds in history religion remains a mystery. Its career is the swath of an agency immense, invisible, paradoxical. If its works are potent, they no more reveal its character than they becloud it. . . .

The position of religion in the world is, and has been, unique; and with the preservation of this distinction its very nature is bound up. The very work done by religion in the course of history has depended—despite her union with the Arts—on the clear eminence, above all her contact with affairs, of a summit which is No-art and touched by no Art. . . .

The whole truth lies surely in this direction—that *all* of our human impulses and loves are akin. . . . The love of God is the one natural instinct of man; worship is the one deed which answers as an echo all other deeds in history.

WILLIAM ERNEST HOCKING

THE FUGITIVES

WE are they that go, that go,
Plunging before the hidden blow.
We run the byways of the earth,
For we are fugitive from birth,
Blindfolded, with wide hands abroad
That sow, that sow the sullen sod.

We cannot wait, we cannot stop
For flushing field or quickened crop;
The orange bow of dusky dawn
Glimmers our smoking swath upon;
Blindfolded still we hurry on.

How do we know the ways we run
That are blindfolded from the sun?
We stagger swiftly to the call,
Our wide hands feeling for the wall.

Oh, ye who climb to some clear heaven,
By grace of day and leisure given,
Pity us, fugitive and driven—
The lithe whip curling on our track,
The headlong haste that looks not back!

FLORENCE WILKINSON

THE FLIGHT

O WILD HEART, track the land's perfume,
  Beach-roses and moor-heather!
All fragrances of herb and bloom
  Fail, out at sea, together.
O follow where aloft find room
  Lark-song and eagle-feather!
All ecstasies of throat and plume
  Melt, high on yon blue weather.

O leave on sky and ocean lost
  The flight creation dareth;
Take wings of love, that mounts the most;
  Find fame, that furthest fareth!
Thy flight, albeit amid her host
  Thee, too, night star-like beareth,
Flying, thy breath on heaven's coast,
  The infinite outweareth.

II

Dead o'er us roll celestial fires;
  Mute stand Earth's ancient beaches;
Old thoughts, old instincts, old desires,
  The passing hour outreaches;
The soul creative never tires—
  Evokes, adores, beseeches;
And that heart most the god inspires
  Whom most its wildness teaches.

For I will course through falling years,
  And stars and cities burning;
And I will march through dying cheers
  Past empires unreturning;
Ever the world-flame reappears
  Where mankind power is earning,
The nations' hopes, the people's tears,
  One with the wild heart yearning.

GEORGE EDWARD WOODBERRY

HEARKEN TO THE HAMMERS!

HEARKEN to the hammers, endlessly hammering,
The din of wheels, the drone of wheels, the furnaces
Panting, where Man as in a demon-palace toils
  To forge the giant creatures of his brain.

He has banished the spring and the innocence of leaves
From the blackened waste he has made; the infected sky
Glooms with a sun aghast, and the murk of the night
  Is peopled with tall flames like spirits insane.

He strips himself to the heat, not of the jovial sun,
But of the scorch of furnaces; with naked breast
Sweating beneath the iron and blear glass, amid
  The hammers' hammering and the wheels' roar.

Not with grapes of October trodden underfoot
Spurting juices of ripeness in runnels, his vats
Brim, but with gushes flickered-over and blinding,
  Unshapen spilth and blaze of molten ore.

With a finger he lifts the weight of mountainsides
Poised; the metal mass he shears red-hot in a trice;
He gives to the animate iron thews of force,
  A Titan's pulse, and breath of fiery draught.

Monsters mightier far than himself he creates
To swim storming seas, and to mount in miles of air,
To deride Space and the old opposition of Time:
  Their speed is like strong drink that he has quaffed.

He has the tamed lightning to do his bidding, draws
Energies out of the veins of earth; he is armed
From all elements, woven as in a magic web;
  He has stolen seeds of Death, wherewith to fight.

He holds fabled terrors of the ancient gods in his hand—
In a handful of dust, earthquake and pestilence;
He exults to destroy, to obliterate, to be
  Lord of the powers of the engulfing night.

Deafened with the hammers, inebriate with the sound
Of the powers he has raised out of their jealous lair,
He has fever within him, he becomes dizzy,
  And craves, and knows not whither he is bound.

Shall he attain god-like felicity of ease,
Supreme articulate voice of nature's striving,
Or builds he a vast prison for himself, a slave
    With iron of his own strong forging crowned?

O where is now the dew-dropt radiance of morning,
That sistered with him rock and reed and rippling stream,
When simple of heart in the sun with a free body
    He accepted all the boundaries of his mind?

Full of fears he was then, shadowed with helpless need
To propitiate Powers that threatened each footstep.
Has he escaped from those old terrors, to be prey
    Of fears more terrible because less blind?

LAURENCE BINYON

FROM "THE SYSTEM OF ANIMATE NATURE"

WE know the inorganic system of things only in terms of mind, and our first adventure of scientific faith is to believe in its external reality; yet it looms impressively over us, even in our defiance, in its stupendous journeying through space. . . .

The realm of organisms. . . . It is surely a magnificent spectacle that the obviously animate presents. What a gamut of life from the microscopic Infusorian to the giant whale, from the hyssop on the wall to the cedar of Lebanon! What abundance of life is revealed when the dredge comes up, or when the insects rise in a cloud as we walk through the grassland of a warm country. What variety of architecture, what abundance of individuality within the same style! All is suggestive of fertile imagination. How strong the pressure as the waves of life surge up against their shores; how numberless the hand-and-glove fitnesses; how subtle the linkages; how constant the changefulness; how universal the beauty! . . .

Living creatures press up against all barriers; they fill every possible niche all the world over; they show that Nature abhors a vacuum. . . . When we consider the filling of every niche, the finding of homes in extraordinary places, the mastery of difficult conditions, the plasticity that adjusts to out-of-the-way exigencies, the circumvention of space (as in migration) and the conquest of time (as in hibernation), we begin to get an impression of the insurgence of life. We see life persistent and intrusive—spreading everywhere, insinuating itself, adapting itself, resisting everything, defying everything, surviving everything!

The hosts of living organisms are not random creatures, they can be classified in battalions and regiments. Neither are they isolated creatures, for every thread of life is intertwined with others in a complex web. . . . No creature lives or dies to itself; there is no insulation. . . . All things are in flux, there is a ceaseless circulation of matter; . . . and so the stuff of the world goes round from one incarnation to another. . . . The multitudinous unique threads of life become more and more interwoven; the warp and the woof of the web are hunger and love; we get glimpses of a changing pattern becoming ever finer. The web seems to become increasingly coherent, though man often rends the fabric ruthlessly.

It is plain that evolution may be down as well as up, and that the gates of parasitism and other facile slopes of degenerate life are always open. It is a misunderstanding to suppose that . . . evolution is synonymous with progress. . . . Some of the most remarkable achievements of evolution have passed away in their prime without leaving direct descendants. It is probable, however, . . . that the distinctive gains of these lost races are, sometimes at least, conserved along collateral lines. . . . The large fact is certain that on the whole there has been for many millions of years progressive differentiation and integration along diverse lines, an increasingly complex and masterly behavior, a growing emancipation of mind and an approximation to personality. This is the largest fact to be borne in mind in our interpretation of evolution. The process has been on the whole progressive. With Lotze we hear "an onward-advancing melody." . . .

It concerns a developing system, like a great organism, in which the exuberance of one part and the tardiness of another cannot be said to disturb the balanced movement of the whole. . . . Evolution is based on order and works out in order. . . .

We must bear in mind the fact that millions of years are spent in the fashioning of minutiæ of perfection in types which are certainly not near the highway of evolution that led to backboned animals and eventually to man. Nothing is too remote, too minute, too trivial—everything must be finished and refined. Though it takes a million years to make an Argonaut, there is no hurry. . . .

The eyes of Man's understanding have been darkened if he does not see something of the majesty of the great becoming. . . .

The process has had its outcome in personalities, who have discerned something of its magnificent sweep, who are seeking to understand its factors, who are learning some of its lessons, who cannot rest until they interpret it—even though it be mistakenly. . . .

It has been a heartening encouragement to know that it is an ascent, not a descent, that we have behind us, and that if we read the story aright the Cosmos is rather with us than against us. The recognition of our solidarity with the realm of organisms has been of great importance, and we cannot go back on it. . . .

Man is the outcome of a persistent trend—towards freedom of mind—which has been characteristic of the process of organic evolution for millions of years. . . .

The plasticity, the adaptations, the progress, the interlinkages, the joy, the happiness, the masterpieces, the note of gentleness, how they make the shadows shrink! Our thesis stands that the facts of an accurate Natural History are not incongruent with an interpretation of Nature in higher terms.

We have, moreover, to bear in mind that the evolution is still in progress, . . . that we in facing and mastering difficulties are sharing in working out a better future for our successors. . . . The main trend of evolution is essentially integrative. Who shall impiously prescribe its limits, especially in the Kingdom of Man, where Personality seems to be beginning to transcend Organism?

It was preeminently Pasteur who . . . convinced every open mind that the days of folded hands and resignation were over, and that it was for Man, with Science as torch, and with Mercy in his heart, to enter courageously into the fuller possession of his Kingdom. . . .

Nature is crowned in Man . . . especially because he is the finest expression of those qualities which mark the main trend of organic evolution,—such as freedom, awareness, mastery. . . . Nature finds herself in Man. . . . But the anomaly is that Man, minister and interpreter of Nature as he is, is subject to inhibitions and disharmonies which are not tolerated in wild nature. If there be an underlying purpose or meaning in organic Evolution, is not Man hindering it by his slowness to understand and fall in with the principles of its accomplishment? If the central fact in Evolution be "the slowly wrought-out dominance of mind in things," it is surely man's fundamental task to use this expounding mind to control his own life. If the process of Evolution suggests any lesson, it is surely that "the sharpened life commands its course,"—by brains, correlation, organization. . . . What the evolution process points to with firmness is that Brains pay—Brains that include Love as well as Logic. . . .

A study of the evolution-process discloses a multitude of cases in which the reward of success is given to types which are careful parents, devoted mates, friendly kinsfolk. . . . The objectively altruistic type succeeds. Nature stamps not only the beautiful, but the other-regarding with the only approval which is hers to bestow—success in surviving. And, unless they are uncommonly good hypocrites, many of Life's children behave as if they found living good.

Thus Nature speaks to our moral as well as to our intellectual ear. Singling and sifting never cease, but Nature has certainly another counsel besides whetting teeth and sharpening claws. . . . As a matter of fact, an extraordinarily large part of the energy of organisms is spent not on themselves, but for others. Nature, we think, stamps not only the beautiful but the good with her approval; and when we carefully consider the process of Natural Selection itself, do we not get from it a deep and ancient ethical message— that the individual must be content to subordinate himself to the species, even to lose himself in its progressive life? There is an ethical undertone.

It is not a small thing, forsooth, that we are part and parcel of an Order of Nature which has evolved for millions of years like a long-drawn-out drama to finer and finer issues; that the process of evolution has in the main "the unity of an onward advancing melody"; that all through the ages, apart from blind alleys, life has been slowly creeping—and sometimes quickly leaping—upwards; that while there have been many mysterious losses even of branches from the great arbor vitæ, the flowers have become consistently finer . . . each age transcending its predecessor.

As we look back, then, on the world-becoming, we see that finer and finer actors have appeared from epoch to epoch on the crowded stage, and the situations have become more and more intricate. A great web has been passing for incomputable ages from the loom of time—hunger and love its warp and woof—but the pattern has become more and more subtle, and it sometimes seems as if it were picturing a story. . . . In any case, the big fact is that men, bent on making much of their life, have behind them an organic momentum which is in part in line with what the best in us regards as best. . . .

It is difficult to shut out the impression that Nature is Nature for a purpose. We do not think any longer of a "directive power" outside of the evolving organisms, but of a directive power which is bone of their bone and flesh of their flesh,—a directive power analogous to that which we ourselves know when we command our course or send an arrow to its mark. What we must particularly take account of is the main trend in evolution, making persistently for the dominance of mentality and the establishment eventually of personality.

J. ARTHUR THOMSON

WE DEAD! AWAKE!

WE dead! awake!
Kiss the beloved past good-by,
Go leave the love-house of the betrayed self,
And through the dark of birth go and enter the soul's bleak
    weather. . . .
And I, I will not stay dead, though the dead cling to me.
I will put away the kisses and the soft embraces and the
    walls that encompass me,
And out of this womb I will surely move to the world of my
    spirit.
I will lose my life to find it, as of old,
Yea! I will turn from the life-lie I lived to the truth I was
    wrought for;
And I will take the creator within, sower of the seed of the
    race,
And make him a god, shaper of civilizations. . . .

Now on my soul's imperious surge,
Taking the risk, as of death, and in deepening twilight,

I ride on the darkening flood and go out on the waters
Till over the tide comes music, till over the tide the breath
Of the song of my far off soul is wafted and blown,
Murmuring commandments. . . .

Oh, Life, of which I am part; Life, from the depths of the
    heavens,
That ascended like a water-spring into David of Asia on the
    eastern hills in the night,
That came like a noose of golden shadow on Joan in the
    orchard,
That gathers all life: the binding of brothers into sheaves:
That of old kneelers in the dust
Named, glorying: Allah, Jehovah, God.

JAMES OPPENHEIM

THE VOICE OF THE UNBORN

FROM the Unseen I come to you to-night,
The Hope and Expectation of your world.
I am Omniscience that seeks of you
A tongue to utter the eternal thought.
I am Omnipotence that claims of you
The tools whereby my power may profit earth.
All Love am I, that seeks to spend itself
Embodied in a human sacrament,
For I have heard the wailing of the world,
Not faint and far away as in a dream,
But very near—and lo, I understood
It need not be. Wherefore I come to you.

O You to whom my tenderness goes out,
To whom I fain would bring an end of groans
And blind, bewildered tears, a cloudless dawn
Of unimagined joy and strength unguessed,
What welcome will you give to me, O World?

Since I whose dwelling is the universe
Will stoop to walls and rafters for your sake,
What is the home you have prepared for me?
O Men and Women, is it beautiful,
A place of peace, a house of harmony?
Will you be glad, who know me as I am,
To see me make my habitation there?
Since I will hamper my divinity
With weight of mortal raiment for your sake,
What vesture have you woven for my wear?
O Man and Woman who have fashioned it
Together, is it fine and clean and strong,
Made in such reverence of holy joy,
Of such unsullied substance, that your hearts
Leap with glad awe to see it clothing me,
The glory of whose nakedness you know?

Oh, long, long silence of the wakening years!
Thus have I called since man took shape as man;
Thus will I call till all mankind shall heed
And know me, who to-day am one with God,
And whom to-morrow shall behold, your child.

From the Unseen I come to you to-night . . .

AMELIA JOSEPHINE BURR

SUMMONS

THE eager night and the impetuous winds,
The hints and whispers of a thousand lures,
And all the swift persuasion of the Spring,
Surged from the stars and stones, and swept me on. . . .
The smell of honeysuckles, keen and clear,
Startled and shook me, with the sudden thrill
Of some well-known but half-forgotten voice.
A slender stream became a naked sprite,

Flashed around curious bends, and winked at me
Beyond the turns, alert and mischievous.
A saffron moon, dangling among the trees,
Seemed like a toy balloon caught in the boughs,
Flung there in sport by some too-mirthful breeze . . .
And as it hung there, vivid and unreal,
The whole world's lethargy was brushed away;
The night kept tugging at my torpid mood
And tore it into shreds. A warm air blew
My wintry slothfulness beyond the stars;
And over all indifference there streamed
A myriad urges in one rushing wave . . .
Touched with the lavish miracles of earth,
I felt the brave persistence of the grass;
The far desire of rivulets; the keen,
Unconquerable fervor of the thrush;
The endless labors of the patient worm;
The lichen's strength; the prowess of the ant;
The constancy of flowers; the blind belief
Of ivy climbing slowly toward the sun;
The eternal struggles and eternal deaths—
And yet the groping faith of every root!
Out of old graves arose the cry of life;
Out of the dying came the deathless call.
And, thrilling with a new sweet restlessness,
The thing that was my boyhood woke in me—
Dear, foolish fragments made me strong again;
Valiant adventures, dreams of those to come,
And all the vague, heroic hopes of youth,
With fresh abandon, like a fearless laugh,
Leaped up to face the heaven's unconcern. . . .
And then—veil upon veil was torn aside—
Stars, like a host of merry girls and boys,
Danced gaily 'round me, plucking at my hand;
The night, scorning its stubborn mystery,
Leaned down and pressed new courage in my heart;

The hermit-thrush, throbbing with more Song,
Sang with a happy challenge to the skies;
Love and the faces of a world of children
Swept like a conquering army through my blood.
And Beauty, rising out of all its forms,
Beauty, the passion of the universe,
Flamed with its joy, a thing too great for tears,
And, like a wine, poured itself out for me
To drink of, to be warmed with, and to go
Refreshed and strengthened to the ceaseless fight;
To meet with confidence the cynic years;
Battling in wars that never can be won,
Seeking the lost cause and the brave defeat.

LOUIS UNTERMEYER

NOTE VIII

THERE is an intensity, a sustained enthusiasm, about this group of writings which sets it quite apart from the others in this second main division. At times the movement hurries lightly along like the dawn of morning, like the growing color of the rose, or the movement of a cricket or a grasshopper. Again it sways forward in rapt ecstasy or bitter grief. Then the massiveness, the oppressing weight, of Life seems to bear down upon the writer. And sometimes the rush and passion of the storm, of the battle, of the breaking heart, carry the sympathetic reader forward until he is amazed at the depths of emotion which have been stirred within him. Here the passionateness of the Life-Urge is experienced at its best.

1. In "Earth," one finds a quiet, but intense, joy in the fact that all life has sprung from the heart of Mother Earth. From the humblest to the noblest order of being, all have a common origin, all are developments from the great primal urge of being. The human soul—as yet in its merest beginnings—is the clear prophecy of all the wonderful future toward which this Power is surely leading us. The author shows remarkable faith, and yet great reserve, in his handling of this supreme theme.

2. "Threads" and "The Greater Birth," though changing the figure, follow much the same thought as above, striking also the notes of fellow feeling and reverence, the joy of sharing with others, and the bliss of partaking of the ultimate Life which, in turn, impels one to express appreciation through brotherhood. This second poem might be called "The Soul's Awakening"—to its great relationships in life.

3. Voices, music, forces terrific and glorious at the same time, cosmic pageants with the eternal drive of progress and conquest in all their make-up—these are a few of the amazing qualities Angela Morgan ("Kinship"), finds in the humdrum cares and pursuits of the average day. In the light of this thought, every task becomes significant; every life a universe of divine activities.

4. *Clondesley Brereton* ("Life"), pays a splendid tribute to the immensity and the tireless urge and variability of Life. Issuing from the presence of the Unseen Spirit, whose will pervades all things, pours a flood of life which carries everything before it with irresistible energy. It touches every portion of the universe—which lives only because of its vivifying power—returning ultimately to the Divine Fountain of being whence started its miraculous career. Only the Eternal Heart of all things remains unchanged and sure of the great Future which is slowly developing.

5. *Mary Raymond Shipman Andrews* traces the sweep of this universal Life through the many forms of existence, especially showing how humanity is trying to give adequate expression to this Divine Urge felt in joy and in sorrow, in art and in literature, in heart-break and in laughter. But always one is conscious of his utter inability to tell the whole story of Power so transcendent, so all-compelling. Every day and hour has its new Creation narrative to pour forth.

6. In "The Wild Ride" and "Unrest," the authors picture Life as a breathless ride and a fierce climb toward the goal of being. The former feels the guiding hand of God; the latter sees only the blind, irresistible Urge and the progress of an unwilling but fate-driven humanity. *Florence Wilkinson* ("The Fugitives"), also describes this same desperate side of life and calls for an understanding of this period of uncertainty on the part of those more highly favored.

7. *Henry Frank* ("The Last Enigma"), finds in his scientific study of man and Nature the mystic secret of being. Life and Death are only passing features of that Soul of Being which dominates all things for the common good. Six writers all feel the tremendous drive of this Life, but seem to have more faith in its kindness and guidance. *Bland* is carried away by the beauty of his great California scenery. *Hocking* reaches his conclusions as to the unique power and naturalness of Religion through psychology and philosophy, and *J. Arthur Thomson* writes a great biological peroration upon the directive power of Nature. *Woodberry* leans on the great human experience of the race, daring to believe that man is achieving the best in life by responding to the urgent calls for progress within him. It remains for *Laurence*

Binyon and *Florence Wilkinson* to present the side of the workman caught up in the whirl of modern industry. Can he save his nobler self under the strain and drive of soulless business?

8.   The last three of this strenuous group of writers summon humanity to look upon this imperious, surging Life as a tremendous blessing, the one chance of a whole Eternity, with not a moment to lose lest the opportunity be withdrawn or passed on to others. And in this closing group of poems ("We Dead! Awake!", "The Voice of the Unborn," and "Summons"), the authors attempt to show the practical uses of this Power as it seeks to function through human channels.

IX

ODE

WE are the music-makers,
    And we are the dreamers of dreams,
Wandering by lone sea-breakers,
    And sitting by desolate streams;
World-losers and world-forsakers,
    On whom the pale moon gleams:
Yet we are the movers and shakers
    Of the world forever, it seems.

With wonderful deathless ditties,
We build up the world's great cities,
    And out of a fabulous story
    We fashion an empire's glory:
One man with a dream, at pleasure,
    Shall go forth and conquer a crown;
And three with a new song's measure
    Can trample a kingdom down.

We, in the ages lying
    In the buried past of the earth,
Built Nineveh with our sighing,
    And Babel itself in our mirth;
And o'erthrew them with prophesying
    To the old of the new world's worth;
For each age is a dream that is dying
    Or one that is coming to birth.

A breath of our inspiration
Is life of each generation;
    A wondrous thing of our dreaming,
    Unearthly, impossible seeming—

The soldier, the king, and the peasant
  Are working together in one,
Till our dream shall become their present
  And their work in the world be done.

They had no vision amazing
Of the goodly house they are raising;
  They had no divine foreshowing
  Of the land to which they are going;
But on one man's soul it hath broken,
  A light that doth not depart;
And his look, or a word he hath spoken,
  Wrought flame in another man's heart.

And therefore to-day is thrilling
With a past day's late fulfilling;
  And the multitudes are enlisted
  In the faith that their fathers resisted,
And, scorning the dream of to-morrow,
  Are bringing to pass, as they may,
In the world, for its joy or its sorrow,
  The dream that was scorned yesterday.

But we, with our dreaming and singing,
  Ceaseless and sorrowless we!
The glory about us clinging
  Of the glorious futures we see,
Our souls with high music ringing:
  O men! it must ever be
That we dwell, in our dreaming and singing,
  A little apart from ye.

For we are afar with the dawning
  And the suns that are not yet high,
And out of the infinite morning
  Intrepid you hear us cry—
How, spite of your human scorning,

Once more God's future draws nigh,
And already goes forth the warning
That ye of the past must die.

Great hail! we cry to the comers
From the dazzling unknown shore;
Bring us hither your sun and your summers,
And renew our world as of yore;
You shall teach us your song's new numbers;
And things that we dreamed not before:
Yea, in spite of a dreamer who slumbers,
And a singer who sings no more.

ARTHUR O'SHAUGHNESSY

SONG OF PALMS

(The second half of the original poem is omitted.)

MIGHTY, luminous, and calm
Is the country of the palm,
Crowned with sunset and sunrise,
Under blue unbroken skies,
Waving from green zone to zone,
Over wonders of its own;
Trackless, untraversed, unknown,
Changeless through the centuries.

Who can say what thing it bears?
Blazing bird and blooming flower,
Dwelling there for years and years,
Hold the enchanted secret theirs:
Life and death and dream have made
Mysteries in many a shade,
Hollow haunt and hidden bower
Closed alike to sun and shower.

Who is ruler of each race
Living in each boundless place,
  Growing, flowering, and flying,
  Glowing, reveling, and dying?
Wave-like, palm by palm is stirred,
And the bird sings to the bird,
And the day sings one rich word,
  And the great night comes replying.

ARTHUR O'SHAUGHNESSY

BEAUTY'S BIRTH

SUCH is the wonder of the procreant earth,
  Whereon we go with eyes unmarvelling;
Such the vast miracle of Beauty's birth
  Up from the earth in every living thing.

Oh when an emerald April pipes her note,
  And walks thin-clad upon the tinted hills,
When the returning thrush pours from his throat
  The cosmic joy that in the atom thrills.

When in the mind leaps up the high desire,
  Flinging aside a diadem for thorns,
I know that I have found the hidden fire,
  Clothed in the flesh and which the flesh adorns.

O life of me, born of that ordering
That mingles sand and sunlight till they sing!

HUGH ROBERT ORR

IT IS ENOUGH

I KNOW the little earth on which I go,
  Is but a smallest speck of cosmic dust,
And I—dust of the driven dust—I know
  I shall return again as all things must.

I know the song I sing is but the rush
  Of some cell energy, that the desire
Of my prayer is an atomic hush,
  And love is but a chemistry of fire.

And yet I sing, I cherish what is fair,
  And drink the brimming cup that Beauty gives;
Free as a dream, unbidden, moves my prayer,
  Love like a thing immortal in me lives.

O dust, O earth, child of a wandering star,
It is enough, remain what thing you are!

HUGH ROBERT ORR

CATHEDRAL EXPRESSION

So long as sin-stained souls stagger under the burden of
conscious guilt, so long as life is torn by passion, so long as
babes are born into loving homes and open graves mock the
joys that clustered around the cradle, so long will religion
seek for expression and the spirit of man reach out for the
spirit of fellow man.

JENKIN LLOYD JONES

TRUE RELIGION

TRUE religion carries health and strength into the soul.
Religion is only another word for the right use of man's whole
self. It gives them direction for the achievement of duty;
it opens to them the coming world.

HENRY WARD BEECHER

BY AN EVOLUTIONIST

THE Lord let the house of a brute to the soul of a man,
  And the man said, 'Am I your debtor?'
And the Lord—'Not yet: but make it as clean as you can,
  And then I will let you a better.'

I

If my body come from brutes, my soul uncertain, or a fable,
    Why not bask amid the senses while the sun of morning
        shines,
I, the finer brute rejoicing in my hounds, and in my stable,
    Youth and Health, and birth and wealth, and choice of
        women and of wines?

II

What hast thou done for me, grim Old Age, save breaking
    my bones on the rack?
    Would I had past in the morning that looks so bright
        from afar!

OLD AGE

Done for thee? starved the wild beast that was linkt with
    thee eighty years back.
    Less weight now for the ladder-of-heaven that hangs on a
        star.

I

If my body come from brutes, tho' somewhat finer than
    their own,
    I am heir, and this my kingdom. Shall the royal voice
        be mute?
No, but if the rebel subject seek to drag me from the
    throne,
    Hold the sceptre, Human Soul, and rule thy Province of
        the brute.

II

I have climb'd to the snows of Age, and I gaze at a field in
    the Past,
    Where I sank with the body at times in the sloughs of a
        low desire,

But I hear no yelp of the beast, and the Man is quiet at
    last
  As he stands on the heights of his life with a glimpse of
    a height that is higher.

TENNYSON

[From " The Works of Tennyson," The Macmillan Co.]

WHEN THE FIRST MOTHER AWOKE

WHEN the first Mother awoke to her first tenderness and
warmed her loneliness at her infant's love, when for a moment
she forgot herself and thought upon its weakness or its pain,
when by the most imperceptible act or sign or look of sympathy she expressed the unutterable impulse of her Motherhood, the touch of a new creative hand was felt upon the
world. However short the earliest infancies, however feeble
the sparks they fanned, however long heredity took to gather
fuel enough for a steady flame, it is certain that once this
fire began to warm the cold hearth of Nature and give
humanity a heart, the most stupendous task of the past was
accomplished.

HENRY DRUMMOND

HOW MUCH OF GODHOOD

How much of Godhood did it take—
   What purging epochs had to pass,
Ere I was fit for leaf and lake
   And worthy of the patient grass?

What mighty travails must have been,
   What ages must have moulded me,
Ere I was raised and made akin
   To dawn, the daisy and the sea.

In what great struggles was I felled,
   In what old lives I labored long,

Ere I was given a world that held
A meadow, butterflies, and song?

But oh, what cleansings and what fears,
What countless raisings from the dead,
Ere I could see Her, touched with tears,
Pillow the little weary head.

LOUIS UNTERMEYER

ALTRUISM

"THE God of things as they are"
Is the God of the highest heaven;
The God of the morning star,
Of the thrush that sings at even;

The God of the storm and sunshine,
Of the wolf, the snail, and the bee,
Of the Alp's majestic silence,
Of the soundless depths of the sea;

The God of the times and the nations,
Of the planets as they roll,
Of the numberless constellations,
Of the limitless human soul.

And there is nothing small,
And nought can mighty be;
Archangels and atoms all
Embodiments of Thee!

A single thought divine
Holds stars and suns in space;
A dream of man is Thine,
And history finds its place.

When the universe was young,
  Thine was the perfect thought
That life should be bound in one
  By the strand of Love inwrought.

In the life of the fern and the lily,
  Of the dragon and the dove,
Still through the stress and struggle
  Waxes the bond of Love.

Out from the ruthless ages
  Rises, like incense mild,
The love of the man and the woman,
  The love of mother and child.

DAVID STARR JORDAN

WORLD VOICES

Out of the shadows of forgotten years,
Across the deeps from unremembered times,
Voices are swelling; varied lands and climes
Joining their echoes as each age appears
And, down the war-swept centuries, there nears
This mystic music, pure as vesper chimes,
Which melts our strange discordances, and rhymes
With all the whispers of the whirling spheres.
It floats past Babylon, the proud, the great;
Past ancient Egypt, tapestried with gold;
Past crumbling walls and Culture's rusted Gate
Where flowered world kingdoms, in the days of old.
These voices, now grown clear, articulate,
Proclaim Love's triumph, which the dawns foretold.

CHARLES RUSSELL WAKELEY

FROM "IF WINTER COMES"

. . . THE web and the tangle and the amenities of a minute fragment of human existence. Life. An odd business. Into life we come, mysteriously arrived, are set on our feet and on we go: functioning more or less ineffectively, passing through permutations and combinations; meeting the successive events, shocks, surprises of hours, days, years; becoming engulfed, submerged, foundered by them; all of us on the same adventure yet retaining nevertheless each his own individuality, as swimmers carrying each his undetachable burden through dark, enormous and cavernous seas. Mysterious journey! Uncharted, unknown, and finally— but there *is* no finality! Mysterious and stunning sequel— not end—to the mysterious and tremendous adventure! Finally, of this portion, death, disappearance,—gone! Astounding development! Mysterious and hapless arrival, tremendous and mysterious passage, mysterious and alarming departure. No escaping it; no volition to enter it or to avoid it; no prospect of defeating it or solving it. Odd affair! Mysterious and baffling conundrum to be mixed up in! . . . Life!

"Hapgood, the remedy's the old remedy. The old God. But it's more than that. It's Light: more light. The old revelation was good for the old world, and suited to the old world, and told in terms of the old world's understanding. Mystical for ages steeped in the mystical; poetic for minds receptive of nothing beyond story and allegory and parable. We want a new revelation in terms of the new world's understanding. We want light, light!" . . .

"I tell you, Hapgood, that plumb down in the crypt and abyss of every man's soul is a hunger, a craving for other food than this earthy stuff. . . . Light, light—that's what he wants." . . .

"I've got the secret. I've got the key to the riddle that's been puzzling me all my life. I've got the new revelation in terms good enough for me to understand. Light, more light. Here it is: God is . . . *love*. Not this, that, nor the other that the intelligence revolts at, and puts aside, and goes away, and goes on hungering, hungering and unsatisfied; nothing like that; but just this: plain for a child, clear as daylight for grown intelligence: God is . . . *love*. . . . 'He that dwelleth in love dwelleth in God and God in him; for God *is* love.' Ecstasy, Hapgood, ecstasy! It explains everything to me. I can reduce all the mysteries to terms of that."

"I tell you . . . old Sabre, when he was telling me that, was a pretty first-class advertisement for his own revelation. He'd found it all right. The look on him was nearer the divine than anything I've ever come near seeing. It certainly was."

A. S. M. HUTCHINSON

IT WILL NOT BE CONTEMNED

It will not be contemned of any one;
    Who thwarts it loses, and who serves it gains;
The hidden good it pays with peace and bliss,
    The hidden ill with pains.

It knows not wrath or pardon; utter-true
    Its measures mete, its faultless balance weighs;
Times are as naught, tomorrow it will judge,
    Or after many days.

Such is the Law which moves to Righteousness,
    Which none at last can turn aside or stay;
The heart of it is Love, the end of it
    Is Peace and Consummation sweet.

Obey!   EDWIN ARNOLD

"IN MY FLESH SHALL I SEE GOD"

I HAVE been fain of heaven; all my soul
Reached out to it in longing; all my heart
Sang with its sweetness; all my thoughts were filled
With visions wonderful that heaven alone
Could match the truth to; and I looked on Death
But as the angel with the flaming sword
Who guards the portals of God's paradise,
August discoverer of a land sublime.
Now all is changed; I think of heaven no more.

I dreamed of heaven's music, how the songs
Of choired seraphim reverberate
Through wide sky-sweeps of high-resounding air,
Tuned to the tall archangel's trumpet-notes.
But once I stood alone upon the shore,
And for the first time listened to the sea.
I heard it thunder on the bare, brown rocks,
That resonant roar back stupendous bass;
I heard the breakers bellow up the beach,
The following half-hush, the long, slow hiss,
When the unwilling waters seaward turn.

I came away; but since that time my dreams
Of heaven's music are become as naught.
I hear alone that grave and God-voiced sea.

I dreamed of heaven's glory, how the light
Would burst unspeakable upon mine eyes,
That never could be dazzled or dismayed
By all its perfect brightness; and I saw
The tree of life beside the crystal sea,
The many-tinted wings of angel-hosts,
The sparkling walls begemmed, the gates of pearl,
The streets of unstained gold, and at the last
Behind all these glowed out the Great White Throne.
But once I stood beside an inland lake

When autumn was abroad in all the land,
And earth drew nigh to sunset; and I saw
Fair armies of tall forest-trees decked out
As for some sweet and high solemnity,
Clothed on with color in a comely way—
The flaring yellow of the lithe, white birch,
The oak-tree's russet-brown or sober red,
And, best of all, those flame-imperial robes
Wherein the maple stands incarnadined.
Nor less in glory shone the radiant sky:
In the far east deep tints of purple-blue,
Ruby and violet clouds, and nearer west
A paler azure and a shy rose-pink,
And streaks of yellow-gold and dull red-gold
And gold that merged to blue and gold on gold,
And low above the trees one ball of gold,
Supreme, resplendent, building out broad paths
Across the smooth, unruffled lake, where lay
Each slightest color of the far-off sky.

I came away; but since that time my dreams
Of heaven's glory are become as naught
Before that wonder-sunset by the lake.

I dreamed of heaven's peace, how all the folk
Abiding there forever dwell in peace;
How never one discordant note might break
The harmony of that most rare delight;
How sweet tranquillity must needs abound
Under the eyes of God, which always smile.
But once I stood upon a mountain-top
Just after sunset, though the little moon
Had climbed up half her hill-way; and I saw
The great gray peaks about me loom up big.
Deep down below, the white clouds crept through all
The crevices, and topped the lower hills;
And leagues away, above that milk-white sea,
High sister-mountains shouldered up their heads,

Lifting themselves against the star-bright sky,
Which in the west yet held faint hints of gold,
And yet shone pale with looking on the sun.
And, oh! the night was still beyond all nights,
That ever hushed the hurried world to sleep.
Below the billowy mist shut out that world,
With all its wise old ways and foolish frets,
And left the eternal silence of the stars,
The eternal silence of the stable hills,
That have most peace of all created things.

I came away; but since that time my dreams
Of heaven's peace are all become as naught,
Because I met with peace upon the hills.

I dreamed of heaven's love, of such a love
As earth with all her sweetness could not know,
And found no image in my inmost soul
To figure forth that dream, but only felt
A high-exalting aspiration born
Of God's own whisper deep within my heart.
But once I stood beside a little bed
Whereon a child lay sleeping; one pink hand
With bits of fingers clutched the coverlid,
And one was pressed beneath a rosy cheek
That silken lashes swept; the wee, sweet mouth
Curved in a smile at gentle presences
By wiser heads perceived not. O'er the child
Hovered a woman, and I looked and saw
A light within her eyes that never yet
I saw the like of; 'twas the light of love,
Of such a love as made me reverent.

I turned away; but ever since my dreams
Of heaven's love are all become as naught.
I see no higher than those mother-eyes.

IRENE PETTIT McKEEHAN

THE TRUMPET OF THE LAW

Music is dead. An age, an age is dying.
Shreds of Uranian song, wild symphonies
Tortured with moans of butchered innocents,
Blow past us on the wind. Chaos resumes
His kingdom. All the visions of the world,
The visions that were music, being shaped
By law, moving in measure, treading the road
That suns and systems tread, O who can hear
Their music now? Urania bows her head.
Only the feet that move in order dance.
Only the mind attuned to that dread pulse
Of law throughout the universe can sing.
Only the soul that plays its rhythmic part
In that great measure of the tides and suns
Terrestrial and celestial, till it soar
Into the absolute melodies of heaven,
Only that soul, climbing the splendid road
Of law from height to height, may walk with God,
Shape its own sphere from chaos, conquer death,
Lay hold on life and liberty, and sing.

. . . .

Murmurs reach it still,
Rumours of that vast music which resolves
Our discords, and to this, to this attuned,
Though blindly, it responds. . . .

Ah, though beneath unpitying spheres
    Unreckoned seems our human cry,
In Thy deep law, beyond the years,
    Abides the Eternal memory.
Thy law is light, to eyes grown dull
    Dreaming of worlds like bubbles blown;
And Mercy that is merciful
    Shall keep Thy law and find its own.

Unchanging God, by that one Light
   Through which we grope to Truth and Thee,
Confound not yet our day with night,
   Break not the measures of Thy sea.
Hear not, though grief for chaos cry
   Or rail at Thine unanswering throne.
Thy law, Thy law, is liberty,
   And in Thy law we find our own.

.   .   .   .

      For in an hour
When, by the law of might, mankind could rise
No higher, into the deepening music stole
A loftier theme, a law that gathered all
The laws of earth into its broadening breast
And moved like one full river to the sea,
The law of Love. . . .

      O land, O beautiful land of Freedom,
Hold fast the faith which made and keeps you great.
With you, with you abide the faith and hope,
In this dark hour, of agonized mankind.
Hold to that law whereby the warring tribes
Were merged in nations, hold to that wide law
Which bids you merge the nations, here and now,
Into one people. Hold to that deep law
Whereby we reach the peace which is not death
But the triumphant harmony of Life,
Eternal Life, immortal Love, the Peace
Of worlds that sing around the throne of God.

                    ALFRED NOYES

THE MYSTIC TRUMPETER

I

HARK, some wild trumpeter, some strange musician,
Hovering unseen in air, vibrates capricious tunes to-night.

I hear thee trumpeter, listening alert I catch thy notes,
Now pouring, whirling like a tempest round me,
Now low, subdued, now in the distance lost.

.   .   .   .

III

Blow trumpeter free and clear, I follow thee,
While at thy liquid prelude, glad, serene,
The fretting world, the streets, the noisy hours of day with-
    draw,
A holy calm descends like dew upon me,
I walk in cool refreshing night the walks of Paradise,
I scent the grass, the moist air and the roses;
Thy song expands my numb'd imbonded spirit, thou freest,
    launchest me,
Floating and basking upon heaven's lake.

.   .   .   .

V

Blow again trumpeter! and for thy theme,
Take now the enclosing theme of all, the solvent and the
    setting,
Love, that is pulse of all, the sustenance and the pang,
The heart of man and woman all for love,
No other theme but love—knitting, enclosing, all-diffusing
    love.
O how the immortal phantoms crowd around me!
I see the vast alembic ever working, I see and know the
    flames that heat the world,
The glow, the blush, the beating hearts of lovers,
So blissful happy some, and some so silent, dark, and nigh
    to death;
Love, that is all the earth to lovers—love, that mocks time
    and space,

Love, that is day and night—love, that is sun and moon
and stars,
Love, that is crimson, sumptuous, sick with perfume,
No other words but words of love, no other thought but love.

VI

Blow again trumpeter—conjure war's alarums.
Swift to thy spell a shuddering hum like distant thunder rolls,
Lo, where the arm'd men hasten—lo, mid the clouds of dust
the glint of bayonets,
I see the grime-faced cannoneers, I mark the rosy flash amid
the smoke, I hear the cracking of the guns;
Nor war alone—thy fearful music-song, wild player, brings
every sight of fear,
The deeds of ruthless brigands, rapine, murder—I hear the
cries for help!
I see ships foundering at sea, I behold on deck and below
deck the terrible tableaus.

VII

O trumpeter, methinks I am myself the instrument thou
playest,
Thou melt'st my heart, my brain—thou movest, drawest,
changest them at will;
And now thy sullen notes send darkness through me,
Thou takest away all cheering light, all hope,
I see the enslaved, the overthrown, the hurt, the opprest of
the whole earth,
I feel the measureless shame and humiliation of my race, it
becomes all mine,
Mine too the revenges of humanity, the wrongs of ages,
baffled feuds and hatreds,
Utter defeat upon me weighs—all lost—the foe victorious,
(Yet 'mid the ruins Pride colossal stands unshaken to the
last,
Endurance, resolution to the last.)

VIII

Now trumpeter for thy close,
Vouchsafe a higher strain than any yet,
Sing to my soul, renew its languishing faith and hope,
Rouse up my slow belief, give me some vision of the future,
Give me for once its prophecy and joy.

O glad, exulting, culminating song!
A vigor more than earth's is in thy notes,
Marches of victory—man disenthral'd—the conqueror at
    last,
Hymns to the universal God from universal man—all joy!
A reborn race appears—a perfect world, all joy!
Women and men in wisdom innocence and health—all joy!
Riotous laughing bacchanals fill'd with joy!
War, sorrow, suffering gone—the rank earth purged—nothing
    but joy left!
The ocean fill'd with joy—the atmosphere all joy!
Joy! joy! in freedom, worship, love! joy in the ecstasy of
    life!
Enough to merely be! enough to breathe!
Joy! joy! all over joy!

                                        WHITMAN

NOTE IX

In this group perhaps we may find a still more mature, certainly a more confident, type of experience described. There is the same urgent pressure of Life evident here, although, on the whole, this fact is taken more philosophically, more joyously even. The moods of desperation and of a life-and-death struggle hitherto so prominent, recede into the background. Hope and love, victory and happiness, peace and the deep sense of the reality of God now prevail. The trend of life is more than ever consciously upward and forward.

1. *Arthur O'Shaughnessy* ("Ode"), lauds the creative power of the poet, the dreamer, the man of vision. Is he not in line with the very world-movement itself? The mightiest dreams of the men of greatest faith are all too small for the actual fulfilments of history. God is working out a vast world-harmony for all to enjoy. Those who scorn the vision of a noble future must be crowded aside to die in their smallness. Those who believe in God and Man and Life—call them dreamers, if you will—shall see their hopes more than realized.

In "Song of Palms," the same author draws a picture of luxurious tropical life. But the steady upward evolution of life is the keynote, as before.

2. The author of "Beauty's Birth" presents Life as Beauty—marvelous, intricate, orderly, and ravishing to the mind that obeys high impulses. In "It Is Enough," the same writer refuses to be oppressed by the all-too-prevalent mechanistic philosophy of our times. Pessimism fades before the surging and altogether natural impulse from within, which bids one rejoice in life, love, and prayer, and continue to dream of still greater experiences unfailing down the years.

3. The next ten writers pay a wonderful tribute to the power of Love and Religion as the inward urge of the divine life. Their own lives illustrate most truly the depths of their

conviction. The brief selection from *Hutchinson's* popular novel cleverly, and very dramatically, sums up the theme of his entire book. Spring, satisfaction of soul, light, and love cannot be far behind for those who seek for them, even in the bitter trials of life.

4. The author of "In My Flesh Shall I See God" gives a timely and very reverent illustration of the way in which the Life-Urge leads one to develop from the lower to the higher and more satisfactory views of life and duty. Developing the great longing expressed by the author of Job, she shows how one may seem to find full temporary satisfaction of soul— as in a literalistic interpretation of a great dramatic book like "The Revelation." Then gradually, and not without many misgivings, the ardent follower of the Urge finds (to his surprise) that Heaven may be found here in human experience; and the wonderful music and glory and peace and love discovered here, in Nature and in human hearts, so satisfy the inner longings that nothing remains to be desired. One need not climb the starry steeps, nor await a dim and distant Day, to experience the best which Life so freely offers.

5. *Alfred Noyes* ("The Trumpet of the Law"), and *Walt Whitman* ("The Mystic Trumpeter"), bring this group of writings to a fitting close with their songs of sturdy optimism. Out of the chaos of the Great World War *Noyes* sees the master hand of the Universe at work producing peace and order once more. The law of love divine shall win the great victory. Even now the listening ear can catch the sweet trumpet-notes which prophesy the ultimate triumph of goodness. *Whitman's* notes rise to the heights of extreme ecstasy as he, too, sees the mighty Power and Love of God ruling all, unifying all, turning all other forms of power into the permanent channels of joyous brotherhood.

III

GOD—THE INFINITE LIFE OF THE UNIVERSE

X

THE LOOM OF YEARS

In the light of the silent stars that shine on the struggling sea,
In the weary cry of the wind and the whisper of flower and
  tree,
Under the breath of laughter, deep in the tide of tears,
I hear the Loom of the Weaver that weaves the Web of Years.

The leaves of the winter wither and sink in the forest mould
To colour the flowers of April with purple and white and gold:
Light and scent and music die and are born again
In the heart of a grey-haired woman who wakes in a world of
  pain.

The hound, the fawn and the hawk, and the doves that croon
  and coo,
We are all one woof of the weaving and the one warp threads
  us through,
One flying cloud on the shuttle that carries our hopes and
  fears
As it goes thro' the Loom of the Weaver that weaves the
  Web of Years.

The crosiers of the fern, and the crown, the crown of the rose,
Pass with our hearts to the Silence where the wings of music
  close,
Pass and pass to the Timeless that never a moment mars,
Pass and pass to the Darkness that made the suns and stars.

Has the soul gone out in the Darkness? Is the dust sealed
  from sight?
Ah, hush, for the woof of the ages returns thro' the warp of
  the night!

Never that shuttle loses one thread of our hopes and fears,
As it comes thro' the Loom of the Weaver that weaves the
    Web of Years.

O, woven in one wide Loom thro' the throbbing weft of the
    whole,
One in spirit and flesh, one in body and soul,
The leaf on the winds of autumn, the bird in its hour to die,
The heart in its muffled anguish, the sea in its mournful cry,

One with the flower of a day, one with the withered moon,
One with the granite mountains that melt into the noon,
One with the dream that triumphs beyond the light of the
    spheres,
We come from the Loom of the Weaver that weaves the
    Web of Years.

ALFRED NOYES

THOU ART THE SKY

THOU art the sky and thou art the nest as well.

O thou beautiful, there in the nest it is thy love that en-
closes the soul with colours and sounds and odours.

There comes the morning with the golden basket in her
right hand bearing the wreath of beauty, silently to crown
the earth.

And there comes the evening over the lonely meadows
deserted by herds, through trackless paths, carrying cool
draughts of peace in her golden pitcher from the Western
ocean of rest.

But there, where spreads the infinite sky for the soul to
take her flight in, reigns the stainless white radiance. There
is no day nor night, nor form nor colour, and never, never a
word.

RABINDRANATH TAGORE

[From "Gitanjali," The Macmillan Co.]

THE HEART OF THE ETERNAL

THERE'S a wideness in God's mercy,
  Like the wideness of the sea;
There's a kindness in his justice,
  Which is more than liberty.

For the love of God is broader
  Than the measures of man's mind;
And the heart of the Eternal
  Is most wonderfully kind.

If our love were but more simple,
  We should take him at his word,
And our lives would be all sunshine
  In the sweetness of our Lord.

FREDERICK W. FABER

PRAISE

WHAT do they know of penitence
  Who never wrought Him wrong?
How can the sinless lift to him
  Redemption's triumph-song?

There lies an eloquence of praise
  Imprisoned in a tear
And crushed within a broken heart
  That God bends low to hear.

EDITH DALEY

THE LITTLE WORDS

WE are weary of little words,
  They seem so very small;
And yet they weave the river-song,
  Brook ripple and bird call.

Nor proud philosophy has found
 A straighter trail to God
Than all the faithful followers
 Of worn old words have trod.

For "love" and "home" are little words;
 And "flower" and "sea" and "star";
And yet they help the heart to find
 Where God and glory are!

      EDITH DALEY

WHEREVER THROUGH THE AGES

WHEREVER through the ages rise
The altars of self-sacrifice,
Where love its arms hath opened wide,
Or man for man has calmly died,

I see the same white wings outspread
That hovered o'er the Master's head;
And the great marvel of his death
To the one order witnesseth.

Up from undated time they come,
The martyr-souls of heathendom,
And to his cross and passion bring
Their fellowship of suffering;

Each in his measure but a part
Of the unmeasured Over-Heart,—
Guide, Comforter, and inward Word,
The eternal Spirit of the Lord!

      WHITTIER

SOMETIMES COMES TO SOUL AND SENSE

SOMETIMES comes to soul and sense
The feeling which is evidence

That very near about us lies
The realm of spiritual mysteries;
That all our sorrow, pain, and doubt,
A great compassion clasps about,
And law and goodness, love and force,
Are wedded fast beyond divorce.

WHITTIER

OUR DWELLING–PLACE

O GOD, our Help in ages past,
  Our Hope for years to come,
Our Shelter from the stormy blast,
  And our eternal Home!

Under the shadow of thy throne
  Thy saints have dwelt secure;
Sufficient is thine arm alone,
  And our defense is sure.

Before the hills in order stood,
  Or earth received her frame,
From everlasting thou art God,
  To endless years the same.

A thousand ages in thy sight
  Are like an evening gone;
Short as the watch that ends the night
  Before the rising sun.

The busy tribes of flesh and blood,
  With all their lives and cares,
Are carried downward by thy flood,
  And lost in following years.

O God, our Help in ages past,
  Our Hope for years to come,
Be thou our Guard while troubles last,
  And our eternal Home.

ISAAC WATTS

O LOVE, THAT DOST WITH GOODNESS CROWN

O Love, that dost with goodness crown
The years through all the ages down,
Our highest faith, our deepest cheer,
Is that thy life is ever near!

From planets singing on their way
To flowers that fear the eye of day,
From rivers that rejoicing go
To brooks that murmur sweet and low,

Well know I that the pageant vast,
So beautiful from first to last,
Is but the smile upon thy face,
The sign of love's unmeasured grace.

The seasons roll at thy command;
'Tis in thy strength the mountains stand;
And rooted are all things that bless
Deep in thy everlastingness.

Within thy circling arms we lie,
Safe-lapped in thine infinity,
O Love, who dost with goodness crown
The moments and the ages down!

JOHN W. CHADWICK

RHAPSODY OF THE WAVES

O, haste with me
To the sunny sea
Which God's great "fiat" made for thee!
Leave cankering care
That chains you there,
And fret and moil and drudgery:
Away! Away! From care and strife

To the sea a-teeming with finny life
All clad in gorgeous silver mail
Gliding through coral grove and dale,
Or sweeping on in circling play
'Mid ocean plants and bowers gay,
That graceful wave o'er Neptune's bed
Of pearly sands in beauty spread.

> Away, and flee
> To the glorious sea
> With its wild, wild waves,
> Not made for slaves
> Of pelf and self and vanity—

To the bounding and the swaying,
To the dashing and the spraying
And the ever-tireless playing:
To the rhythm and the singing,
And the deep diapason of the waves;
To the care-effacing soul-uplifting waves—
To the fierce wild rapture of the waves.

II

In the witching hour when the weary sun
Seeks his ocean bed, his day's work done;
In the wave he laves his brows that burn—
And, lo! to gold the bright waves turn.
'Tis the "Good-night" kiss of the King of Day,
As he seeks his couch, till Aurora's ray
His eyelids touch, to bid him arise
And run his course in the purple skies.
But when fast he closes his eyes in sleep,
The Queen of Night steals over the deep;
And the waves that had lost their burnished gold
Show silver bright in their every fold.
Then the twinkling stars peep down in glee
To mirror themselves in the silver sea.

When, lo! fair Dian for a space,
Draws a misty veil o'er her radiant face,
And sable darkness grows apace.

III

As from flinty rock the living spark,
Sudden—from out the waters dark—
Bursts forth a brightly flashing light
To chase the growing gloom of night.
Phosphoric sparks from crest to crest
Fly wild along the ocean's breast;
Kindling to flame the ocean wide,
Like burning Etna's molten tide;
The billows burn—the breakers glow—
Tossing flame to heaven as on they go.
The answering heavens flash back the light,
The welkin round is dazzling bright;
While rainbow tints their charms entwine—
Fit climax to a scene divine.
The Polar Lights, have they frisked away
From allotted bounds, like elfs at play,
To gambol free 'mid the breakers' foam,
Too gay to think of returning home?
Or have sea-nymphs gathered in sportive glee
To make a gladsome jubilee?
Or is it a host of angels bright
That have stolen out in the silent night
Thro' the pearly gates of the vaulted skies;
To dance on the foam in their silver attire
And sing "Glory to God!" on their heavenly lyre—
To hearten us mortals to arise
And sunder all unholy ties
And lift our souls to heaven above
Where reign unbounded joy and love?

IV

O, Mortal Man! whosoe'er thou be,
In rapture gaze on the glorious sea—
On the sea, and the moon, and the starry night,
With sparkling glory rich bedight;
Then, with swelling breast lift thy soul above
Till it burns and glows with a seraph's love,
And pour it forth in an endless flood
Of ardent praise to the Boundless Good,
Whose Infinite Might hath all things made,
From ocean vast to tiniest blade;
Tinting with beauty every one—
The faintest reflex of His own—
　　Then each bright gift to man hath given
　　To light him home to his native Heaven.

JOHN D. WALSHE

A SONG OF JOY

Joy! Joy! Infinite joy!
Wild as the fire in the heart of a boy;
Clean as the soul of the laughing breeze;
Pure as the heart of the dryad trees!

The sky is mine, the earth is mine,
The air and the sea and all that is;
But when I shall pass I shall walk divine
In ways more starry fair than this!

I say I have lived in a joyous world;
Where every loving dream comes true;
With comfort and plenty around me curled;
Where every moment is fresh and new.

It's great!—this life on the hills of Time,—
To follow the gleam and still endure,
To strive in joy for the High Sublime,
And know that the way of love is sure.

HENRY MEADE BLAND

FROM "SAUL"

o .   .   .   .

THEN the truth came upon me. No harp more—no song
   more! outbroke—

"I have gone the whole round of creation: I saw and I spoke:
I, a work of God's hand for that purpose, received in my brain
And pronounced on the rest of his handwork—returned him
   again
His creation's approval or censure: I spoke as I saw:
I report, as a man may of God's work—all's love, yet all's
   law.
Now I lay down the judgeship he lent me. Each faculty
   tasked
To perceive him, has gained an abyss, where a dewdrop was
   asked.
Have I knowledge? confounded, it shrivels at Wisdom laid
   bare.
Have I forethought? how purblind, how blank, to the Infinite
   Care!
Do I task any faculty highest, to image success?
I but open my eyes,—and perfection, no more and no less,
In the kind I imagined, full-fronts me, and God is seen God
In the star, in the stone, in the flesh, in the soul and the
   clod.
And thus looking within and around me, I ever renew
(With that stoop of the soul which in bending upraises it
   too)
The submission of man's nothing-perfect to God's all-com-
   plete,
As by each new obeisance in spirit, I climb to his feet.
Yet with all this abounding experience, this deity known,
I shall dare to discover some province, some gift of my own.

.   .   .   .

Do I find love so full in my nature, God's ultimate gift,
That I doubt his own love can compete with it? Here, the
    parts shift?
Here, the creature surpass the Creator,—the end, what
    Began?
Would I fain in my impotent yearning do all for this man,
And dare doubt he alone shall not help him, who yet alone
    can?

. . . .

"I believe it! 'Tis thou, God, that givest, 'tis I who receive:
In the first is the last, in thy will is my power to believe.
All's one gift: thou canst grant it moreover, as prompt to my
    prayer
As I breathe out this breath, as I open these arms to the air.
From thy will stream the worlds, life and nature, thy dread
    Sabaoth:
I will?—the mere atoms despise me! Why am I not loth
To look that, even that in the face too? Why is it I dare
Think but lightly of such impuissance? What stops my
    despair?
This;—'tis not what man Does which exalts him, but what
    man Would do!
See the King—I would help him but cannot, the wishes fall
    through.
Could I wrestle to raise him from sorrow, grow poor to enrich,
To fill up his life, starve my own out, I would—knowing
    which,
I know that my service is perfect. Oh, speak through me now!
Would I suffer for him that I love? So wouldst thou—so wilt
    thou!
So shall crown thee the topmost, ineffablest, uttermost
    crown—
And thy love fill infinitude wholly, nor leave up nor down
One spot for the creature to stand in! It is by no breath,
Turn of eye, wave of hand, that salvation joins issue with
    death!

As thy Love is discovered almighty, almighty be proved
Thy power, that exists with and for it, of being Beloved!
He who did most, shall bear most; the strongest shall stand
    the most weak.
'Tis the weakness in strength, that I cry for! my flesh, that
    I seek
In the Godhead! I seek and I find it. O Saul, it shall be
A Face like my face that receives thee; a Man like to me,
Thou shalt love and be loved by, forever: a Hand like this
    hand
Shall throw open the gates of new life to thee! See the
    Christ stand!"

BROWNING

THE MARSHES OF GLYNN

. . . .

O BRAIDED dusks of the oak and woven shades of the vine,
While the riotous noon-day sun of the June-day long did
    shine
Ye held me fast in your heart and I held you fast in mine;
But now when the noon is no more, and riot is rest,
And the sun is a-wait at the ponderous gate of the West,
And the slant yellow beam down the wood-aisle doth seem
Like a lane into heaven that leads from a dream,—
Ay, now, when my soul all day hath drunken the soul of the
    oak,
And my heart is at ease from men, and the wearisome sound
    of the stroke
  Of the scythe of time and the trowel of trade is low,
   And belief overmasters doubt, and I know that I know,
    And my spirit is grown to a lordly great compass within,
That the length and the breadth and the sweep of the
    Marshes of Glynn
Will work me no fear like the fear they have wrought me of
    yore

When length was fatigue, and when breadth was but bitter-
    ness sore,
And when terror and shrinking and dreary unnamable pain
Drew over me out of the merciless miles of the plain,—
Oh, now, unafraid, I am fain to face
    The vast sweet visage of space.

To the edge of the wood I am drawn, I am drawn,
Where the gray beach glimmering runs, as a belt of the dawn,
    For a mete and a mark
      To the forest-dark:—
          ·So:
Affable live-oak, leaning low,—
Thus—with your favor—soft, with a reverent hand
(Now lightly touching your person, Lord of the land!),
Bending your beauty aside, with a step I stand
On the firm-packed sand,
          Free
By a world of marsh that borders a world of sea.
    Sinuous southward and sinuous northward the shimmering
      band
    Of the sand-beach fastens the fringe of the marsh to the
      folds of the land.
Inward and outward to northward and southward the beach-
    lines linger and curl
As a silver-wrought garment that clings to and follows the
    firm sweet limbs of a girl.
Vanishing, swerving, evermore curving again into sight,
Softly the sand-beach wavers away to a dim gray looping of
    light.
And what if behind me to westward the wall of the woods
    stands high?
The world lies east: how ample, the marsh and the sea and
    the sky!
A league and a league of marsh-grass, waist-high, broad in
    the blade,

Green, and all of a height, and unflecked with a light or a
    shade,
Stretch leisurely off, in a pleasant plain,
To the terminal blue of the main.

Oh, what is abroad in the marsh and the terminal sea?
    Somehow my soul seems suddenly free
From the weighing of fate and the sad discussion of sin,
By the length and the breadth and the sweep of the marshes
    of Glynn.

Ye marshes, how candid and simple and nothing-withholding
    and free
Ye publish yourselves to the sky and offer yourselves to the
    sea!
Tolerant plains, that suffer the sea and the rains and the
    sun,
Ye spread and span like the catholic man who hath mightily
    won
God out of knowledge and good out of infinite pain
And sight out of blindness and purity out of a stain.
As the marsh-hen secretly builds on the watery sod,
Behold I will build me a nest on the greatness of God:
I will fly in the greatness of God as the marsh-hen flies
In the freedom that fills all the space 'twixt the marsh and
    the skies:
By so many roots as the marsh-grass sends in the sod
I will heartily lay me a-hold on the greatness of God:
Oh, like to the greatness of God is the greatness within
The range of the marshes, the liberal marshes of Glynn.

. . . .

SIDNEY LANIER

TINTERN ABBEY

. . . THESE beauteous forms,
Through a long absence, have not been to me

As is a landscape to a blind man's eye:
But oft, in lonely rooms, and 'mid the din
Of towns and cities, I have owed to them
In hours of weariness, sensations sweet,
Felt in the blood, and felt along the heart;
And passing even into my purer mind,
With tranquil restoration:—feelings too
Of unremembered pleasure: such, perhaps,
As have no slight or trivial influence
On that best portion of a good man's life,
His little, nameless, unremembered acts
Of kindness and of love. Nor less, I trust,
To them I may have owed another gift,
Of aspect more sublime; that blessèd mood,
In which the burthen of the mystery,
In which the heavy and the weary weight
Of all this unintelligible world,
Is lightened:—that serene and blessèd mood,
In which the affections gently lead us on,—
Until, the breath of this corporeal frame
And even the motion of our human blood
Almost suspended, we are laid asleep
In body, and become a living soul:
While with an eye made quiet by the power
Of harmony, and the deep power of joy,
We see into the life of things.

   . . . I have learned
To look on nature, not as in the hour
Of thoughtless youth; but hearing oftentimes
The still, sad music of humanity,
Nor harsh, nor grating, though of ample power
To chasten and subdue. And I have felt
A presence that disturbs me with the joy
Of elevated thoughts; a sense sublime
Of something far more deeply interfused,

Whose dwelling is the light of setting suns,
And the round ocean and the living air,
And the blue sky, and in the mind of man;
A motion and a spirit, that impels
All thinking things, all objects of all thought,
And rolls through all things. Therefore am I still
A lover of the meadows and the woods,
And mountains; and of all that we behold
From this green earth; of all the mighty world
Of eye, and ear,—both what they half create,
And what perceive; well pleased to recognize
In nature and the language of the sense,
The anchor of my purest thoughts, the nurse,
The guide, the guardian of my heart, and soul
Of all my moral being.

  .   .   .   .

Knowing that Nature never did betray
The heart that loved her; 'tis her privilege,
Through all the years of this our life, to lead
From joy to joy: for she can so inform
The mind that is within us, so impress
With quietness and beauty, and so feed
With lofty thoughts, that neither evil tongues,
Rash judgments, nor the sneers of selfish men,
Nor greetings where no kindness is, nor all
The dreary intercourse of daily life,
Shall e'er prevail against us or disturb
Our cheerful faith, that all which we behold
Is full of blessings.

WORDSWORTH

THE HIGHER PANTHEISM

THE sun, the moon, the stars, the seas, the hills and the
    plains—
Are not these, O Soul, the Vision of Him who reigns?

Is not the Vision He? tho' He be not that which He seems?
Dreams are true while they last, and do we not live in dreams?

Earth, these solid stars, this weight of body and limb,
Are they not sign and symbol of thy division from Him?

Dark is the world to thee: thyself art the reason why;
For is He not all but that which has power to feel 'I am I'?

Glory about thee, without thee; and thou fulfillest thy doom
Making Him broken gleams, and a stifled splendour and
    gloom.

Speak to Him thou for He hears, and Spirit with Spirit
    can meet—
Closer is He than breathing, and nearer than hands and feet.

God is law, say the wise; O soul, and let us rejoice,
For if He thunder by law the thunder is yet His voice.

Law is God, say some: no God at all, says the fool;
For all we have power to see is a straight staff bent in a pool;

And the ear of man cannot hear, and the eye of man cannot
    see;
But if we could see and hear, this Vision—were it not He?

TENNYSON

[From "The Works of Tennyson," The Macmillan Co.]

FLOWER IN THE CRANNIED WALL

FLOWER in the crannied wall,
I pluck you out of the crannies,
I hold you here, root and all, in my hand,
Little flower—but *if* I could understand
What you are, root and all, and all in all,
I should know what God and man is.

TENNYSON

[From "The Works of Tennyson," The Macmillan Co.]

THE SINGER OF THE STILLNESS

I AM the great Singer in the Stillness;
Those who listen at dawn in the High Places may hear me;
My voice is the wind as it sweeps over the prairies,
And at night, when the stars sing in the heavens,
My song mingles with the music of the spheres.
The bare oak branches in the winter are my harp strings,
And my words are heard in the throbbing of the moon-
    haunted sea.
Great things have I to tell to those who hark to me;
I lift them above the world and they see life spread out be-
    fore them,
For I am the Wisdom of the ages, I am the great Singer in
    the Stillness.

                BERTHA TEN EYCK JAMES

IMMANENCE

I COME in the little things,
  Saith the Lord;
Not borne on morning wings
Of majesty; but I have set my feet
Amidst the delicate and bladed wheat
That springs triumphant in the furrowed sod—
There do I dwell, in weakness and in power;
Not broken or divided, said our God!
In your straight garden plot I come to flower;
  About your porch my vine,
  Meek, fruitful, doth entwine,
Waits, at the threshold, Love's appointed hour.

I come in the little things,
  Saith the Lord;
Yea, on the glancing wings
Of eager birds, the soft and pattering feet

Of furred and gentle beasts, I come to meet
Your hard and wayward heart. In brown bright eyes
That peep from out the brake, I stand confest.
On every nest
Where feathery Patience is content to brood
And leaves her pleasure for the high emprise
Of motherhood—
There does my Godhead rest.

I come in the little things,
Saith the Lord;
My starry wings I do forsake,
Love's highway of humility to take;
Meekly I fit my stature to your need.
In beggar's part
About your gates I shall not cease to plead
As man, to speak with man
Till by such art
I shall achieve my immemorial plan;
Pass the low lintel of the human heart.

EVELYN UNDERHILL

OUT OF THE VAST

THERE'S part of the sun in an apple,
   There's part of the moon in a rose;
There's part of the flaming Pleiades
   In every leaf that grows.
Out of the vast comes nearness;
   For the God whose love we sing
Lends a little of his heaven
   To every living thing.

AUGUSTUS WRIGHT BORNBERGER

GOD IS NOT DUMB

GOD is not dumb, that he should speak no more!
If thou hast wanderings in the wilderness
And findest not Sinai—'tis thy soul is poor!
There towers the mountain of the Voice no less,
Which whoso seeks shall find—but he who bends
Intent on manna still and mortal ends,
Sees it not,—neither hears its thundered lore.

JAMES RUSSELL LOWELL

OH! THE EARTH AND THE AIR!

OH! the earth and the air!
Honeysuckle and rose:
Fir trees tapering high
Into the deep repose
Of the fleckless sky:
Hills that climb and are strong,
Basking contented plain:
Sunlight poured out along
The sea of the grass like rain:
Spice-burdened winds that rise,
Whisper, wander and hush;
And the caroling harmonies
Of robin and quail and thrush.
O God! Thy world is fair!

And this but the place of his feet!
I had cried, "Let me see, let me hear,
Show me the ways of thy hands."
For it all was a riddle drear
And I fainted to understand.
Canopy close curtained round,
Part not nor lift from the ground;

Move not your finger tips,
Firs, from the heaven's lips.
When this is the place of his feet
How should I bear to raise
My blasted vision to meet
The inconceivable blaze
Of his majesty complete!

JAMES T. MCKAY

DAY

I WAKE.
A new day pours over me its blossom,
Fragrant with sun-thoughts.

My ears are opened
To the poesy of winds and waves
Echoing with the song of jubilant birds.

My eyes are opened.
The vault of heaven spans the world
In its vaulted core, the sun.

I was asleep.
My soul adventured I know not whither—
No sun was there.

When darkness came, I trembled.
Death was there,
Death and hissing tongues.

Now is earth's day.
Insects throng from her lap,
Gambol in the blithesome air.

Whither is passed that uncouth darkness?
Whither has it fled away?
Day-beams now are everywhere,
A world built all of day-beams.

To bathe my hair in that sea of light,
Which floods the grass,
And kisses the dust
So that it bourgeons in myriad hues!

To catch the scent of creative winds,
That dance on my forehead,
Play upon my nostrils!

Sparkling day!
You are God's laughing eye,
The mirror of His soul.

His thoughts
Flash out from the abysses,
From the crypts of heaven, from constellations,
A fiery host of seraphim.

SIGBJÖRN OBSTFELDER

ABOVE THE HEAVENS

ABOVE the gold the sunbeams fling
    With bird-songs drifting through,
God's glory is a richer thing,
    And sweeter singing too.

Above the azure wide and high
    The steady, candid blue,
God's glory is a vaster sky,
    Illimitably true.

Above the faintest, farthest star
    In distant chaos wrought,
God's glory, infinitely far
    Transcends our feeble thought.

Yet God's rich glow, and God's great song,
　　And God's vast heaven of blue;
And God's far starlight ages long,
　　Comes down to me and you!

AMOS R. WELLS

BLIND

"Show me your God!" the doubter cries.
I point him out the smiling skies;
I show him all the woodland greens;
I show him peaceful sylvan scenes;
I show him winter snows and frost;
I show him waters tempest-tossed;
I show him hills rock-ribbed and strong;
I bid him hear the thrush's song;
I show him flowers in the close—
The lily, violet and rose;
I show him rivers, babbling streams;
I show him youthful hopes and dreams;
I show him stars, the moon, the sun;
I show him deeds of kindness done;
I show him joy, I show him care,
And still he holds his doubting air,
And faithless goes his way, for he
Is blind of soul, and cannot see!

JOHN KENDRICK BANGS

FROM "THE SPELL OF THE YUKON"

But the stars throng out in their glory,
　　And they sing of the God in man;
They sing of the Mighty Master,
　　Of the loom his fingers span,

Where a star or a soul is a part of the whole,
And weft in the wondrous plan.

Here by the camp-fire's flicker,
Deep in my blanket curled,
I long for the peace of the pine-gloom,
Where the scroll of the Lord is unfurled,
And the wind and the wave are silent,
And world is singing to world.

ROBERT SERVICE

THE SPACIOUS FIRMAMENT ON HIGH

THE spacious firmament on high,
With all the blue ethereal sky,
And spangled heavens, a shining frame,
Their great Original proclaim.
The unwearied sun from day to day
Does his Creator's power display,
And publishes to every land
The work of an Almighty hand.

Soon as the evening shades prevail
The moon takes up the wondrous tale,
And nightly to the listening earth
Repeats the story of her birth;
Whilst all the stars that round her burn,
And all the planets in their turn,
Confirm the tidings as they roll,
And spread the truth from pole to pole.

What though in solemn silence all
Move round the dark terrestrial ball?
What though no real voice nor sound
Amid their radiant orbs be found?
In reason's ear they all rejoice

And utter forth a glorious voice,
Forever singing as they shine,
"The hand that made us is divine."

JOSEPH ADDISON

GOD OF THE EARTH, THE SKY, THE SEA

GOD of the earth, the sky, the sea,
Of all above and all below,
Creation lives and moves in thee,
Thy present life through all doth flow.

Thy love is in the sunshine's glow,
Thy life is in the quickening air;
When lightnings flash and storm-winds blow,
There is thy power, thy law is there.

We feel thy calm at evening's hour,
Thy grandeur in the march of night;
And when the morning breaks in power,
We hear thy word, "Let there be light!"

But higher far, and far more clear,
Thee in man's spirit we behold;
Thine image and thyself are there,—
The indwelling God, proclaimed of old.

SAMUEL LONGFELLOW

GOD IS AT THE ORGAN

GOD is at the organ;
I can hear
A mighty music echoing,
Far and near.

God is at the organ
  And the keys
Are storm-strewn billows,
  Moorlands, trees.

God is at the organ,
  I can hear
A mighty music, echoing
  Far and near.

JOYCE KILMER

EXALTATION

REJOICE with wonder, O my soul, rejoice!
  And you, ye starry heavens, thou vast hush,
That art so far thou hast for us no voice,
  Lend me your silent rapture! With a rush
Come, ye Æolian winds that bring the blush
  Of holy morning to the eastern sky!
And you, ye springs and fountains that forth gush
  To seek the sea! Sweet flowers that smile and die,
And O, thou glorious majesty on high,
  Which art the life of all this beauteous Earth!
Come and possess me as the birds that fly,
  And lift my being into vocal birth,
Deep on wide wings ascending, till I tell
The glory of our God, that ye have told so well!

PAUL SHIVELL

THE FIRST CAUSE

. . . .

DOUBTLESS we think the Being who made man,
The visible world, space powdered thick with stars,
The golden fruit whose core is curious life,
Created all things—love, and law, and death;
Fate, the crowned forehead; Will, the sceptred hand.

Perchance—perchance: yet need it be that He
Who planted us is the Head-gardener? What
If beyond Him rose rank on rank, as the bulb
Is higher than the crystals of its food,
And he who sets it, higher than the flower,
And he that owns the garden, more than all?

The great Cause works through lesser ones. . . .
Know we the limit of the power He gives
To lesser Wills to will imperfectly?
Is earth that limit? Is the last link man,
Between the finite and the infinite? . . .

O mother world! we stammer at thy knee
Vainly our childish questions. 'Tis enough
For such as we to know, that on His throne,
Nearer than we can think, and farther off
Than any mind can fathom, sits the One,
And sees to it—though pain and evil come,
And all may not be good—that all is well.

EDWARD ROWLAND SILL

THE HOUNDS OF GOD

THE hounds of God across the years
Are running swift and true.
Far and away they seem to play,
But they're tracking me and you.

The king is seated on his throne,
His courtiers all around him,
They see him start and grasp his heart,—
The hounds of God have found him.

At low midnite the wastrel wakes
Afraid upon his bed,
For the hollow sounds of the baying hounds
Are ringing in his head.

The wicked woman wipes her lips
And says, " 'Tis naught! 'Tis naught!"
Yet the velvet feet of the hounds so fleet
Whisper behind her thought.

They have torn great empires limb from limb;
They have conquered the conquerors;
And their teeth have hurt for sins of dirt,
In plagues that are worse than wars.

They have cruelly taken the old man down,
They have bitten the babe at the breast;
For there's never a sin of kith or kin
Can escape their fateful quest.

Before us goes God's angel tall
Flying upon the wind,
And sweet as the dawn he beckons us on—
But the hounds of God are behind!

FRANK CRANE

THE ETERNAL SPIRIT

O Thou that weavest sun and stars
 Upon Thine everlasting loom,
Whose pattern makes of Earth and Mars
 But glittering spots of flame—to whom
Save Thee, Thou source of soul and fire,
Shall I, unkindled dust, aspire?

The universe that thrills with Thee
 Is half Thyself yet is not Thou,
Behind the quivering mask I see,
 With them of old, Thy face and brow;
Like Moses on the awful height,
I all but touch Thee day and night!

. . . .

Their flames are one with those that shine
   In Sirius and the Milky Way,
Both share the Energy divine,
   Nor mind nor matter knows decay—
Stars fall, force changes, men must bow,
Yet all is life, and life is—*Thou!*

FREDERIC L. KNOWLES

NOTE X

For many thousands of years man has felt himself related to, and subject to, certain mystic Powers of Nature which have defied definition but which have become ever more real and mighty with expanding human experience. The poems of this tenth section suggest the overwhelming results of man's earnest outreaching for a knowledge of these environing Powers. As varied as the hues and voices of Nature herself are the crowding impressions which puzzle one who persists in asking: What is this Power? Especially when one realizes the unity of Nature and when all of these characteristics are felt to belong to the One rather than to the many, does the questioner resort to such terms as *Infinite* and *Universal* to describe the tremendous might and astounding versatility of this Being of beings, and the Heart of all sentient life. The fact that language exhausts itself in endeavoring to express human-divine relationships makes the chastened phrases, and even the reverent pauses, in such poetry to reflect the most sincere moods of the inmost life of man.

1. In "The Loom of Years," *Alfred Noyes* very clearly represents the monotony and the eternal pressure of Life by the steady hum of the loom. The swift movement of the shuttle, with its swish and whir and chug, suggests the successive acts of creation as Nature moves forward in fulfilment of her studied plan of life. All experiences of life, sad and glad, and all the glory and decadence of life, have their destined part in the pattern which, act by act, moves forward to ultimate completion. Back of all, guiding all, are the steady hand and the master mind of the Weaver, God. The poet gives one confidence in the final outcome, even though for the moment the jar of machinery and the snap of threads seem to spell discord and defeat. And above all is felt the grand unity of the entire pattern of experience.

2. With true Eastern delicacy and reverence, *Tagore* ("Thou Art the Sky"), finds the Nameless One in all Nature; suggesting a very riot of color and restful beauty and love as

the divine environment which invites the human soul to try its powers of flight.

3. The seven succeeding poems pay tribute to the unfailing interest and love of God—sufficient for every human need.

4. In "Rhapsody of the Waves" and "A Song of Joy," two of our newer Western poets have drawn upon all the sensuous beauty and joy of Nature to picture their sense of man's happy relationship to the Divine.

5. *Browning's* "Saul" is one of our greatest classics on the subject of divine love and power. When man (represented by David) fails, at his desperate best, to bring back love and happiness to the stolid face of a King Saul, it is the all-victorious love of God which turns human defeat into divine success. Humanity can never fail as long as it co-operates with God.

6. "The Marshes of Glynn," "Tintern Abbey," and "The Higher Pantheism" are three more classic poems devoted to this same great theme. *Lanier*, worn out with a hopeless struggle against the disease which led to his untimely death, and thoroughly disgusted with the futile theological and sectarian controversies between the churches of his home town, turns with a great sigh of relief to the noble marshes which remind him so forcefully of the breadth and humanity of the all-inclusive God.

With less desperation, and with more of the meditative spirit of the artist, *Wordsworth* derives his supreme inspiration from the beauty of England's fields and streams.

Tennyson defends his experience in finding God in the universe and its laws against the narrow theologians and the devotees of mechanistic science who regard his views as too pantheistic, or too mystical. He finds God in all Nature's processes, and in the quiet communion of man's aspiring spirit with its greater Counterpart, which both fills the universe with its glory and power and also enters the portals of human life in ways simple enough to be apprehended by all earnest souls.

7. The following fourteen little poems emphasize, in varying detail, the ever-present and friendly nature of God, who

appeals to man's nobler self in quiet and natural ways. To appreciate truly the gift of such fellowship is to enter into an experience of rapturous joy akin to Nature's own.

8. Through the symbol of a hierarchy of divine beings, the author of "The First Cause" attempts to lead men's thoughts beyond the ordinary paltry conceptions of deity to One of cosmic grandeur; and yet is He master of his worlds and victor over all of life's ills.

9. In "The Hounds of God," two clear forces are seen at work in men's lives: (1) Man's native tendency to avoid the road of upward struggle and to choose the lower road of passion and sensual delight. (2) The seeking Love of God, always luring man by kindness; but, failing in that, driving him by sting of conscience to rise to his true heights of greatness. Divine Love cannot allow any man to fail of his high purpose in life.

10. Finally, in "The Eternal Spirit," we are reminded of both Tennyson and Noyes. God is the Life Complete which informs and shapes the progress of the whole, and yet enters, in generous measure, into the limited experience of mankind.

THE PILGRIM

It is so long a way that I must go,
  A pilgrim in a kingdom that is strange!
Only my Distant City do I know,
  And all the rest is changelessness—and change.

The changeless way that all my fathers trod,
  The way of Life, that is so old, so old!
And yet so changeful that each travelled rod
  Discloses alterations manifold!

It is so strange a way that I must go,
  I scarcely know how I might best prepare.
Only my Distant City do I know,
  And all my heart is willed to conquer there!

O, brave to tread the way as yet untrod,
  Undaunted by the dangers that I see,
This is the spirit I would show the God
  Who showed my Distant City unto me!

CHARLES M. LUCE

THE SABBATH OF THE SOUL

Work is not all, however much we need
The stress of toil, the sobering hand of care,
Compulsion strong, enforcing us to bear
The heavier burden with the lesser meed.
Shall work be all? Shall man no longer heed
The whisper of the help from otherwhere
Of vibrant strength the weakest soul may share?
Shall toil-dimmed eyes God's promise fail to read?

The soul must keep its Sabbaths and renew
The inner life that makes the outer strong,
By finding in the Infinite its rest.
Let not the good obscure the best, its due;
The hours of work if they be not too long
Are good. The Sabbath of the soul is best.

LAURA BELL EVERETT

O POWER, WHOSE VISION BLINDED

O POWER, whose vision blinded Paul and shone through
  Christ, on thee we call.
Hail, soul of Man's fine harmonies which subtly blend to
  gladness calm.
Hail, ruler here beneath the skies: Hail, fire and flight of
  Hebrew's psalm;
Mid creeds and temples' ruin strown, lead us by thy still
  light alone.
Faiths old and dead have vanished before the splendors of
  thy flame,
Thine impulse thrills to strength the social heart and warms
  the palest hope to life;
It makes the coldest spirit smart in anguish for our human
  strife.
Thou mouldest states and Gods like clay, and every shape
  attests thy sway.
Old laws expire, new minds desire the quickening which thou
  sendest forth.
New meanings thrill through threadbare forms.
New life inspires old melodies: still the heavens sought not
  in vain, say, "God is Man's sublimest pain."
Radiant now are Reason's eyes, relieved at last from anxious
  quest,
As seeing from a crowd arise a long sought face beloved best.
O soul of Man's fine harmonies, mysterious more the better
  known—we thee adore.

ALFRED CLOAKE

WHAT IS NATURE'S SELF?

NAY, what is Nature's
Self, but an endless
Strife toward music,
Euphony, rhyme?

Trees in their blooming,
Tides in their flowing,
Stars in their circling,
Tremble with song.

God on His throne is
Eldest of poets;
Unto His measures
Moveth the whole.

WILLIAM WATSON

PENETRALIA

I AM a part of all you see
In Nature; part of all you feel:
I am the impact of the bee
Upon the blossom; in the tree
I am the sap,—that shall reveal
The leaf, the bloom,—that flows and flutes
Up from the darkness through its roots.

I am the vermeil of the rose,
The perfume breathing in its veins;
The gold within the mist that glows
Along the west and overflows
With light the heaven; the dew that rains
Its freshness down and strings with spheres
Of wet the webs and oaten ears.

I am the egg that folds the bird;
The song that beaks and breaks its shell;

The laughter and the wandering word
The water says; and, dimly heard,
The music of the blossom's bell
When soft winds swing it; and the sound
Of grass slow-creeping o'er the ground.

I am the warmth, the honey-scent
That throats with spice each lily-bud
That opens, white with wonderment,
Beneath the moon; or, downward bent,
Sleeps with a moth beneath its hood:
I am the dream that haunts it too,
That crystallizes into dew.

I am the seed within the pod;
The worm within its closed cocoon:
The wings within the circling clod,
The germ that gropes through soil and sod
To beauty, radiant in the noon:
I am all these, behold! and more—
I am the love at the world-heart's core.

MADISON CAWEIN

PURPOSE

DEEPLY and long the sap must flow
Ere the merest layer of elm can grow.

Many a wave's recurrent shock
Is needed to smooth the tiniest rock.

Thousands of leaves must fade and fall
To make the mould by the garden wall.

Thus, as the patient seasons roll,
Slowly is fashioned a human soul.

Purpose and failure and purpose still,
Steadily moved by a quiet will—

Layer on layer in sturdy way,
Hardly seen the growth of a day—

Times of failure, and fear and fall,
But one strong tendency through it all—

God and purpose and sun by sun
Reach the stars before they are done!

AMOS R. WELLS

RELIANCE ON GOD

IF thou hast ever felt that all on earth
Is transient and unstable, that the hopes
Which man reposes on his brother man
Are but broken reeds; if thou hast seen
That life itself "is but a vapor," sprung
From time's upheaving ocean, decked, perhaps
With here and there a rainbow, but full soon
To be dissolved and mingled with the vast
And fathomless expanse that rolls its waves
On every side around thee; if thy heart
Has deeply felt all this, and thus has learned
That earth has no security, then go
And place thy trust in God.

The bliss of earth
Is transient as the colored light that beams
In morning dewdrops. Yet a little while,
And all that earth can show of majesty,
Of strength, or loveliness, shall fade away
Like vernal blossoms. From the conqueror's hand
The sceptre and the sword shall pass away;

The mighty ones of earth shall lay them down
In their low beds, and Death shall set his seal
On Beauty's marble brow, and cold and pale,
Bloomless and voiceless, shall the lovely ones
Go to the "congregation of the dead."

Yea, more than this: the mighty rocks that lift
Their solemn forms upon the mountain heights,
Like time's proud citadels, to bear the storms
And wrecks of ages,—these, too, shall decay,
And Desolation's icy hand shall wave
O'er all that thou canst see; blot out the suns
That shed their glory o'er uncounted worlds;
Call in the distant comets from their wild
And devious course, and bid them cease to move;
And clothe the heavens in darkness. But the power
Of God, his goodness, and his grace, shall be
Unchanged, when all the worlds that he hath made
Have ceased their revolutions. When the suns
That burn in yonder sky have poured their last,
Their dying glory o'er the remains of space,
Still, God shall be the same, the same in love,
In majesty, in mercy: then rely
In faith on him, and thou shalt never find
Hope disappointed, or reliance vain.

CASKET

WHO CAN TELL?

Great Nature, with what wonders fraught,
Thy secrets we with subtlest thought,
    In vain essay;
We see thy face, we know in part,
But may not pierce thy inner heart
    With reason's ray.

We watch with constant efforts new,
The stars afloat in liquid blue;
      But how unfold
Of what these shining orbs are made,
Whence luminous, or when to fade,
      Or how controlled?

The regal sun that never tires—
What fount supplies his ceaseless fires
      And golden light?
And whence the silver of the sphere,
Which wanders calm her pathway clear,
      To rule the night?

How gauge her finest influence wide
On mortal man and swelling tide
      And verdant dale?
Or tell how clouds from middle air,
Enormous though the weight they bear
      In gauzy veil,

In crystal drop or folded flake
Of snow, descend on mountain lake
      And torrent free;
Or riding on the northern gale,
Come charging down in deadly hail
      On flower and tree?

What laws confine the rolling seas,
'Mid tempest mild or softest breeze,
      To ebb and flow?
To boom in wrath 'gainst jutting rock
Or lave the strand with gentler shock
      And murmur low?

The struggling winds, who chains them fast,
Or swings them loose in sweeping blast;
      Then bids them back

To darksome cave, like conquered steeds,
While zephyrs play among the reeds
    That escaped their wrack?

Who bids the avalanche at rest,
Speed merciless from mountain crest
    On vale below?
Or Ætna burst his rocky band,
And fiercely burning, o'er the land
    Destructive flow?

Ah! none save Him, who great and small
From naught to being called them all;
    All comprehends;
'Tis He, the one Eternal Cause
Who guideth each with wisest laws
    To wisest ends.

JOHN D. WALSHE

A VALEDICTION

GOD be with thee, my belovèd,—GOD be with thee!
    Else alone thou goest forth,
    Thy face unto the north,
Moor and pleasance all around thee and beneath thee
    Looking equal in one snow;
    While I, who try to reach thee,
    Vainly follow, vainly follow
    With the farewell and the hollo,
    And cannot reach thee so.
    Alas, I can but teach thee!
GOD be with thee, my belovèd,—GOD be with thee!

II

Can I teach thee, my belovèd,—can I teach thee?
    If I said, 'Go left or right,'
    The counsel would be light,

The wisdom, poor of all that could enrich thee;
      My right would show like left;
      My raising would depress thee,
      My choice of light would blind thee,
      Of way—would leave behind thee,
      Of end—would leave bereft.
      Alas, I can but bless thee!
May GOD teach thee, my belovèd,—may GOD teach thee!

III

Can I bless thee, my belovèd,—can I bless thee?
      What blessing word can I
      From mine own tears keep dry?
What flowers grow in my field wherewith to dress thee?
      My good reverts to ill;
      My calmnesses would move thee,
      My softnesses would prick thee,
      My bindings up would break thee,
      My crownings curse and kill.
      Alas, I can but love thee!
May GOD bless thee, my belovèd,—may GOD bless thee!

IV

Can I love thee, my belovèd,—can I love thee?
      And is *this* like love, to stand
      With no help in my hand,
When strong as death I fain would watch above thee?
      My love-kiss can deny
      No tear that falls beneath it;
      Mine oath of love can swear thee
      From no ill that comes near thee,
      And thou diest while I breathe it,
      And *I*—I can but die!
May GOD love thee, my belovèd,—may GOD love thee!

ELIZABETH BARRETT BROWNING

WHERE IS HEAVEN?

WHERE is Heaven? Is it not
Just a friendly garden plot,
Walled with stone and roofed with sun,
Where the days pass one by one
Not too fast and not too slow,
Looking backward as they go
At the beauties left behind
To transport the pensive mind.

Does not Heaven begin that day
When the eager heart can say,
Surely God is in this place,
I have seen Him face to face
In the loveliness of flowers,
In the service of the showers,
And His voice has talked to me
In the sunlit apple tree.

BLISS CARMAN

HYMN OF TRUST

O LOVE Divine, that stooped to share
   Our sharpest pang, our bitterest tear,
On Thee we cast each earth-born care,
   We smile at pain while Thou art near!

Though long the weary way we tread,
   And sorrow crown each lingering year,
No path we shun, no darkness dread,
   Our hearts still whispering, Thou art near!

When drooping pleasure turns to grief,
   And trembling faith is changed to fear,
The murmuring wind, the quivering leaf,
   Shall softly tell us, Thou art near!

On Thee we fling our burdening woe,
    O Love Divine, forever dear,
Content to suffer while we know,
    Living and dying, Thou art near!

OLIVER WENDELL HOLMES

NOTE XI

THESE eleven poems represent the interplay of sunshine and shadow in human experience. Each writer shows a different way to the realization of God. Now it is a heroic pilgrimage toward the City Ideal; again, it is attained through the restfulness and renewing vigor of meditation. Now it is the struggle upward from beast to manhood, with many a failure on the long, trying road, but with the fruits of victory already assured; again, it is the mysterious but almighty power which masters and moulds, thrills and attunes, man's inharmonious life until his whole nature breaks forth into the divine harmonies. Found in all Nature's varied forms of progress and decay, and most of all in the love of man for his kind, human faith in the active presence and goodness of God is both justifiable and inevitable.

XII

AND YET I KNOW

AND yet I know when all my faiths had fled,
  And every god that men had made through years
In their own image from their hope and dread,
  To give them comfort in their faith and fears—

When all these seemed to me a fairy tale,
  And man's utopias a fairy land,
You came, as now again when all things fail,
  You came and touched me, Beauty, with your hand.

And so when man has failed the thousandth time
  To make in his own likeness what shall last,
When from utopias of bread and wine
  He wakes as from a dream when it is past,

Oh touch the untouched, the unbroken string,
Till in the mind sings the immortal thing!

                                    HUGH ROBERT ORR

DISILLUSIONMENT

YET while in disillusionment I sit
  Turning the pages of that yesterday,
While through my memory old fancies flit
  Like the bright colored dragon flies in May,

Although I would not one false stone replace
  Of all man's shattered shrines that round me lie,
I know somewhere there is a living grace,
  Some glory that awaits the seeing eye.

I know there is a Beauty that abides,
　And makes as one the living and the dead;
Born of the dust, within the mind it hides
　The while I sing or break my bitter bread.

It is as if some god plucked at my sleeve,
And cried, "Behold my wound, believe, believe!"

HUGH ROBERT ORR

SO WERE WE BORN TO DREAD

So were we born to dread and to despise
　Our common days, ignore the commonplace,
To seek some unguessed haunt where on our eyes
　Beauty shall fall with her redeeming grace.

Looking to some to-morrow for our hope,
　We reach athwart this living hour our hands
Into the unlit, the unknown, to grope
　Like blind men wandering in unknown lands,

Until at last we know they seek in vain,
　Who find no wonder in the trodden place,
The naked hill flower beaten by the rain,
　The pathos of the ages in man's face.

Oh then the seeker after God returns
To kiss the common clay where Beauty burns.

HUGH ROBERT ORR

THE IDEA OF GOD

IF the idea of God is the supreme achievement of man, it
is also his supreme comfort. Without God life is too much
for the genuine man. It is infinite and it cries out for the

support of the Infinite. . . . Indeed it would seem that the sanity of the educated mind is ultimately dependent upon faith in God. Knowledge is chiefly a revelation of the Infinite. With every advance of science the universe grows more complicated. The torch of discovery leads only farther in upon the Eternal mystery. The shoreless universe surrounds man, and as he advances in civilization his own humanity becomes to him of infinite concern. Love is the crown of life, and as it comes to its coronation it is with the gravest solicitude. To allow love to take its way, to permit the heart to mellow, to throw out a thousand tendrils, to involve its peace with the welfare of kindred, with the happiness of communities and peoples, with the fortune of humanity, is to run a fearful risk. Love must go mad or it must go to God. Without God humanity must break down; it cannot, in a godless universe, support the burden of its own heart.

GEORGE A. GORDON

PROOF OF GOD'S BEING

. . . .

WHAT is the proof of God's being to which one may come who longs to rest only upon ascertained reality? The answer to this question is both close at hand and of infinite significance. God is known as the ideal strength of the soul; and thus he comes to be known as the ideal strength of the world.

. . . .

Human history is the blank landscape of the blind, the mute world of the deaf, the unsuspected intellectual treasure of the race to the dormant mind, until the moral ideal takes possession of the individual soul.

. . . .

Without this interior personal discovery of God the discussions about his being are infinite in their dreary unproductiveness. The key to the universe lies in personality, otherwise there is no key. The key to the moral universe is in the moral personality, or again there is no key. Nature is but a sphinx, and human history a tragedy until the eyes of the lover and doer of righteousness rest upon them. It is the God within who finds the God without, and in the calling of deep to deep the voice that breaks the silence and that begins and that sustains the divine dialogue is the voice of the dutiful soul. . . . The pursuit of the moral ideal is the path to certainty about God. Where the universe has become helper in the struggle to overtake the moral best, one can run no risk in calling the universe God. And where one is a successful pursuer of ideal ends, one can appreciate nature in so far as she lives in the pursuit of an ideal end; one can, further, appreciate the grand historic movement of mankind upon an ideal end. Thus ideal ends explain both nature and human history, and God is given in the grand pursuit, in the strength that makes it possible, in the achievement that makes it noble, and yet more in the light that guides it.

GEORGE A. GORDON

GOD, THE NECESSITY OF HUMANITY

GOD is the necessity of humanity. If we did not need him, we should not seek him. If God were not essential to man's life, even were his existence forced upon the mind, man would take no vital interest in him. The God who does not answer to man's needs can never satisfy man's reason. Reason is the supreme servant of life, and in the service of life reason hears the footsteps of the advancing God, and goes onward to meet him. Power may account for much, wisdom and power may account for more; but both together cannot account for man. It should always be borne in mind that the quest for God is essentially the search for the full account and final meaning of human life. Before they can suffice as the maker of man, wisdom and power must rise into love. For the genuine life of mankind is love; as it comes to itself, that life comes to love. The love of man seeks for the origin of itself in the love of God.

GEORGE A. GORDON

THIS IS NOT GOD!

This is not God—this shape, this wood
With its eyes adream, its placid mood.
For God is alive, awake, aware,
Somehow or where I sense His infinite care.
This is not God,—this body, this head,
God is not passionless, unresponsive, dead!

This is not God—this image of fear,
Set in the heavens so cold, so drear.
For I feel His breath on my burning face,
I lean back breathless in his strong embrace.
I can die unafraid, as I live at peace
In my new-found trust, my sorrow's surcease.

This is my God—this pulsing, creative *Life*
Which makes me akin to all ages of strife;
This Infinite *Power* which nerves and inspires
Me with visions of hope, and pours its fires
Into my waiting will to lighten my load.
Life, Power, Love—here I find God!

ANON.

GOD WITH US

THERE were three lights that night:
The star above the darkness, crystal fair,
The foremost angel's garment flaming white,
        The baby's circled hair.

Three sounds: upon the hill
A sudden song; low drawn, a woman's sigh;
And, when the midnight deepened gray and chill,
    A little, little cry.

Three woes: a witless lamb
Lost from the scattered flock; its mother's grieving;
The long, deep slumber of the townfolk—blind
    And deaf and unbelieving.

Three wonders: dark-browed kings
Riding from far; young shepherds' lifted faces;
The silver beauty raining from the star
    On Bethlehem's dark places.

There were Faith, Hope and Love:
Faith that had known, Hope that had waited well,
Love that had wrought; and in their trembling midst,
    Immanuel!

NANCY BYRD TURNER

[By permission of the Author and *Good Housekeeping*.]

TRUTH

THE Truth is large—
    No man hath seen the whole.
Vaster than speech
    It brooks not the control
Of Creed or Custom.

No book can hold it—
    No device of speech or language.
Truth is the sun
    And reason is the prism—
Your life before it,
    Through which the radiance
Falls in various colors.

If this man takes the red
　　As you the blue,
Is yours the whole of truth?
　　Is his not true?
Spirit is Truth,
　　Howe'er the colors fall.
The fact goes back
　　To Spirit after all.

ANON.

VESTIGIA

I TOOK a day to search for God,
And found Him not. But as I trod
　　By rocky ledge, through woods untamed,
　　Just where one scarlet lily flamed,
I saw His footprint in the sod.

Then suddenly, all unaware,
Far off in the deep shadows, where
　　A solitary hermit thrush
　　Sang through the holy twilight hush—
I heard His voice upon the air.

And even as I marvelled how
God gives us Heaven here and now,
　　In a stir of wind that hardly shook
　　The poplar leaves beside the brook—
His hand was light upon my brow.

At last with evening as I turned
Homeward, and thought what I had learned
　　And all that there was still to probe—
　　I caught the glory of His robe
Where the last fires of sunset burned.

Back to the world with quickening start
I looked and longed for any part
  In making saving Beauty be. . . .
  And from that kindling ecstasy
I knew God dwelt within my heart.

                       BLISS CARMAN

THE FIRE–BRINGER

I STOOD within the heart of God;
It seemed a place that I had known:
(I was blood-sister to the clod,
Blood-brother to the stone.)

I found my love and labor there,
My house, my raiment, meat and wine,
My ancient rage, my old despair,—
Yea, all things that were mine.

I saw the spring and summer pass,
The trees grow bare, and winter come;
All was the same as once it was
Upon my hills at home.

Then suddenly in my own heart
I felt God walk and gaze about;
He spoke; His words seemed held apart
With gladness and with doubt.

"Here is my meat and wine," He said,
"My love, my toil, my ancient care;
Here is my cloak, my book, my bed,
And here my old despair."

"Here are my seasons: winter, spring,
Summer the same, and autumn spills
The fruits I look for; everything
As on my heavenly hills."

              WILLIAM VAUGHN MOODY

THE HOUND OF HEAVEN

I FLED Him, down the nights and down the days;
  I fled Him, down the arches of the years;
I fled Him, down the labyrinthine ways
  Of my own mind; and in the mist of tears
I hid from Him, and under running laughter.
        Up vistaed hopes I sped;
        And shot, precipitated,
Adown Titanic glooms of chasmèd fears,
  From those strong Feet that followed, followed after.
        But with unhurrying chase,
        And unperturbèd pace,
  Deliberate speed, majestic instancy,
        They beat—and a Voice beat
        More instant than the Feet—
'All things betray thee, who betrayest Me.'

        I pleaded, outlaw-wise,
By many a hearted casement, curtained red,
  Trellised with intertwining charities;
(For, though I knew His love Who followèd,
        Yet was I sore adread
Lest, having Him, I must have naught beside).
But, if one little casement parted wide,
  The gust of His approach would clash it to:
  Fear wist not to evade, as Love wist to pursue.

.   .   .   .

  I was heavy with the even,
  When she lit her glimmering tapers
  Round the day's dead sanctities.
  I laughed in the morning's eyes.
I triumphed and I saddened with all weather,
  Heaven and I wept together,
And its sweet tears were salt with mortal mine;

Against the red throb of its sunset-heart
 I laid my own to beat,
 And share commingling heat;
But not by that, by that, was eased my human smart.
In vain my tears were wet on Heaven's grey cheek.

 . . . .

   Nigh and nigh draws the chase,
   With unperturbèd pace,
  Deliberate speed, majestic instancy;
    And past those noisèd Feet
    A voice comes yet more fleet—
 'Lo! naught contents thee, who content'st not Me.'

 . . . .

That Voice is round me like a bursting sea:
   'And is thy earth so marred,
   Shattered in shard on shard?
 Lo, all things fly thee, for thou fliest Me!
 Strange, piteous, futile thing!

 . . . .

   Alack, thou knowest not
How little worthy of any love thou art!
Whom wilt thou find to love ignoble thee,
   Save Me, save only Me?

 . . . .

  Ah, fondest, blindest, weakest,
  I am He Whom thou seekest!
Thou dravest love from thee, who dravest Me.'

FRANCIS THOMPSON

FROM "SONG OF THE UNIVERSAL"

And thou America,
For the scheme's culmination, its thought and its reality,
For these (not for thyself) thou hast arrived.

Thou too surroundest all,
Embracing carrying welcoming all, thou too by pathways
    broad and new,
To the ideal tendest.

The measur'd faiths of other lands, the grandeurs of the past,
Are not for thee, but grandeurs of thine own,
Deific faiths and amplitudes, absorbing, comprehending all,
All eligible to all.

All, all for immortality,
Love like the light silently wrapping all,
Nature's amelioration blessing all,
The blossoms, fruits of ages, orchards divine and certain,
Forms, objects, growths, humanities, to spiritual images
    ripening.

Give me O God to sing that thought,
Give me, give him or her I love this quenchless faith,
In Thy ensemble, whatever else withheld withhold not from
    us
Belief in pıan of Thee enclosed in Time and Space,
Health, peace, salvation universal.

Is it a dream?
Nay but the lack of it the dream,
And failing it life's lore and wealth a dream,
And all the world a dream.

                         WHITMAN

PARACELSUS

.   .   .   .

No, I have naught to fear! Who will may know
The secret'st workings of my soul. What though
It be so?—if indeed the strong desire
Eclipse the aim in me?—if splendor break

Upon the outset of my path alone,
And duskest shade succeed? What fairer seal
Shall I require to my authentic mission
Than this fierce energy?—this instinct striving
Because its nature is to strive?—enticed
By the security of no broad course,
Without success forever in its eyes!
How know I else such glorious fate my own,
But in the restless irresistible force
That works within me? Is it for human will
To institute such impulses?—still less,
To disregard their promptings! What should I
Do, kept among you all; your loves, your cares,
Your life—all to be mine? Be sure that God
Ne'er dooms to waste the strength he deigns impart!
Ask the geier-eagle why she stoops at once
Into the vast and unexplored abyss,
What full-grown power informs her from the first,
Why she not marvels, strenuously beating
The silent boundless regions of the sky!
Be sure they sleep not whom God needs! Nor fear
Their holding light his charge, when every hour
That finds that charge delayed, is a new death.

.   .   .   .

I was restless, nothing satisfied,
Distrustful, most perplexed. I would slur over
That struggle; suffice it, that I loathed myself
As weak compared with them, yet felt somehow
A mighty power was brooding, taking shape
Within me; and this lasted till one night
When, as I sat revolving it and more,
A still voice from without said—"Seest thou not,
Desponding child, whence spring defeat and loss?
Even from thy strength. Consider: hast thou gazed
Presumptuously on wisdom's countenance,

No veil between; and can thy faltering hands,
Unguided by the brain the sight absorbs,
Pursue their task as earnest blinkers do
Whom radiance ne'er distracted? Live their life
If thou wouldst share their fortune, choose their eyes
Unfed by splendor. Let each task present
Its petty good to thee. Waste not thy gifts
In profitless waiting for the gods' descent,
But have some idol of thine own to dress
With their array. Know, not for knowing's sake,
But to become a star to men forever;
Know, for the gain it gets, the praise it brings,
The wonder it inspires, the love it breeds:
Look one step onward, and secure that step!"
And I smiled as one never smiles but once,
Then first discovering my own aim's extent,
Which sought to comprehend the works of God,
And God himself, and all God's intercourse
With the human mind; I understood, no less,
My fellows' studies, whose true worth I saw,
But smiled not, well aware who stood by me.
And softer came the voice—"There is a way:
'Tis hard for flesh to tread therein, imbued
With frailty—hopeless, if indulgence first
Have ripened inborn germs of sin to strength:
Wilt thou adventure for my sake and man's,
Apart from all reward?" And last it breathed—
"Be happy, my good soldier; I am by thee,
Be sure, even to the end!"—I answered not,
Knowing him. As he spoke, I was endued
With comprehension and a steadfast will;
And when he ceased, my brow was sealed his own.
If there took place no special change in me,
How comes it all things wore a different hue
Thenceforward?—pregnant with vast consequence,
Teeming with grand result, loaded with fate?

So that when, quailing at the mighty range
Of secret truths which yearn for birth, I haste
To contemplate undazzled some one truth,
Its bearings and effects alone—at once
What was a speck expands into a star,
Asking a life to pass exploring thus,
Till I near craze. I go to prove my soul!
I see my way as birds their trackless way.
I shall arrive! what time, what circuit first,
I ask not: but unless God send his hail
Or blinding fireballs, sleet or stifling snow,
In some time, his good time, I shall arrive:
He guides me and the bird. In his good time!

. . . .

BROWNING

NOTE XII

CAN the thought of God endure the light of Science, Philosophy, and all the daily tests of personal need? We have the positive answer in this group of writings. However much man may delve into this question, even though the search lead him into temporary despair or utter loss of faith in God and goodness; yet time, and human hunger, and the insistence of divine love must win the day—to man's infinite advantage.

1. The author of the first three poems rises to sublime heights of faith because the vision of Life in its perfection, its symmetry, has prevailed over the shadow cast by the tombs of lost hopes and lurking fears. Beauty—the appealing Whole—makes all things beautiful, and the larger faith results.

2. In the three selections from Doctor Gordon's facile pen one feels the irresistible plea of the poet, the philosopher, and the lover of men. The argument from practical experience appeals to many, where even philosophic proof might utterly fail. God enters every life through humble portals. Philosophers' minds are few and difficult of access. Apart from God, human life is meaningless. In the love of God— and there alone—man finds his true origin, sustenance, and his destiny.

3. The next four poems stress the larger and nobler conception of God which lies close at hand in daily experience. "God gives us Heaven here and now."

4. "The Fire-Bringer," drawing its striking parallel from Æschylus' classic poem, "Prometheus Bound," and "The Hound of Heaven" are two of our finest expressions of the conviction that man and God are by destiny fitted for eternal partnership. Where human frailty might allow man to miss the Great Plan, the inescapable love of God effects this happy union. Man must not fail of his high mission.

5. *Whitman* and *Browning* close the section with their ardent cries of faith in this Greater God who guides both the individual man, and life as a whole, toward the ultimate goal of perfection and love. *Browning* thinks of God as ever waiting, in the hour of man's perplexity and bitterness, to reveal the supremacy of love over philosophic doubt, over knowledge, and even over the lust of power. The human soul rises through struggle to full self-realization only by the power of Love.

XIII

LOVE'S VIGIL

Love will outwatch the stars, and light the skies
   When the last star falls, and the silent dark devours;
   God's warrior, he will watch the allotted hours,
And conquer with the look of his sad eyes:
He shakes the kingdom of darkness with his sighs,
   His quiet sighs, while all the Infernal Powers
   Tremble and pale upon their central towers,
Lest, haply, his bright universe arise.

All will be well if he have strength to wait,
   Till his lost Pleiad, white and silver-shod,
Regains her place to make the perfect Seven;
Then all the worlds will know that Love is Fate—
That somehow he is greater even than Heaven—
   That in the Cosmic Council he is God.

EDWIN MARKHAM

FROM "THE ANCIENT SAGE"

Thou canst not prove the Nameless, O my son,
Nor canst thou prove the world thou movest in,
Thou canst not prove that thou art body alone,
Nor canst thou prove that thou art spirit alone,
Nor canst thou prove that thou art both in one:
Thou canst not prove thou art immortal, no
Nor yet that thou art mortal—nay my son,
Thou canst not prove that I, who speak with thee,
Am not thyself in converse with thyself,
For nothing worthy proving can be proven,

Nor yet disproven: wherefore thou be wise,
Cleave ever to the sunnier side of doubt,
And cling to Faith beyond the forms of Faith!
She reels not in the storm of warring words,
She brightens at the clash of 'Yes' and 'No,'
She sees the Best that glimmers thro' the Worst,
She feels the Sun is hid but for a night,
She spies the summer thro' the winter bud,
She tastes the fruit before the blossom falls,
She hears the lark within the songless egg,
She finds the fountain where they wail'd 'Mirage!'

TENNYSON

[From "The Works of Tennyson," The Macmillan Co.]

DOUBT

If I lay waste and wither up with doubt
    The blessed fields of heaven where once my faith
    Possessed itself serenely safe from death;
If I deny the things past finding out;
Or if I orphan my own soul of One
    That seemed a Father, and make void the place
    Within me where He dwelt in power and grace,
What do I gain by what I have undone?

WILLIAM D. HOWELLS

UNMANIFEST DESTINY

To what new fates, my country, far
    And unforeseen of foe or friend,
Beneath what unexpected star,
    Compelled to what unchosen end,

Across the sea that knows no beach
The Admiral of Nations guides

Thy blind obedient keels to reach
  The harbor where thy future rides!

The guns that spoke at Lexington
  Knew not that God was planning then
The trumpet word of Jefferson
  To bugle forth the rights of men.

To them that wept and cursed Bull Run,
  What was it but despair and shame?
Who saw behind the cloud the sun?
  Who knew that God was in the flame?

Had not defeat upon defeat,
  Disaster on disaster come,
The slave's emancipated feet
  Had never marched behind the drum.

There is a Hand that bends our deeds
  To mightier issues than we planned;
Each son that triumphs, each that bleeds,
  My country, serves Its dark command.

I do not know beneath what sky
  Nor on what seas shall be thy fate;
I only know it shall be high,
  I only know it shall be great.

RICHARD HOVEY

GOD CALLED UP FROM DREAMS

God called up from dreams a man into the vestibule of
heaven, saying, "Come thou hither and see the glory of my
house." And to the servants that stood around his throne
he said, "Take him and undress him from his robes of flesh;
cleanse his vision and put a new breath into his nostrils;
only touch not with any change his human heart—the heart

that weeps and trembles." And it was done; and, with a mighty angel for his guide, the man stood ready for his infinite voyage, and from the terraces of heaven, without sound of farewell, at once they wheeled away into endless space. Sometimes with the solemn flight of angel wing they fled through Zaarahs of darkness, through wildernesses of death, that divided the worlds of life; sometimes they swept over frontiers that were quickening under prophetic motions from God. Then, from distance that is counted only in heaven, light dawned for a time through a sleepy film; by unutterable pace the light swept to *them*, they by unutterable pace to the light: in a moment the rushing of planets was upon them; in a moment the blazing of suns was around them. Then came eternities of twilight, that revealed, but were not revealed. To the right hand and to the left towered mighty constellations, that by self-repetitions and answers from afar, that by counter positions, built up triumphal gates, whose architraves, whose archways,—horizontal, upright,—rested, rose,—at altitudes, by spans,—that seemed ghostly from infinitude. Without measure were the architraves, past number were the archways, beyond memory the gates. Within were stairs that scaled the eternities above, that descended to the eternities below: above was below, below was above, to the man stripped of gravitating body: depth was swallowed up in height insurmountable, height was swallowed up in depth unfathomable. Suddenly, as thus they rode from infinite to infinite, suddenly, as thus they tilted over abysmal worlds, a mighty cry arose, that systems more mysterious, that worlds more billowy,—other heights and other depths,— were coming, were nearing, were at hand. Then the man sighed and stopped, shuddered and wept. His overladen heart uttered itself in tears, and he said, "Angel, I will go no farther; for the spirit of man aches with this infinity. Insufferable is the glory of God. Let me lie down in the grave from the persecutions of the infinite; for end, I see, there is none." And from all the listening stars that shone around issued a choral voice, "The man speaks truly; end there is none that ever yet we heard of." "End is there none?" the angel solemnly demanded. "Is there, indeed, no end? and is this the sorrow that kills you?" But no voice answered, that he might answer himself. Then the angel threw up his glorious hands to the heaven of heavens, saying, "End is there none to the universe of God? Lo, also, there is no beginning."

JEAN PAUL RICHTER

THE WORLD-PURPOSE

MEN sadly say that Love's high dream is vain,
    That one force holds the heart—the hope of gain.
Are, then, the August Powers behind the veil
    Weary of watch and powerless to prevail?
Have they grown palsied with the creep of age,
    And do they burn no more with pallid rage?
Are the shrines empty and the altars cold,
    Where once the saints and heroes knelt of old?

Not so: the vast inbrothering of man—
    The glory of the universe—began
When first the heart of the Mother Darkness heard
    The Whisper, and the ancient chaos stirred.
Ever the feet of Christ were in events,
    B idging the seas, shaking the continents.

His feet are heard in the historic march
    Under the whirlwind, under the starry arch.
Forever the Great Purpose presses on,
    From darkness unto darkness, dawn to dawn,
Resolved to lay the rafter and the beam
    Of Justice—the imperishable Dream.

This is the voice of Time against the Hours;
    This is the witness of the Cosmic Powers;

This is the Music of the Ages—this
   The song whose first note broke the First Abyss.

All that we glory in was once a dream;
   The World-Will marches onward, gleam by gleam,
New voices speak, dead paths begin to stir;
   Man is emerging from the sepulchre!
Let no man dare, let no man ever dare
   To mark on Time's great way, 'No Thoroughfare.'

EDWIN MARKHAM

THE PARADOX

ALL that is broken shall be mended;
   All that is lost shall be found;
   I will bind up every wound
When that which is begun shall be ended.
Not peace I brought among you but a sword
   To divide the night from the day,
When I sent My worlds forth in their battle-array
   To die and to live,
   To give and to receive,
     Saith the Lord.

.   .   .   .

Consider the troubled waters of the sea
   Which never rest;
As the wandering waves are ye;
   Yet assuaged and appeased and forgiven,
   As the seas are gathered together under the infinite glory
     of heaven,
   I gather you all to my breast.
But the sins and the creeds and the sorrows that trouble the
     sea
   Relapse and subside,

Chiming like chords in a world-wide symphony
  As they cease to chide;
For they break and they are broken of sound and hue,
And they meet and they murmur and they mingle anew,
Interweaving, intervolving, like waves: they have no stay:
They are all made as one with the deep, when they sink and
    are vanished away;
  Yea, all is toned at a turn of the tide
  To a calm and golden harmony. . . .

I am the End to which the whole world strives:
  Therefore are ye girdled with a wild desire and shod
With sorrow; for among you all no soul
Shall ever cease or sleep or reach its goal
Of union and communion with the Whole,
  Or rest content with less than being God.

. . . .

      My love contrives
That ye should have the glory of this
  For ever; yea, that life should blend
  With life and only vanish away
  From day to wider wealthier day,
Like still increasing spheres of light that melt and merge in
    wider spheres
Even as the infinite years of the past melt in the infinite
    future years.
  Each new delight of sense,
  Each hope, each love, each fear,
  Widens, relumes and recreates each sphere,
From a new ring and nimbus of pre-eminence.
I am the Sphere without circumference:
I only and for ever comprehend
All others that within me meet and blend.
  Death is but the blinding kiss
  Of two finite infinities;

Two finite infinite orbs
The splendour of the greater of which absorbs
The less, though both like Love have no beginning and
no end.

ALFRED NOYES

NOTE XIII

THE deification of love has long been a fruitful theme with poets, but never more than in recent days when unprecedented human crises have revealed characters of exceptional beauty and forcefulness. These eight selections are among the choicest expressions of faith in the ultimate goodness of life. Whether, with *Markham*, we are thinking in terms of universal struggle; or of national destiny, as *Hovey* dreams; or whether we are facing intellectual doubt and repeated defeats of the soul in its aspiration to attain the highest, as *Tennyson*, *Howells*, and *Browning* suggest; yet the outcome is certain and happy in the extreme.

As *Richter* and *Noyes* develop the great theme, the very infinite Power and Love are in themselves overwhelming guarantees that the universe—and certainly humanity, then —is in the keeping of One who both sees and is the End of all existence. The great verities, Life and Death and Love, find wonderfully new meaning in the light of this eternity of being.

IV

THE DIVINE POSSIBILITIES OF MAN

XIV

FROM "PARACELSUS"

PROGRESS is
The law of life, man is not Man as yet.
Nor shall I deem his object served, his end
Attained, his genuine strength put fairly forth,
While only here and there a star dispels
The darkness, here and there a towering mind
O'erlooks its prostrate fellows: when the host
Is out at once to the despair of night,
When all mankind alike is perfected,
Equal in full-blown powers—then, not till then,
I say, begins man's general infancy.

. . . .

So in man's self arise
August anticipations, symbols, types
Of a dim splendor ever on before
In that eternal circle life pursues.
For men begin to pass their nature's bound,
And find new hopes and cares which fast supplant
Their proper joys and griefs; they grow too great
For narrow creeds of right and wrong, which fade
Before the unmeasured thirst for good: while peace
Rises within them ever more and more.

BROWNING

A DEATH IN THE DESERT

. . . .

FOR life, with all it yields of joy and woe,
And hope and fear,—believe the aged friend,—

181

Is just our chance o' the prize of learning love,
How love might be, hath been indeed, and is;
And that we hold thenceforth to the uttermost
Such prize despite the envy of the world,
And, having gained truth, keep truth: that is all.

. . . .

I say that man was made to grow, not stop;
That help, he needed once, and needs no more,
Having grown but an inch by, is withdrawn:
For he hath new needs, and new helps to these.
This imports solely, man should mount on each
New height in view; the help whereby he mounts,
The ladder-rung his foot has left, may fall,
Since all things suffer change save God the Truth.
Man apprehends him newly at each stage
Whereat earth's ladder drops, its service done . . .

. . . .

—Man is not God but hath God's end to serve,
A master to obey, a course to take,
Somewhat to cast off, somewhat to become?
Grant this, then man must pass from old to new,
From vain to real, from mistake to fact,
From what once seemed good, to what now proves best.
How could man have progression otherwise?

. . . .

BROWNING

GRADATIM

HEAVEN is not gained at a single bound;
   But we build the ladder by which we rise
   From the lowly earth to the vaulted skies,
And we mount to its summit round by round.

I count this thing to be grandly true,
  That a noble deed is a step toward God—
  Lifting the soul from the common sod
To a purer air and a broader view.

We rise by things that are 'neath our feet;
  By what we have mastered of good and gain;
  By the pride deposed and the passion slain,
And the vanquished ills that we hourly meet.

We hope, we aspire, we resolve, we trust,
  When the morning calls us to life and light,
  But our hearts grow weary, and, ere the night,
Our lives are trailing the sordid dust.

We hope, we resolve, we aspire, we pray,
  And we think that we mount the air on wings
  Beyond the recall of sensual things,
While our feet still cling to the heavy clay.

Wings for the angels, but feet for men!
  We may borrow the wings to find the way—
  We may hope, and resolve, and aspire, and pray,
But our feet must rise, or we fall again.

Only in dreams is a ladder thrown
  From the weary earth to the sapphire walls;
  But the dream departs, and the vision falls,
And the sleeper wakes on his pillow of stone.

Heaven is not reached at a single bound:
  But we build the ladder by which we rise
  From the lowly earth to the vaulted skies,
And we mount to its summit round by round.

J. G. HOLLAND

AFTER

I HAVE lived and rejoiced in the living,
I have loved and accepted the pain,
I have given for joy of the giving
And counted the gift as a gain—
Like music that melts into laughter,
And laughter that trembles to tears,
I have waked every chord—but hereafter
How mute are the years!

They are dim with the fear of forgetting,
And numb with a joy that is cold,
They are wan from a sun that is setting,
And blank as a tale that is told.
No thrill in the rush of the river,
No throb in the hush of the seas,
In the wound of Grief's guarding, no quiver,
For drained are Life's lees!

CORINNE ROOSEVELT ROBINSON

CLOSING THE DOORS

I HAVE closed the door on Doubt.
I will go by what light I can find,
And hold up my hands and reach them out
To the glimmer of God in the dark, and call,
"I am Thine, though I grope and stumble and fall.
I serve, and Thy service is kind."

I have closed the door on Fear.
He has lived with me far too long.
If he were to break forth and reappear,
I would lift my eyes and look at the sky,
And sing aloud and run lightly by;
He will never follow a song.

I have closed the door on Gloom.
His house has too narrow a view.
I must seek for my soul a wider room,
With windows to open and let in the sun,
And radiant lamps when the day is done,
And the breeze of the world blowing through.

IRENE PETTIT MCKEEHAN

THE ROAD–SONG OF THE RACE

I HAVE lived in the Garden with Adam,
And eaten the fruit of the tree;
I have hidden ashamed from the face of God,
For I dreamed that he could not see.
The flaming sword of the Angel of Wrath
Has driven me over the earth;
I am marked with the brand of the murderer Cain;
I have travailed at death and at birth.
With patriarch, priest, and prophet
I seek for the Promised Land:—
Lead me, brother; follow me, brother;
Brother, O take my hand!
I am moving onward and ever on;
O brother, I may not stand.

I have found my king in a little Child
And knelt in a manger-room;
But I sold the Master for silver coin;
With a kiss I sealed his doom.
I hung on the cross with Christ the Lord,
I suffered his pain and scorn;
But mine were the hands that drove the nails
And wove him the crown of thorn.
I track the light of my guiding star
Through the snow and the desert sand:—

Lead me, brother; follow me, brother;
  Brother, O take my hand!
I am but a pilgrim, O brother;
  And woe is me if I stand.

I have made my children the slaves of Trade
  And scarred their backs with the rod;
For a bag of gold with a sword of steel
  I have broken the laws of God.
But whenever a Call demands my life,
  I have laid it down with a will;
For honor and love and a heartwrung cry
  I can play the hero still.
My feet are firm on the steep, strait way—
  Though I doubt if I understand:—
Lead me, brother; follow me, brother;
  Brother, O take my hand!
And stay not behind, O brother of mine!
  On the road to the Promised Land.

IRENE PETTIT MCKEEHAN

THE HERITAGE

No matter what my birth may be,
  No matter where my lot is cast,
I am the heir in equity
  Of all the precious Past.

The art, the science, and the lore
  Of all the ages long since dust,
The wisdom of the world in store,
  Are mine, all mine in trust.

The beauty of the living earth,
  The power of the golden sun,
The Present, whatsoe'er my birth,
  I share with every one.

As much as any man am I
  The owner of the working day;
Mine are the minutes as they fly
  To save or throw away.

And mine the Future to bequeath
  Unto the generations new;
I help to shape it with my breath,
  Mine as I think or do.

Present and Past my heritage,
  The Future laid in my control;—
No matter what my name or age,
  I am a Master-soul!

ABBIE FARWELL BROWN

A. M. D. G.

THE CHRISTIAN HERO

Yon lowly shrub that skirts the mountain way—
I passed it all the Summer, day by day;
Nor heeded it, though fair enough it grew
Mid plant and flower offered to the view;
For all alike seemed beautiful and gay
In the bright sunshine of the Summer's day.

King Winter comes and scatters o'er the land
Hoar frost and icicles with generous hand;
He builds his frosty palace on the hill
Where stands the shrub, hard by a frozen rill.
Then came the thought, the plant he noted there
Might yet be made more beautiful and fair.

The background chosen is a field of snow;
With frosty brush he touches leaf and bough
In rainbow tints, and colors bright and gold—
What varied hues his cunning strokes unfold

Till stands it there in richer splendor clad,
Than Solomon in all his glory had.
Who now could overlook that charming plant?
Who could approach, and in his heart not want
To gaze enraptured on the change unsought
In common shrub, by Winter's pencil wrought?

Thus oft of one who seems of common mould
No note we take; within his breast the gold
Of character is locked from human view;
In Spring's balm clime and Summer's ease he grew—
His face all smiles, his heart one merry chime
From morn to night.—'Tis yet his summer time.

II

But Winter comes,—and bitter is the hour;
The Sun grows dim, the skies begin to lower;
The thunder-clouds roll fast athwart the sky—
Prepare thy soul for wrathful tempest nigh!
Now fierce assail the blasts of suffering rude;
The biting frost of Man's ingratitude;
From Slander's leaden clouds each fiery dart
Speeds, deadly aimed at his devoted heart:
'Twould seem the storm, as on his ruin bent,
On him alone its gathered fury spent.

Before such stress the meaner soul might cower;
Ne'er flinches he;—with noble Christian power
He bears the storm of wrong, and all the pain,
For love of Him, the suffering Nazarene.
As woe's dark form, which on her ceaseless frowned,
The peerless Virgin, Queen of Martyrs crowned;
So suffering has evoked his latent worth,
And from the gold removed the dross of earth.

Thus comes he forth ennobled from the storm—
Thus takes he on a new and glorious form,

The form of Christ—'tis viewed in every line—
His countenance less human than divine.
Wise Providence it was that limned the face,
And chose the storm to add each nobler grace.
Tho' noted not before the Winter came,
Deserves he now a Christian hero's name.
How high he towers o'er those who on him trod,
The admired of men, of angels, and of God!

JOHN D. WALSHE

SUB PONDERE CRESCIT

THE hope of Truth grows stronger, day by day;
I hear the soul of Man around me waking,
Like a great sea, its frozen fetters breaking,
And flinging up to heaven its sunlit spray,
Tossing huge continents in scornful play,
And crushing them, with din of grinding thunder,
That makes old emptinesses stare in wonder;
The memory of a glory passed away
Lingers in every heart, as, in the shell,
Resounds the bygone freedom of the sea,
And every hour new signs of promise tell,
That the great soul shall once again be free,
For high, and yet more high, the murmurs swell
Of inward strife for truth and liberty.

JAMES RUSSELL LOWELL

TO M. O. S.

.   .   .   .

OUR love is not a fading, earthly flower:
Its wingëd seed dropped down from Paradise,
And, nursed by day and night, by sun and shower,
Doth momently to fresher beauty rise:

To us the leafless autumn is not bare,
Nor winter's rattling boughs lack lusty green.
Our summer hearts make summer's fulness, where
No leaf, or bud, or blossom may be seen:
For nature's life in love's deep life doth lie,
Love,—whose forgetfulness is beauty's death,
Whose mystic key these cells of Thou and I
Into the infinite freedom openeth,
And makes the body's dark and narrow grate
The wide-flung leaves of Heaven's own palace-gate.

JAMES RUSSELL LOWELL

FROM "THE HIGHER CATECHISM"

WHAT is the world's true Bible—'tis the highest thought of man,
The thought distilled through ages since the dawn of thought began.
And each age adds its word thereto, some psalm or promise sweet—
And the canon is unfinished and forever incomplete.
O'er the chapters that are written long and lovingly we pore—
But the best is yet unwritten, for we grow from more to more.

Let us heed the Voice within us and its messages rehearse;
Let us build the growing Bible—for we too must write a verse.
What is the purport of the scheme towards which all time is gone?
What is the great æonian goal? The joy of going on.
And are there any souls so strong, such feet with swiftness shod,
That they shall reach it, reach some bourne, the ultimate of God?

There is no bourne, no ultimate. The very farthest star
But rims a sea of other stars that stretches just as far.
There's no beginning and no end. As in the ages gone,
The greatest joy of joys shall be the joy of going on.

SAM WALTER FOSS

I SAID: "LET ME WALK"

I SAID: "Let me walk in the fields."
He said: "No, walk in the town."
I said: "There are no flowers there."
He said: "No flowers, but a crown."

I said: "But the skies are black;
There is nothing but noise and din."
And He wept as He sent me back—
"There is more," He said: "There is sin."

I said: "But the air is thick,
And fogs are veiling the sun."
He answered: "Yet souls are sick,
And souls in the dark undone!"

I said: "I shall miss the light,
And friends will miss me, they say."
He answered: "Choose tonight
If I am to miss you or they."

I pleaded for time to be given.
He said: "Is it hard to decide?
It will not seem so hard in heaven
To have followed the steps of your Guide."

I cast one look at the fields,
Then set my face to the town;
He said: "My child, do you yield:
Will you leave the flowers for the crown?"

Then into His hand went mine;
And into my heart came He;
And I walk in a light divine,
The path I had feared to see.

GEORGE MACDONALD

FROM "SĀDHĀNA"

MAN must realise the wholeness of his existence, his place in the infinite. . . . Essentially man is not a slave either of himself or of the world; but he is a lover. His freedom and fulfilment is in love, which is another name for perfect comprehension. By this . . . permeation of his being, he is united with the all-pervading Spirit, who is also the breath of his soul . . . it is the practice of realising and affirming the presence of the Infinite (Brahma) in all things which has been its constant inspiration. . . . We are immersed in his consciousness body and soul. . . . Our soul can realise itself truly only by denying itself. . . . Man is . . . abroad to satisfy needs which are more to him than food and clothing. He is out to find himself. Man's history is the history of his journey to the unknown in quest of the realisation of his immortal self—his soul . . . whose onward course is never checked by death or dissolution. . . .

Really, there is no limit to our powers, for we are not outside the universal power which is the expression of universal law.

. . . Our life, like a river, strikes its banks not to find itself closed in by them, but to realise anew every moment that it has its unending opening towards the sea. It is as a poem that strikes its metre at every step not to be silenced by its rigid regulations, but to give expression every moment to the inner freedom of its harmony. . . . Our roots must go deep down into the universal if we would attain the greatness of personality. . . . We must know that it is only the revelation of the Infinite which is endlessly new and eternally beautiful in us, and which gives the only meaning to our self. . . . When a man feels the rhythmic throb of the soul-life, the whole world in his own soul, then is he free.

. . . O worker of the universe! We would pray to thee to let the irresistible current of thy universal energy come like the impetuous south wind of Spring, let it come rushing over the vast field of the life of man. . . . Let our newly awakened powers cry out for unlimited fulfilment in leaf and flower and fruit.

RABINDRANATH TAGORE

[Copyright by The Macmillan Co.]

THE SUPERMAN

HE will come;

I know not when, or how;

But he will walk breast-high with God, stepping among the stars.

Clothed in light and crowned with glory he will stride down the Milky Way,

Creating with a thought, building with a word.

A hundred million ages it may be until he comes, what does it matter?

Consider the deliberate stars—how eternity awaits their fulfilments.

A hundred million ages, and yet, sometimes,

Here and now, in these small primeval days—in this dull gloaming of creation's dawn—

Here and now, sometimes, there crackles out a tiny shimmering spark,

Some hint in our blind, protoplasmic lives,

Of that far, infinite torch

Whose ray shall one day touch the utmost reaches of space

Where life is borne.

One that has made brotherhood with the eagle and the hawk:
One that has made voices speak across the emptiness;
One that has laid cheer and comfort to the tired heart—
These and a thousand others are the prophecy;
These tell of the day
When the poor expedient of birth and the trouble of dying
    have been dismissed,
And all the sad advantages of the body are long forgot.
Walking as the angels walk, but greater than the angels,
He that will come will know not space or time, nor any limi-
    tation,
But will step across the sky, infinite, supreme, one with God.

ALBERT BIGELOW PAINE

FROM "THE PRESENT CRISIS"

ONCE to every man and nation comes the moment to decide,
In the strife of Truth with Falsehood, for the good or evil
    side;
Some great cause, God's new Messiah, offering each the bloom
    or blight,
Parts the goats upon the left hand, and the sheep upon the
    the right,
And the choice goes by forever 'twixt that darkness and that
    light.

Hast thou chosen, O my people, on whose party thou shalt
    stand,
Ere the Doom from its worn sandals shakes the dust against
    our land?
Though the cause of Evil prosper, yet 'tis Truth alone is
    strong,
And, albeit she wander outcast now, I see around her throng
Troops of beautiful, tall angels, to enshield her from all wrong.

Backward look across the ages and the beacon-moments see,
That, like peaks of some sunk continent, jut through Ob-
livion's sea;
Not an ear in court or market for the low foreboding cry
Of those Crises, God's stern winnowers, from whose feet
earth's chaff must fly;
Never shows the choice momentous till the judgment hath
passed by.

Careless seems the great Avenger; history's pages but record
One death-grapple in the darkness 'twixt old systems and
the Word;
Truth forever on the scaffold, Wrong forever on the throne,—
Yet that scaffold sways the future, and behind the dim
unknown,
Standeth God within the shadow, keeping watch above his
own.

We see dimly in the Present what is small and what is
great,
Slow of faith how weak an arm may turn the iron helm of
fate,
But the soul is still oracular; amid the market's din,
List the ominous stern whisper from the Delphic cave
within,—
"They enslave their children's children who make com-
promise with sin."

Slavery, the earth-born Cyclops, fellest of the giant brood,
Sons of brutish Force and Darkness, who have drenched the
earth with blood,
Famished in his self-made desert, blinded by our purer
day,
Gropes in yet unblasted regions for his miserable prey;—
Shall we guide his gory fingers where our helpless children
play?

Then to side with Truth is noble when we share her wretched
    crust,
Ere her cause bring fame and profit, and 'tis prosperous to
    be just;
Then it is the brave man chooses, while the coward stands
    aside,
Doubting in his abject spirit, till his Lord is crucified,
And the multitude make virtue of the faith they had de-
    nied.

Count me o'er earth's chosen heroes,—they were souls that
    stood alone,
While the men they agonized for hurled the contumelious
    stone,
Stood serene and down the future saw the golden beam in-
    cline
To the side of perfect justice, mastered by their faith divine,
By one man's plain truth to manhood and to God's supreme
    design.

By the light of burning heretics Christ's bleeding feet I
    track,
Toiling up new Calvaries ever with the cross that turns not
    back,
And these mounts of anguish number how each generation
    learned
One new word of that grand *Credo* which in prophet-hearts
    hath burned
Since the first man stood God-conquered with his face to
    heaven upturned.

For Humanity sweeps onward: where to-day the martyr
    stands,
On the morrow crouches Judas with the silver in his hands;
Far in front the cross stands ready and the crackling fagots
    burn,

While the hooting mob of yesterday in silent awe return
To glean up the scattered ashes into History's golden urn.

'Tis as easy to be heroes as to sit the idle slaves
Of a legendary virtue carved upon our fathers' graves,
Worshippers of light ancestral make the present light a
   crime;—
Was the Mayflower launched by cowards, steered by men
   behind their time?
Turn those tracks toward Past or Future, that make Plym-
   outh Rock sublime?

They were men of present valor, stalwart old iconoclasts,
Unconvinced by axe or gibbet that all virtue was the Past's;
But we make their truth our falsehood, thinking that hath
   made us free,
Hoarding it in mouldy parchments, while our tender spirits
   flee
The rude grasp of that great Impulse which drove them across
   the sea.

They have rights who dare maintain them; we are traitors
   to our sires,
Smothering in their holy ashes Freedom's new-lit altar-
   fires;
Shall we make their creed our jailer? Shall we, in our haste
   to slay,
From the tombs of the old prophets steal the funeral lamps
   away
To light up the martyr-fagots round the prophets of to-
   day?

New occasions teach new duties; Time makes ancient good
   uncouth;
They must upward still, and onward, who would keep abreast
   of Truth;

Lo, before us gleam her camp-fires! we ourselves must Pilgrims be,
Launch our Mayflower, and steer boldly through the desperate winter sea,
Nor attempt the Future's portal with the Past's blood-rusted key.

JAMES RUSSELL LOWELL

THE COMMON STREET

THE common street climbed up against the sky,
Gray meeting gray; and wearily to and fro
I saw the patient, common people go,
Each with his sordid burden trudging by.
And the rain dropped; there was not any sigh
Or stir of a live wind; dull, dull and slow
All motion; as a tale told long ago
The faded world; and creeping night drew nigh.
Then burst the sunset, flooding far and fleet,
Leavening the whole of life with magic leaven.
Suddenly down the long wet glistening hill
Pure splendor poured—and lo! the common street,
A golden highway into golden heaven,
With the dark shapes of men ascending still.

HELEN GRAY CONE

BROADWAY

How like the stars are these white, nameless faces—
    These far innumerable burning coals!
This pale procession out of stellar spaces,
    This Milky Way of souls!
Each in its own bright nebulæ enfurled,
Each face, dear God, a world!

I fling my gaze out through the silent night:
  In those far stars, what gardens, what high halls,
Has mortal yearning built for its delight,
  What chasms and what walls?
What quiet mansions where a soul may dwell?
What heaven and what hell?

HERMANN HAGEDORN

[From "Poems and Ballads," The Macmillan Co.]

THE CRY OF THE CHILDREN

I

Do ye hear the children weeping, O my brothers,
  Ere the sorrow comes with years?
They are leaning their young heads against their mothers,
  And *that* cannot stop their tears.
The young lambs are bleating in the meadows,
  The young birds are chirping in the nest,
The young fawns are playing with the shadows,
  The young flowers are blowing toward the west—
But the young, young children, O my brothers,
  They are weeping bitterly!
They are weeping in the playtime of the others,
  In the country of the free.

II

Do you question the young children in the sorrow
  Why their tears are falling so?
The old man may weep for his to-morrow
  Which is lost in Long Ago;
The old tree is leafless in the forest,
  The old year is ending in the frost,
The old wound, if stricken, is the sorest,
  The old hope is hardest to be lost:

But the young, young children, O my brothers,
  Do you ask them why they stand
Weeping sore before the bosoms of their mothers,
  In our happy Fatherland?

III

They look up with their pale and sunken faces,
  And their looks are sad to see,
For the man's hoary anguish draws and presses
  Down the cheeks of infancy;
'Your old earth,' they say, 'is very dreary,
  Our young feet,' they say, 'are very weak;
Few paces have we taken, yet are weary—
  Our grave-rest is very far to seek:
Ask the aged why they weep, and not the children,
  For the outside earth is cold,
And we young ones stand without, in our bewildering,
  And the graves are for the old.'

.   .   .   .

V

Alas, alas, the children! they are seeking
  Death in life, as best to have:
They are binding up their hearts away from breaking,
  With a cerement from the grave.
Go out, children, from the mine and from the city,
  Sing out, children, as the little thrushes do;
Pluck your handfuls of the meadow-cowslips pretty.
  Laugh aloud, to feel your fingers let them through!
But they answer, 'Are your cowslips of the meadows
  Like our weeds anear the mine?
Leave us quiet in the dark of the coal-shadows,
  From your pleasures fair and fine!

VI

'For oh,' say the children, 'we are weary,
    And we cannot run or leap;
If we cared for any meadows, it were merely
    To drop down in them and sleep.
Our knees tremble sorely in the stooping,
    We fall upon our faces, trying to go;
And, underneath our heavy eyelids drooping
    The reddest flower would look as pale as snow.
For, all day, we drag our burden tiring
    Through the coal-dark, underground;
Or, all day, we drive the wheels of iron
    In the factories, round and round.

VII

'For all day the wheels are droning, turning;
    Their wind comes in our faces,
Till our hearts turn, our heads with pulses burning,
    And the walls turn in their places:
Turns the sky in the high window, blank and reeling,
    Turns the long light that drops adown the wall,
Turn the black flies that crawl along the ceiling:
    All are turning, all the day, and we with all.
And all day the iron wheels are droning,
    And sometimes we could pray,
"O ye wheels" (breaking out in a mad moaning),
    "Stop! be silent for to-day!"'

VIII

Ay, be silent! Let them hear each other breathing
    For a moment, mouth to mouth!
Let them touch each other's hands, in a fresh wreathing
    Of their tender human youth!
Let them feel that this cold metallic motion
    Is not all the life God fashions or reveals:

Let them prove their living souls against the notion
  That they live in you, or under you, O wheels!
Still, all day, the iron wheels go onward,
  Grinding life down from its mark;
And the children's souls, which God is calling sunward,
  Spin on blindly in the dark.

IX

Now tell the poor young children, O my brothers,
  To look up to Him and pray;
So the blessèd One who blesseth all the others,
  Will bless them another day.
They answer, 'Who is God that He should hear us,
  While the rushing of the iron wheels is stirred?
When we sob aloud, the human creatures near us
  Pass by, hearing not, or answer not a word.
And *we* hear not (for the wheels in their resounding)
  Strangers speaking at the door:
Is it likely God, with angels singing round Him,
  Hears our weeping any more?

X

'Two words, indeed, of praying we remember,
  And at midnight's hour of harm,
"Our Father," looking upward in the chamber,
  We say softly for a charm.
We know no other words except "Our Father,"
  And we think that, in some pause of angels' song,
God may pluck them with the silence sweet to gather,
  And hold both within his right hand which is strong.
"Our Father!" If He heard us, He would surely
  (For they call Him good and mild)
Answer, smiling down the steep world very purely,
  "Come and rest with me, my child."

XI

'But, no!' say the children, weeping faster,
  'He is speechless as a stone:
And they tell us, of His image is the master
  Who commands us to work on.
Go to!' say the children,—'up in Heaven,
  Dark, wheel-like, turning clouds are all we find.
Do not mock us; grief has made us unbelieving:
  We look up for God, but tears have made us blind.'
Do you hear the children weeping and disproving,
  O my brothers, what ye preach?
For God's possible is taught by his world's loving,
  And the children doubt of each.

XII

And well may the children weep before you!
  They are weary ere they run;
They have never seen the sunshine, nor the glory
  Which is brighter than the sun.
They know the grief of man, without its wisdom;
  They sink in man's despair, without its calm;
Are slaves, without the liberty in Christdom,
  Are martyrs, by the pang without the palm:
Are worn as if with age, yet unretrievingly
  The harvest of its memories cannot reap,—
Are orphans of the earthly love and heavenly.
  Let them weep! let them weep!

XIII

They look up with their pale and sunken faces,
  And their look is dread to see,
For they mind you of their angels in high places,
  With eyes turned on Deity.
'How long,' they say, 'how long, O cruel nation,

Will you stand, to move the world, on a child's heart,—
Stifle down with a mailèd heel its palpitation,
  And tread onward to your throne amid the mart?
Our blood splashes upward, O gold-heaper,
  And your purple shows your path!
But the child's sob in the silence curses deeper
  Than the strong man in his wrath.'

                              ELIZABETH BARRETT BROWNING

THE CHILDREN OF THE NIGHT

For those that never know the light,
    The darkness is a sullen thing;
And they, the Children of the Night,
    Seem lost in Fortune's winnowing.

But some are strong and some are weak,—
    And there's the story. House and home
Are shut from countless hearts that seek
    World-refuge that will never come.

And if there be no other life,
    And if there be no other chance
To weigh their sorrow and their strife
    Than in the scales of circumstance,

'Twere better, ere the sun go down
    Upon the first day we embark,
In life's imbittered sea to drown,
    Than sail forever in the dark.

But if there be a soul on earth
    So blinded with its own misuse
Of man's revealed, incessant worth,
    Or worn with anguish, that it views

No light but for a mortal eye,
   No rest but of a mortal sleep,
No God but in a prophet's lie,
   No faith for "honest doubt" to keep;

If there be nothing, good or bad,
   But chaos for a soul to trust,—
God counts it for a soul gone mad,
   And if God be God, He is just.

And if God be God, He is Love;
   And though the Dawn be still so dim,
It shows us we have played enough
   With creeds that make a fiend of Him.

There is one creed, and only one,
   That glorifies God's excellence;
So cherish, that His will be done,
   The common creed of common sense.

It is the crimson, not the gray,
   That charms the twilight of all time;
It is the promise of the day
   That makes the starry sky sublime;

It is the faith within the fear
   That holds us to the life we curse;—
So let us in ourselves revere
   The Self which is the Universe!

Let us, the Children of the Night,
   Put off the cloak that hides the scar!
Let us be Children of the Light,
   And tell the ages what we are!

EDWIN ARLINGTON ROBINSON

FROM "THE SPIRIT OF MAN"

(A PSALM OF CONFIDENCE)

THE spirit of Man shall triumph and reign o'er all the earth.

The earth was made for Man, he is heir to all that therein is.

He is the end of creation. the purpose of the ages since the dawn of time.

He is the fulfillment of all prophecy and in himself the goal of every great hope born in high desire.

Who art Thou, O Spirit of Man?

Thou art the Child of the Infinite, in thy nostrils is the breath of God.

Thou didst come at Love's behest, yea! to fulfill the Love of the Eternal didst Thou come.

Yet Man's beginnings were in lowliness, in nature akin to that of the brute.

His body and appetite bore the marks of the beast, yet in his soul was the unquenchable Spark of Divine Fire.

His ascending hath been with pain, with struggle and conflict hath he marched towards the Ideal.

At times he hath turned his face away from the Promise of Destiny.

He hath given reins to the lust of the brute; he hath appeared at times as the Child of Hate.

He hath forgotten his Divine Origin, he hath forsaken the dream of Eternal Love.

Then hath he lifted his hands against his fellows and war and bloodshed have dwelt upon the earth.

In moments of blind passion he hath destroyed the work of his own hands, the fruit of the centuries hath he cast to the winds.

He hath marred the Divine Image, deaf to the call of the Promise of God.

Upon the altars of Self hath he sacrificed Brotherhood, and ruled by avarice and greed he hath slain Justice and Right.

Thus have wickedness and sin dwelt in his midst, and his
  soul hath been chained in the bondage of low desires.
Yet all this could not destroy the unquenchable Spark of
  Divine Fire.
For it belongs to the Eternal and that which is Eternal can-
  not die.
Therefore, great though Thy shortcomings, manifold
  though Thy failures, wicked though Thy crimes;
I will not despair, O Spirit of Man!
Thou canst not forever deny the God that is within Thee,
  nor turn Thy back upon the Ideal
Though Thou destroyest fairest hopes yet shall they live
  again.
Though Thou returnest to the level of the beast Thou shalt
  arise to the heights of Thy Divine Humanity.
For the Spirit of Man breathes the untiring purpose of the
  Living God and to the fulfillment of that purpose the
  whole creation moves.

STANTON COIT

FROM "THE GREAT HUNGER"

Now it was that I began to realize how every great sorrow
leads us farther and farther out on the promontory of existence. I had come to the outermost point now—there was
no more. . . .

I sat alone on the promontory of existence, with the sun
and the stars gone out, and ice-cold emptiness above me,
about me, and in me, on every side.

But then, my friend, by degrees it dawned on me that there
was still something left. There was one little indomitable
spark in me, that began to glow all by itself—it was as if I
were lifted back to the first day of existence, and an eternal
will rose up in me, and said: Let there be light!

This will it was that by and by grew and grew in me, and
made me strong.

I began to feel an unspeakable compassion for all men upon earth, and yet in the last resort I was proud that I was one of them.

I understood how blind fate can strip and plunder us of all, and yet something will remain in us at the last, that nothing in heaven or earth can vanquish. Our bodies are doomed to die, and our spirit to be extinguished, yet still we bear within us the spark, the germ of an eternity of harmony and light both for the world and for God.

And I knew now that what I had hungered after in my best years was neither knowledge, nor honour, nor riches; nor to be a priest or a great creator in steel; no, friend, but to build temples; not chapels for prayers or churches for wailing penitent sinners, but a temple for the human spirit in its grandeur, where we could lift up our souls in an anthem as a gift to heaven.

. . . standing upon the ruins of my life, I felt a vast responsibility. Mankind must arise, and be better than the blind powers that order its ways; in the midst of its sorrows it must take heed that the godlike does not die. The spark of eternity was once more aglow in me, and said: Let there be light.

And more and more it came home to me that it is man himself that must create the divine in heaven and on earth—that that is his triumph over the dead omnipotence of the universe. . . .

We are flung by the indifferent law of the universe into a life that we cannot order as we would; we are ravaged by injustice, by sickness and sorrow, by fire and flood. Even the happiest must die. In his own home he is but on a visit. He never knows but that he may be gone to-morrow. And yet man smiles and laughs in the face of his tragic fate. In the midst of his thraldom he has created the beautiful on earth; in the midst of his torments he has had so much surplus energy of soul that he has sent it radiating forth into the cold depths of space and warmed them with God.

So marvellous art thou, O spirit of man! So godlike in thy very nature! Thou dost reap death, and in return thou sowest the dream of everlasting life. In revenge for thine evil fate thou dost fill the universe with an all-loving God.

We bore our part in his creation, all we who now are dust; we who sank down into the dark like flames gone out;— we wept, we exulted, we felt the ecstasy and the agony, but each of us brought our ray to the mighty sea of light, each of us, from the negro setting up the first mark above the grave of his dead to the genius raising the pillars of a temple towards heaven. We bore our part, from the poor mother praying beside a cradle, to the hosts that lifted their songs of praise high up into boundless space.

Honour to thee, O spirit of man. Thou givest a soul to the world, thou settest it a goal, thou art the hymn that lifts it into harmony; therefore turn back into thyself, lift high thy head and meet proudly the evil that comes to thee. Adversity can crush thee, death can blot thee out, yet art thou still unconquerable and eternal.

JOHAN BOJER

NOTE XIV

THAT man has limitless powers of development, the greater natures among us have always believed; and faith always tends to beget character of forward-looking types.

1. *Browning* does not forget human weaknesses and absorption in lesser ideals in asserting confidence that man's yearning for self-realization is fully matched by the rich opportunities opened to him in the life of love. With *Holland*, however, he reminds us that it is only by the painful steps of an uphill climb that we ever achieve the truly worthy ends of life.

2. As in "After," human joy sometimes passes into utter eclipse; but "Closing the Doors" and "The Road-Song of the Race" usually represent the sequel when all of the forces of one's life converge to bring back the sense of a common humanity and that reassertion of will which invariably spells moral victory. The hand of progress cannot be stayed.

3. The next ten selections give varied expression to this sense of mastery, the joy of progress, and man's growing sense of powers which Time can by no means measure. His future lies in the realm of the free and the eternal, with a joyous God leading the way.

4. But in the face of pressing social problems—tenements, the jangle of noisy streets, illness of body and spirit, child-labor, and a pessimistic view of life because some have never seen the natural light of happiness—can one be sure of a hopeful future? The very exigencies of life, say our writers in this closing section, yield overwhelming power for victory. Life is actually seen to its best advantage against the black cloud of human sorrow; for sorrow leads to desperation, and desperation to strenuous activity for self-preservation. And the will to conquer finds a greater Will standing by to co-operate and to assure human triumph over all opposing forces.

V

JESUS IN EVERY-DAY LIFE

XV

OUR MASTER

Immortal Love, forever full,
  Forever flowing free,
Forever shared, forever whole,
  A never-ebbing sea!

Our outward lips confess the name
  All other names above;
Love only knoweth whence it came,
  And comprehendeth love.

Blow, winds of God, awake and blow
  The mists of earth away!
Shine out, O Light Divine, and show
  How wide and far we stray!

Hush every lip, close every book,
  The strife of tongues forbear;
Why forward reach, or backward look,
  For love that clasps like air?

We may not climb the heavenly steeps
  To bring the Lord Christ down:
In vain we search the lowest deeps,
  For him no depths can drown.

.   .   .   .

But warm, sweet, tender, even yet
  A present help is he;
And faith has still its Olivet,
  And love its Galilee.

The healing of his seamless dress
  Is by our beds of pain;

We touch him in life's throng and press,
  And we are whole again.

Through him the first fond prayers are said
  Our lips of childhood frame,
The last low whispers of our dead
  Are burdened with his name.

O Lord and Master of us all!
  Whate'er our name or sign,
We own thy sway, we hear thy call,
  We test our lives by thine.

.   .   .   .

Our Friend, our Brother, and our Lord,
  What may thy service be?—
Nor name, nor form, nor ritual word,
  But simply following thee.

We bring no ghastly holocaust,
  We pile no graven stone;
He serves thee best who loveth most
  His brothers and thy own.

Thy litanies, sweet offices
  Of love and gratitude;
Thy sacramental liturgies,
  The joy of doing good.

In vain shall waves of incense drift
  The vaulted nave around,
In vain the minster turret lift
  Its brazen weights of sound.

The heart must ring thy Christmas bells,
  Thy inward altars raise;
Its faith and hope thy canticles,
  And its obedience praise!

                                    WHITTIER

A BALLAD OF TREES AND THE MASTER

INTO the woods my Master went,
Clean forspent, forspent.
Into the woods my Master came,
Forspent with love and shame.
But the olives they were not blind to Him,
The little gray leaves were kind to Him:
The thorn-tree had a mind to Him
When into the woods He came.

Out of the woods my Master went,
And He was well content.
Out of the woods my Master came,
Content with death and shame.
When Death and Shame would woo Him last,
From under the trees they drew Him last:
'Twas on a tree they slew Him—last
When out of the woods He came.

SIDNEY LANIER

REJECTED

THE world denies her prophets with rash breath,
    Makes rich her slaves, her flatterers adorns;
To Wisdom's lips she presses drowsy death,
    And on the brow divine a crown of thorns.
Yet blessèd, though neglected and despised—
    Who for the World himself hath sacrificed,
Who hears unmoved her witless mockery,
    While to his spirit, slighted and misprized,
Whisper the voices of Eternity!

FLORENCE EARLE COATES

THY KINGDOM COME!

Now in the east the morning dies,
　The full light of the splendid sun
Strikes downward on our lifted eyes
　And the long journey is begun:
　　Across the shattered walls
　　A voice prophetic calls,
　　　With tumult and with laughter
　　　We rise and follow after.

The modern world, immense and wide,
　Awaits us, huger than before,
With new stars swimming in the Void,
　And Science broadening evermore
　　The sweep of the limitless Vast,
　　The Past is dead and past;
　　　Yet through it all forever
　　　One voice is silent never.

'Mid iron wheels and planets whirled,
　The clanging city, in the street,
－The machinery of the modern world—
　His lips cry loudly and entreat,
　　Like one that lifts his head
　　For a second time from the dead,
　　　—Out of the Ages' prison
　　　The new Christ re-arisen!

O holy spirit—O heart of man!
　Will you not listen, turn, and bow
To that clear voice, since time began
　Loud in your ears, and louder now!
　　Mankind, the Christ, retried—
　　Recrowned, recrucified;
　　　No god for a gift God gave us,
　　　Mankind alone must save us.

Will you not hear him—reach your hand!—
　From factory, tenement and slum
His voice pleads vainly in the land,
　　Ah, heart of man, the time has come!
　　　The voice of Cain that wailed
　　　Grew sorrowful and failed,
　　　But a new voice rings deeper,
　　　"You *are* your brother's keeper."

O world, grown pitiless and grim!
　O world of men, had you but known
Your brother is your Christ, through him
　　You must be saved and him alone!
　　　Love for his sorrows—love
　　　Alone can lift you above
　　　The pain of your misgiving,
　　　The doom and the horror of living.

Within ourselves we must find the light
　And in ourselves our gods to-be,
Not throned beyond the stars of night;
　　Here, in America, we must see
　　　The love of man for man,
　　　The new world republican,—
　　　A heaven, not superhuman,
　　　Reborn in man and woman.

Forward—! Truth glorifies, not kills
　The ancient marvel of the soul,
Each new progression but fulfills
　　That wonder,—the wheels of the world that roll
　　　Thundering, but proclaim
　　　God with a louder name;
　　　Science, revealing, rehearses
　　　But vaster universes.

Though the dark veil of dusk and doom
　You strip from off the Soul of things,

Though with new torches through the gloom
  You hunt Him on untiring wings,
    And in the starry space,
    You shall not find His face;
    A voice comes following after
    Out of the dust, with laughter.

The Vision—the Ideal—the God—
  Not anything ever may destroy.
Then let us follow, winged and shod
  With love, with courage and with joy;
    Herein alone is the truth,
    The glory and fire of youth,
    Herein all high endeavor,
    Forever and forever!

                  JOHN HALL WHEELOCK

THE SUPREME LOVE OF JESUS

THIS was the greatness of Jesus Christ. He felt, as no other felt, a union of mind with the human race, felt that all had a spark of that same intellectual and immortal flame which dwelt in him. I insist on this view of his character, not only to encourage us to aspire after a likeness to Jesus; I consider it as peculiarly fitted to call forth love toward him. If I regard Jesus as an august stranger, belonging to an entirely different class of existence from myself, having no common thoughts or feelings with me, and looking down upon me with only such a sympathy as I have with an inferior animal, I should regard him with a vague awe; but the immeasurable space between us would place him beyond friendship and affection. But when I feel that all minds form one family, that I have the same nature with Jesus, and that he came to communicate to me, by his teaching, example, and intercession, his own mind, to bring me into communion

with what was sublimest, purest, happiest in himself, then
I can love him as I love no other being, excepting only
him who is the Father alike of Christ and of the Christian.

CHANNING

AN INVOCATION—CHRISTMAS, 1923

O Star of Bethlehem!
Rise o'er the fringèd hem
Of the horizon's bar.
Rise, and with radiance white,
Born of thy path's delight
Lead us away from night
To that poor Manger, lowly and afar.

"Once there were three wise men."
So spake the Scripture.
Wisdom, come again
And lift our blinded eyes.
Open, O threatening skies,
And let the fair star's light
Into our inner sight;
And we shall rise,
As once, in long gone years,
Men, whom we now know wise,
Followed despite of fears.

Scoffers have railed,
And those of ardent faith—
Yea even those—
Say that our Christianity hath failed
Because o'er God's green earth
Rivers of blood have run;
And, done to death, or blank with hollow dearth,
Myriads have grovelled, died beneath a sun,
Which, spite of woes,

Rises immutable, in golden calm,
Indifferent to alarm!

Here on this Christmas night,
When candles deck the fir trees, all a-light,
When Christmas cheer purges our hearts of fear,
And when in some deep cell
Of all our being there sings an undertone that all is well—
We know that Christianity can never fail!
That little Child born in the manger,
Jesus, meek and mild—
That Man divine,
Righteous in wrath, though full of love's rare wine—
That Saviour, suffering because our sin
Ravaged his soul within;
Martyred and pale—
Nay! Christianity can never fail.

But, Fellowmen,
We, we have failed again.—
We, Nations of the world,
Who have unfurled
Standards of selfish greed, or slothful ease—
We, upon bended knees,
Must spread our palms, and joy to feel the nail
Pierce quivering flesh—
Or else our Lord *shall* fail.

Woe, woe betide
Unless each tender side
Shall bare itself to what the Spear may bring
Of quick, sharp sting—
'Tis *we*, O Christ! O Man of Galilee!
We, who have failèd thee!

And now on this thy night,
The night of joy,

When thou didst come, Heaven's promise to the Earth,
When Mary held thee close, a little boy,
Against a Mother's breast
For succor and for rest—
On this still night,
Thy star must shed its light,
Into our hearts, until,
With holy flame,
And in thy name,
We who believe that thou canst never fail,
Must rise, an army clad in steelèd mail,
And pledge ourselves anew to that deep love
Which thou hast died to prove.
Let us give love to all our fellowmen
Who, as we do, falter and fall, yet rise again
If love but faileth not.
O Christ, who standeth at the door,
Craving to enter—knocking as of yore,
Whose love is without blot—
The time has come when we, who know that thou canst never
        fail,
We must prevail.

Jesus, of Calvary and of the Cross,
Ourselves we dedicate
This holy night, when thou for peace wast born;
We, of a world disordered, torn and threatened by grim fate,
Pledge love again, peace and good-will to men,
Against thy loss.
Thou savedst us, who for our sins hast died—
Must we not now save thee, O Crucified!

CORINNE ROOSEVELT ROBINSON

THE UNIQUENESS OF JESUS

It is the singleness of this "life in God" that gave its uniqueness to the personality of Jesus; referring back all his experiences to the infinitely Perfect, all his sorrows to the eternal blessedness, all his disappointments to the living Fountain of hope. The deluding impressions of a drudging and suffering world were habitually checked and transcended by a recovered contact with the one and only Good.

In completely realizing the filial relation to God, he at once glorified the dependent, obedient, suffering life which is assigned to us; and rose to the height of that divine kinship which makes the affections of heaven and earth reciprocal, and identifies the essence of moral perfection in both spheres. The Man of Sorrows is our personal exemplar; the Son of God is our spiritual ideal, in whose harmonious and majestic soul, imperturbable in justice, tender in mercy, stainless in purity, and bending in protection over all guileless truth, an objective reflection of the Divine holiness is given to us, answering and interpreting the subjective revelation of the conscience.

JAMES MARTINEAU

CHRIST OF JUDEA

Christ of Judea, look Thou in my heart:
Do I not love Thee, look to Thee, in Thee
Alone have faith of all the sons of men,
Faith deepening with the weight and woe of years?

Pure soul and tenderest of all that came
Into this world of sorrow, hear my prayer:
Lead me, yes, lead me deeper into life—
This suffering human life wherein Thou liv'st
And breath'st still, and hold'st Thy way divine.

'Tis here, O pitying Christ, where Thee I seek,
Here where the strife is fiercest; where the sun
Beats down upon the highway thronged with men,
And in the raging mart. Oh! deeper lead
My soul into the living world of souls
Where Thou dost move.

RICHARD WATSON GILDER

THE BALLAD OF THE CROSS

MELCHIOR, Gaspar, Balthazar,
  Great gifts they bore and meet;
White linen for His body fair
  And purple for His feet;
And golden things—the joy of kings—
  And myrrh to breathe Him sweet.

It was the shepherd Terish spake,
  "Oh, poor the gift I bring—
A little cross of broken twigs,
  A hind's gift to a king—
Yet, haply, He may smile to see
  And know my offering."

And it was Mary held her Son
  Full softly to her breast,
"Great gifts and sweet are at Thy feet
  And wonders king-possessed,
O little Son, take Thou the one
  That pleasures Thee the best."

It was the Christ-Child in her arms
  Who turned from gaud and gold,
Who turned from wondrous gifts and great,
  From purple woof and fold,
And to His breast the cross He pressed
  That scarce His hands could hold.

'Twas king and shepherd went their way—
  Great wonder tore their bliss;
'Twas Mary clasped her little Son
  Close, close to feel her kiss,
And in His hold the cross lay cold
  Between her heart and His!

THEODOSIA GARRISON

A WORD

A WORD came forth in Galilee, a word like to a star;
It climbed and rang and blessed and burnt wherever brave
    hearts are;
A word of sudden secret hope, of trial and increase
Of wrath and pity fused in fire, and passion kissing peace.
A star that o'er the citied world beckoned, a sword of flame;
A star with myriad thunders tongued: a mighty word there
    came.

The wedge's dart passed into it, the groan of timber-wains,
The ringing of the rivet nails, the shrieking of the planes;
The hammering on the roofs at morn, the busy workshop
    roar;
The hiss of shavings drifted deep along the windy floor;
The heat-browned toiler's crooning song, the hum of human
    worth—
Mingled of all the noise of crafts, the ringing word went
    forth.

The splash of nets passed into it, the grind of sand and shell,
The boat-hook's clash, the boat-oar's jar, the cries to buy
    and sell,
The flapping of the landed shoals, the canvas crackling free,
And through all varied notes and cries, the roaring of the
    sea,
The noise of little lives and brave, of needy lives and high;
In gathering all the throes of earth, the living word went by.

Earth's giant sins bowed down to it, in Empire's huge eclipse,
When darkness sat above the thrones, seven thunders on her lips,
The woe of cities entered it, the clang of idols' falls,
The scream of filthy Cæsars stabbed high in their brazen halls,
The dim hoarse floods of naked men, the world-realms snapping girth,
The trumpets of Apocalypse, the darkness of the earth:

The wrath that brake the eternal lamp and hid the eternal hill,
A world's destruction loading, the word went onward still—
The blaze of creeds passed into it, the hiss of horrid fires,
The headlong spear, the scarlet cross, the hair-shirt and the briars,
The cloistered brethren's thunderous chaunt, the errant champion's song,
The shifting of the crowns and thrones, the tangle of the strong.

The shattering fall of crest and crown and shield and cross and cope,
The tearing of the gauds of time, the blight of prince and pope,
The reign of ragged millions leagued to wrench a loaded debt,
Loud with the many-throated roar, the word went forward yet.
The song of wheels passed into it, the roaring and the smoke,
The riddle of the want and wage, the fogs that burn and choke.
The breaking of the girths of gold, the needs that creep and swell,
The strengthening hope, the dazing light, the deafening evangel,

Through kingdoms dead and empires damned, through
    changes without cease,
With earthquake, chaos, born and fed, rose,—and the word
    was "Peace."

CHESTERTON

THE EVERLASTING MERCY

.   .   .   .

I DID not think, I did not strive,
The deep peace burnt my me alive;
The bolted door had broken in,
I knew that I had done with sin.
I knew that Christ had given me birth
To brother all the souls on earth,
And every bird and every beast
Should share the crumbs broke at the feast.

O glory of the lighted mind.
How dead I'd been, how dumb, how blind.
The station brook, to my new eyes,
Was babbling out of Paradise,
The waters rushing from the rain
Were singing Christ has risen again.
I thought all earthly creatures knelt
From rapture of the joy I felt.
The narrow station-wall's brick ledge,
The wild hop withering in the hedge,
The lights in huntsman's upper storey
Were parts of an eternal glory,
Were God's eternal garden flowers.
I stood in bliss at this for hours.

.   .   .   .

Out of the mist into the light,
O blessèd gift of inner sight.
The past was faded like a dream;
There come the jingling of a team,

A ploughman's voice, a clink of chain,
Slow hoofs, and harness under strain.
Up the slow slope a team came bowing,
Old Callow at his autumn ploughing,
Old Callow, stooped above the hales,
Ploughing the stubble into wales.

. . . .

O wet red swathe of earth laid bare,
O truth, O strength, O gleaming share,
O patient eyes that watch the goal,
O ploughman of the sinner's soul.
O Jesus, drive the coulter deep
To plough my living man from sleep.

Slow up the hill the plough team plod,
Old Callow at the task of God,
Helped by man's wit, helped by the brute,
Turning a stubborn clay to fruit,
His eyes forever on some sign
To help him plough a perfect line.

. . . .

I kneeled there in the muddy fallow,
I knew that Christ was there with Callow,
That Christ was standing there with me,
That Christ had taught me what to be,
That I should plough, and as I ploughed
My Saviour Christ would sing aloud,
And as I drove the clods apart
Christ would be ploughing in my heart,
Through rest-harrow and bitter roots,
Through all my bad life's rotten fruits.

O Christ who holds the open gate,
O Christ who drives the furrow straight,
O Christ, the plough, O Christ, the laughter
Of holy white birds flying after,

Lo, all my heart's field red and torn,
And Thou wilt bring the young green corn,
The young green corn divinely springing,
The young green corn forever singing;
And when the field is fresh and fair
Thy blessèd feet shall glitter there,
And we will walk the weeded field,
And tell the golden harvest's yield,
The corn that makes the holy bread
By which the soul of man is fed,
The holy bread, the food unpriced,
Thy everlasting mercy, Christ.

The share will jar on many a stone,
Thou wilt not let me stand alone;
And I shall feel (thou wilt not fail),
Thy hand on mine upon the hale.

. . . .

O lovely lily clean,
O lily springing green,
O lily bursting white,
Dear lily of delight,
Spring in my heart agen
That I may flower to men.

JOHN MASEFIELD

[From "The Everlasting Mercy," The Macmillan Co.]

CHAOS—AND THE WAY OUT

I

I HEARD a knocking on The Outer Door
That stands betwixt man and the Infinite;
And every knock re-echoed in my heart,
And in the troubled heart-beats of the world.

The Door stood fast, with complex bolts and bars
That could be opened only from within,
And He who knocked stood patiently without,
And knocked . . . and knocked . . . and waited. . . .   But
The bolts were rusted stiff with many a sin,
And no man rose to loosen them
And let Him in.

Within were noises multitudinous,
Confusions vast and endless, hopeless strife;
Earth's millions, swarming like an angry hive,
Fought for their lives but gave no thought to Life.
How should that knocking on the Outer Door
Be heard amid such murderous uproar?

Small thought indeed they gave, and still less heed
To Him who stood so patiently without
And knocked upon The Door, and on their hearts,
Bolted as surely lest He should come in.

And He without;—
His feet were bleeding from the road
That He so hopefully had trod
To lead men back to God.

His brow still bore the scurril thorn,
(—The noblest crown was ever worn—)
His fair white robe was stained and torn;
But yet no suppliant forlorn
Was He
Who waited there so patiently.

His face was sad yet full of loving hope—
The saddest face the world has ever seen.
Yet Love,
That conquered Death, still hopeful strove
With that sore challenge of the close-barred Door,

Nor would surrender smallest shred of hope,
But hoping, lived and loved and hoped the more.
For Love lives on though Hope may droop and die,
Since Christ Himself gave Love her crown
Of Immortality.

The gentle hands that ever wrought man's good
Still bore the wounds of man's ingratitude,
And as He waited there, so great the pain
Of that barred Door, the old wounds bled again.

And . . . ever . . . ever,
More and more
Impassioned, yet all patiently,
The Silent Watcher stood without
And knocked upon the close-barred Door,
Stood ever waiting . . . waiting . . . waiting,
Ever knocking on The Door,
    And no man let Him in.

Has Life e'er known a sweeter, truer,
Nobler, more devoted wooer,
Or Love more loving a pursuer?
    Yet—man would none of Him!

II

Earth's ills waxed more and more; and still The Door,
By which God's Mercy entrance sought, was barred.
The world in torment groaned unceasingly,—
One long unending cry of tortured souls,—
The panting sobs of men who fought for life,
Women in anguish, children's wailing cries,
Laughter of fools, and moans of dying men,
All blent in one hoarse dirge of agony.

For, even where no actual strife was waged,
Where, here and there, the lands at times had peace,—

Yet even there black hidden warfare raged,
Of fouler cast than where the hosts engaged.

—Warfare of commerce grinding men to nought,
Bodies and souls but chattels to be bought
And sold for profit—
Traffic of ghouls with endless evils fraught;

—Warfare of vast self-seeking enterprise,
Which grew distent on others' miseries,
Soul-less and thoughtless save for its own gain,
Its ledgers foul with many a grim red stain;

—Warfare of greed that stole the children's lives;
Warfare of lust that naught could satisfy,
Honour as dust, and women left to die;
—Warfare of class with class, and rancorous hate
That would all save itself annihilate.

.   .   .   .

Earth was no longer earth as God designed;
Perverse and blind, the free-will of mankind
Had made it liker hell. And Faith and Hope
Their draggled wings had spread,
And, sorrowing, fled,
Since Love, that should have ruled the world,
Seemed dead.

And . . . ever . . . ever
More and more
Impassioned, yet all patiently,
The Silent Watcher stood without
And knocked upon the close-barred Door,
Stood ever waiting . . . waiting . . . waiting,
Ever knocking on the Door,
   And no man let Him in.

Has Life e'er known a sweeter, truer,
Nobler, more devoted wooer,

Or Love more loving a pursuer?
  Yet—man would none of Him!

.   .   .   .

Then heard they Him,—and heeded, for their woes
Had grown beyond their bearing, and their needs
Passed their desires.
Storms they had sown, and whirlwinds they had reaped,
Sands they had ploughed, and garnered only dust;
Their mouths were full of ashes—Dead-Sea fruit
That turned within to gall and bitterness.
Their building left a world with wreckage fraught,
Their vast self-strivings all had come to nought,
Their own devices their own ruin wrought.

"Unbar the Door!"—they cried,—*"Unbar the Door,*
And let the Lord Christ in!
All other ways have proved our own ways vain,
His power alone can cleanse the world of sin,
His love alone can give us peace again.
Unbar the Door, and let the Lord Christ in!"

.   .   .   .

The Door swung wide, and wider, wider grew,
Till like the dawn it spread across the sky;
Great seas of new life-giving light welled through,
And spread o'er all the earth a quickening flood,—
Healing and life for all earth's deadly woes,
That larger Life that Love alone bestows—
Life out of death for all the sons of men,
For in the Light Christ came to earth again.

.   .   .   .

No gladder face was ever seen than His,
So full of grace and all high sovereignties,
And all aglow with sweet benignities.
His love-lit eyes shone like the great twin stars,
And on His brow which once had worn,

With patient dignity, the thorn,
Was now a radiant crown of stars,
Which hid and healed the bitter scars
Made by the crown of scorn.

His robe was brighter than the noonday sun,
And in His hand He bore a holy grail,
Clear crystal, brimmed with blessings infinite,—
Pardon and grace for all who would,
And benedictions sweet. . . .

. . . .

Then was earth made anew where'er He went,
For all men's hearts were opened to the Light,
And Christ was King, and Lord Omnipotent.

And everywhere men's hearts turned unto Him
As to the very source and fount of Right,
As flowers turn to the sun, and everywhere
New Life sprang up to greet Him as He went
Dispensing grace to all men everywhere.
And His dispensèd grace changed all men's hearts,
Made His will theirs, and their wills wholly His;
So that they strove no more each for himself,
But each for good of all, and all for Him;
Man's common aim was for the common good;
The age-old feuds were of the past,
And all mankind joined hands at last
In common brotherhood.

. . . .

*And every man in all the whole wide world
Had room, and time, and wherewithal to live
His life at fullest full within the Law—
The Law that has no bounds or bonds for those
Who live it, for it is His Love,—
The great unchanged, unchanging, and unchangeable
Law whose beginning and whose end is—Love.*

JOHN OXENHAM

THE GREATNESS OF JESUS

JESUS CHRIST belonged to the true race of prophets. He saw with open eye the mystery of the soul. Drawn by its severe harmony, ravished with its beauty, he lived in it, and had his being there. Alone in all history, he estimated the greatness of man. One man was true to what was in you and me. He saw that God incarnates himself in man, and evermore goes forth anew to take possession of his world.

The excellence of Jesus, and of every true teacher, is, that he affirms the Divinity in him and in us —not thrusts himself between it and us.

Jesus speaks always from within, and in a degree that transcends all others. In that is the miracle. I believe beforehand that it ought to be so. All men stand continually in the expectation of the appearance of such a teacher.

EMERSON

JESUS THE CARPENTER

IF I could hold within my hand
　The hammer Jesus swung,
Not all the gold in all the land,
Nor jewels countless as the sand,
　All in the balance flung,
Could weigh the value of that thing
Round which his fingers once did cling.

If I could have the table he
　Once made in Nazareth,
Not all the pearls in all the sea,
Nor crowns of kings, or kings to be,
　As long as men have breath,
Could buy that thing of wood he made—
The Lord of Lords who learned a trade.

Yes, but his hammer still is shown
   By honest hands that toil,
And round his table men sit down,
And all are equals, with a crown
   No gold nor pearls can soil.
The shop at Nazareth was bare,
But Brotherhood was builded there.

CHARLES M. SHELDON

THE BETTER PART

LONG fed on boundless hopes, O race of man,
How angrily thou spurn'st all simpler fare!
"Christ," some one says, "was human as we are;
No judge eyes us from heaven, our sin to scan;

We live no more, when we have done our span."
"Well, then, for Christ," thou answerest, "who can care?
From sin which Heaven records not, why forbear?
Live we like brutes our life without a plan!"

So answerest thou; but why not rather say,—
"Hath man no second life? *Pitch this one high!*
Sits there no judge in heaven, our sin to see?

More strictly, then, the inward judge obey!
Was Christ a man like us? *Ah! let us try
If we then, too, can be such men as he!*"

MATTHEW ARNOLD

[By permission of the publishers, The Macmillan Co.]

PEACE ON EARTH

IT came upon the midnight clear,
   That glorious song of old,

From angels bending near the earth
 To touch their harps of gold:
'Peace on the earth, good-will to men,
 From heaven's all-gracious King!'
The world in solemn stillness lay
 To hear the angels sing.

Still through the cloven skies they come,
 With peaceful wings unfurled;
And still their heavenly music floats
 O'er all the weary world:
Above its sad and lowly plains
 They bend on hovering wing,
And ever o'er its Babel-sounds
 The blessed angels sing.

Yet with the woes of sin and strife
 The world has suffered long;
Beneath the angels' strain have rolled
 Two thousand years of wrong;
And man, at war with man, hears not
 The love-song which they bring:
O hush the noise, ye men of strife,
 And hear the angels sing!

For lo, the days are hastening on,
 By prophet-bards foretold,
When with the ever-circling years
 Comes round the age of gold,
When Peace shall over all the earth
 Its ancient splendors fling,
And the whole world give back the song
 Which now the angels sing!

        EDMUND H. SEARS

CHRISTMAS, 1919

SHALL ever a star shine out to men
   As the Bethlehem Star of old?
Shall ever the wise men turn again
   With their frankincense and gold,
And follow the star to the radiant king
   That had come to be stable born?
And, oh, shall ever the angels sing
   As they did on that happy morn?

Shall ever men treasure another day
   For all that it means to them?
Shall ever there be in the far away
   Another such Bethlehem?
Shall ever the bells ring out at dawn
   Such glorious joy for all
As they did when the Savior of men was born
   On the straw of a stable stall?

The days have come from the womb of time,
   Dawned, risen to noon and died,
And some have come when the bells would chime
   And some when the world was tried;
But never through ages old and gray,
   Since ever the world began,
Have mortals witnessed another day
   That has meant so much to man.

Now He that once in a manger lay
   Still lives in the hearts of men,
The world is keeping His Christmas day
   As the wise men kept it then.
For ever the heavens shall ring with song
   And ever the bells shall chime,
And this glorious day that has lived so long
   Shall live to the end of time.

EDGAR A. GUEST

A PARABLE

SAID Christ our Lord, "I will go and see
How the men, my brethren, believe in me."
He passed not again through the gate of birth,
But made himself known to the children of earth.

Then said the chief priests, and rulers, and kings,
"Behold, now, the Giver of all good things;
Go to, let us welcome with pomp and state
Him who alone is mighty and great."

With carpets of gold the ground they spread
Wherever the Son of Man should tread,
And in palace-chambers lofty and rare
They lodged him, and served him with kingly fare.

Great organs surged through arches dim
Their jubilant floods in praise of him;
And in church, and palace, and judgment-hall,
He saw his own image high over all.

But still, wherever his steps they led,
The Lord in sorrow bent down his head,
And from under the heavy foundation-stones,
The son of Mary heard bitter groans.

And in church, and palace, and judgment-hall,
He marked great fissures that rent the wall,
And opened wider and yet more wide
As the living foundation heaved and sighed.

"Have ye founded your thrones and altars, then,
On the bodies and souls of living men?
And think ye that building shall endure,
Which shelters the noble and crushes the poor?

"With gates of silver and bars of gold
Ye have fenced my sheep from their Father's fold;
I have heard the dropping of their tears
In heaven these eighteen hundred years."

"O Lord and Master, not ours the guilt,
We build but as our fathers built;
Behold thine images, how they stand,
Sovereign and sole, through all our land.

"Our task is hard,—with sword and flame
To hold thine earth forever the same,
And with sharp crooks of steel to keep
Still, as thou leftest them, thy sheep."

Then Christ sought out an artisan,
A low-browed, stunted, haggard man,
And a motherless girl, whose fingers thin
Pushed from her faintly want and sin.

These set he in the midst of them,
And as they drew back their garment-hem,
For fear of defilement, "Lo, here," said he,
"The images ye have made of me!"

JAMES RUSSELL LOWELL

L'ENVOI

O Love triumphant over guilt and sin,
My soul is soiled, but Thou shalt enter in;
My feet must stumble if I walk alone,
Lonely my heart till beating by Thine own;
My will is weakness till it rest in Thine,
Cut off, I wither, thirsting for the Vine;
My deeds are dry leaves on a sapless tree,
My life is lifeless till it live in Thee!

FREDERIC L. KNOWLES

"THE CREED OF CREEDS"

AND so the Word had breath, and wrought
　　With human hands the creed of creeds
　　In loveliness of perfect deeds,
More strong than all poetic thought;

Which he may read that binds the sheaf,
　　Or builds the house, or digs the grave,
　　And those wild eyes that watch the wave
In roarings round the coral reef.
　　　　　　　　　　　　　　TENNYSON

[From "The Works of Tennyson," The Macmillan Co.]

GOLGOTHA

OUR crosses are hewn from different trees,
But we all must have our Calvaries;
We may climb the height from a different side,
But we each go up to be crucified;
As we scale the steep another may share
The dreadful load that our shoulders bear,
But the costliest sorrow is all our own—
For on the summit we bleed alone!

　　　　　　　　　　FREDERIC L. KNOWLES

TO JESUS THE NAZARENE

CLOSEST to men, thou pitying Son of man,
And thrilled from crown to foot with fellowship,
Yet most apart and strange and lonely as God—
Dwell in my heart, remote and intimate One!
Brother of all the world, I come to Thee!

Gentle as she who nursed Thee at her breast
(Yet what a lash of lightnings once thy tongue
To scourge the hypocrite and Pharisee!)—

Nerve Thou mine arm, O meek, O mighty One!
Champion of all who fail, I fly to Thee!

O Man of Sorrows with the wounded hands—
For chaplet, for throne, a pagan cross;
Bowed with the woe and agony of time,
Yet loved by children and the feasting guests—
I bring my suffering, joyful heart to Thee!

Chaste as the virginal lily on her stem,
Yet in each lot, full pulse, each tropic vein,
More filled with feeling than the flower with sun;
No anchorite—hale, sinewy, warm with love—
I come in youth's high tide of bliss to Thee!

O Christ of contrasts, infinite paradox,
Yet life's explainer, solvent harmony,
Frail strength, pure passion, meek austerity,
And the white splendor of these darkened years—
I lean my wondering, wayward heart on Thine!

FREDERIC L. KNOWLES

THE OTHER WISE MAN

So—the Other Wise Man—passed through countries
where famine lay heavy upon the land, and the poor were
crying for bread. . . . He visited the oppressed and the afflicted in the gloom of subterranean prisons, and the crowded
wretchedness of slave-markets, and the weary toil of galley-
ships. In all this populous and intricate world of anguish,
though he found none to worship, he found many to help.
He fed the hungry, and clothed the naked, and healed the
sick, and comforted the captive; and his years passed more
swiftly than the weaver's shuttle. . . . It seemed almost
as if he had forgotten his quest.

Three-and-thirty years of the life of Artaban had passed

away, and he was still a pilgrim and a seeker after light. His hair—was now white as the wintry snow. . . .

Worn and weary and ready to die, but still looking for the King, he had come for the last time to Jerusalem . . . at last he might succeed. . . . The multitude . . . flowed unceasingly along the street that leads to the Damascus gate. . . .

"Jesus of Nazareth, a man who has done many wonderful works among the people, so that they love him greatly—Pilate has sent him to the cross because he said that he was the 'King of the Jews.'"

How strangely these familiar words fell upon the tired heart of Artaban. They had led him for a lifetime over land and sea. And now . . . the King . . . was about to perish.

(Artaban) ". . . it may be that I shall find the King . . . and shall come in time to offer my pearl for his ransom before he dies."

And so the old man followed the multitude with slow and painful steps . . . a troop of Macedonian soldiers came down the street, dragging a young girl with torn dress and dishevelled hair. As the Magian paused to look at her with compassion, she broke suddenly from the hands of her tormenters, and threw herself at his feet, clasping him around the knees. She had seen his white cap and the winged circle on his breast.

"Have pity on me," she cried, "and save me, for the sake of the God of Purity! I also am a daughter of the true religion. . . ."

Twice the gift which he had consecrated to the worship of religion had been drawn to the service of humanity. . . .

Was it his great opportunity, or his last temptation? He took the pearl from his bosom. Never had it seemed so luminous, so radiant, so full of tender, living lustre. He laid it in the hand of the slave.

"This is thy ransom, daughter! It is the last of my treasures which I kept for the King."

. . . .

A heavy tile, shaken from the roof, fell and struck the old man on the temple. He lay breathless and pale, with his gray head resting on the young girl's shoulder. . . . As she bent over him, fearing that he was dead, there came a voice through the twilight, very small and still, like music sounding from a distance. . . . The girl turned . . . but saw no one.

Then the old man's lips began to move, as if in answer, and she heard him say in the Parthian tongue:

"Not so, my Lord! For when saw I thee an hungered and fed thee? Or thirsty, and gave thee drink? Three-and-thirty years have I looked for thee; but I have never seen thy face, nor ministered to thee, my King."

He ceased, and the sweet voice came again . . . very faint and far away:

"Verily, I say unto thee, inasmuch as thou hast done it unto one of the least of these my brethren, thou hast done it unto me."

A calm radiance of wonder and joy lighted the pale face of Artaban like the first ray of dawn on a snowy mountain peak. A long breath of relief exhaled gently from his lips.

His journey was ended. His treasures were accepted. The Other Wise Man had found the King.

HENRY VAN DYKE

IF THE CHRIST YOU MEAN

Ah, no! If the Christ you mean
Shall pass from this time, this scene,
These hearts, these lives of ours,
'Tis but as the summer flowers
Pass but return again,
To gladden the world of men
For he,—the only, the true,—
In each age, in each waiting heart,
Leaps into life anew.
Tho' he pass, he shall not depart.

Behold him now where he comes!
Not the Christ of our subtle creeds,
But the lord of our hearts, of our homes,
Of our hopes, our prayers, our needs;
The brother of want and blame,
The lover of women and men,
With a love that puts to shame
All passions of mortal ken,—
Yet of all of women born
His is the scorn of scorn;
Before whose face do fly
Lies and the love of a lie;
Who from the temple of God
And the sacred place of laws
Drives forth, with smiting rod,
The herds of ravening maws.

'Tis he, as none other can,
Makes free the spirit of man,
And speaks, in darkest night,
One word of awful light
That strikes through the dreadful pain
Of life, a reason sane—
That word divine which brought
The universe from naught.

Ah, no! thou life of the heart,
Never shalt thou depart!
Not till the leaven of God
Shall lighten each human clod;
Not till the world shall climb
To thy height serene, sublime,
Shall the Christ who enters our door
Pass to return no more.

RICHARD WATSON GILDER

NOTE XV

JESUS of NAZARETH is just coming to his own in the literature of the past half-century. Either the subject has been too sacred to touch, or possibly men have believed that they could not better the story of the gospels and the traditions of the Church. But the growing demand for human leadership and for practical ideals of living is creating a new place for Jesus in the busy life of our day.

These writings pay a very simple, but most hearty, tribute to Him who, more than any other in history, has made God and religion, mercy and justice, prayer and the need of humility, compellingly vital and attractive.

As the world's most startling and attractive embodiment of devotion to ideals and love for brother man; as the stern Conscience of the race, urging men to endure beyond the power of endurance in order to fulfil the best promises within themselves; and as the Cheer-bringer to worlds of weary and discouraged folk, Jesus has no competitor. He has captured the imagination of the poetic, dramatic few. He has mastered millions by the compelling power of his practical ethics. He will ultimately find his place in the lives of all men; for he belongs by sheer dominance of character, by right of simple living and happy nature, to all races and to all times.

VI

SERVICE AND WORLD-BROTHERHOOD

XVI

SYMPATHY

WHEN a cry is caught on a heart beat,
And sight is a mist of tears,
   When life is a note
   That's an ache in the throat,
And hope fades into fears;
When *Faith is a flame* that flutters,
And strength is a broken wing,
   Then God wakes the note
   That's a hurt in the throat—
And Sympathy learns to sing!

EDITH DALEY

PAIN THE INTERPRETER

PAIN the Interpreter with level eyes
Has bound a crown of thorns upon my brow—
And bids me wear it valiantly, nor bow
A vanquished head before joy's sacrifice.

Pain the Interpreter with searching hand
Has probed my heart to all its pregnant woe
That I may feel the world's titanic throe,
And all the Earth pain fitly understand.

Pain the Interpreter has seared my soul
Until its flame-swept vision may discern
The utter loneliness of souls that yearn
Through some deep anguish toward a distant goal.

CORINNE ROOSEVELT ROBINSON

OURS IS A FAITH

TAUGHT by no priest, but by our beating hearts:
Faith to each other; the fidelity
Of men whose pulse leaps with kindred fire,
Who in the flash of eyes, the clasp of hands,
Nay, in the silent bodily presence, feel
The mystic stirrings of a common life
That makes the many one.

ANON.

THE VISION OF SIR LAUNFAL

. . . .

V

As Sir Launfal made morn through the darksome gate,
    He was 'ware of a leper, crouched by the same,
Who begged with his hand and moaned as he sate;
    And a loathing over Sir Launfal came;
The sunshine went out of his soul with a thrill,
The flesh 'neath his armor 'gan shrink and crawl,
And midway its leap his heart stood still
    Like a frozen waterfall;
For this man, so foul and bent of stature,
Rasped harshly against his dainty nature,
And seemed the one blot on the summer morn,—
So he tossed him a piece of gold in scorn.

VI

The leper raised not the gold from the dust:
"Better to me the poor man's crust,
Better the blessing of the poor,
Though I turn me empty from his door;
That is no true alms which the hand can hold;
He gives only the worthless gold

Who gives from a sense of duty;
But he who gives but a slender mite,
And gives to that which is out of sight,
   That thread of the all-sustaining Beauty
Which runs through all and doth all unite,—
The hand cannot clasp the whole of his alms,
The heart outstretches its eager palms,
For a god goes with it and makes it store
To the soul that was starving in darkness before."

.   .   .   .

PART SECOND

VII

As Sir Launfal mused with a downcast face,
A light shone round about the place;
The leper no longer crouched at his side,
But stood before him glorified,
Shining and tall and fair and straight
As the pillar that stood by the Beautiful Gate,—
Himself the Gate whereby men can
Enter the temple of God in Man.

VIII

His words were shed softer than leaves from the pine,
And they fell on Sir Launfal as snows on the brine,
That mingle their softness and quiet in one
With the shaggy unrest they float down upon;
And the voice that was softer than silence said,
"Lo it is I, be not afraid!
In many climes, without avail,
Thou hast spent thy life for the Holy Grail;
Behold, it is here,—this cup which thou
Didst fill at the streamlet for me but now;
This crust is my body broken for thee,
This water his blood that died on the tree;

The Holy Supper is kept, indeed,
In whatso we share with another's need;
Not what we give, but what we share,
For the gift without the giver is bare;
Who gives himself with his alms feeds three,
Himself, his hungering neighbor, and me."

JAMES RUSSELL LOWELL

"BROTHERHOOD"

O BROTHER man! fold to thy heart thy brother;
Where pity dwells, the peace of God is there;
To worship rightly is to love each other,
Each smile a hymn, each kindly deed a prayer.

Follow with reverent steps the great example
Of Him whose holy work was "doing good";
So shall the wide earth seem our Father's temple,
Each loving life a psalm of gratitude.

Then shall all shackles fall; the stormy clangor
Of wild war music o'er the earth shall cease;
Love shall tread out the baleful fire of anger,
And in its ashes plant the tree of peace!

WHITTIER

RESURGENCE

"ALL truth is crucified," we said;
"The right is crushed. There lifts its head
Evil triumphant and elate.
The forces of the dark await
The final word that Truth is dead."

The Spirit of the Time-to-be,
Of brotherhood, of manhood free,

Spoke to a prostrate world in tears;
"Be not afflicted. Quell thy fears.
Behold the place where over-sea,—
Europe a charnel-house—they laid
And guarded Him. Be not afraid
For He is risen. Every sun
That sees a deed of service done,
A brother's heart by kindness swayed,
Proclaims His resurrection known
Not in gravèd tower of pilèd stone,
But in the every act that can
Bring near the Brotherhood of Man."

LAURA BELL EVERETT

AS I GO ON MY WAY

My life shall touch a dozen lives before this day is done—
Leave countless marks for good or ill ere sets this evening
sun.
Shall fair or foul its imprint prove, on those my life shall
hail?
Shall benison my impress be, or shall a blight prevail?

When to the last great reckoning the lives I meet must go,
Shall this wee, fleeting touch of mine have added joy or woe?
Shall He who looks their records o'er—of name and time
and place—
Say "Here a blessed influence came" or "Here is evil's
trace"?

From out each point of contact of my life with other lives
Flows ever that which helps the one who for the summit strives.
The troubled souls encountered—does it sweeten with its
touch,
Or does it more embitter those embittered overmuch?

Does love in every handclasp flow in sympathy's caress?
Do those that I have greeted know a newborn hopefulness?
Are tolerance and charity the keynote of my song
As I go plodding onward with earth's eager, anxious throng?

My life shall touch a million lives in some way ere I go
From this dear world of struggle to the land I do not know.
So this the wish I always wish, the prayer I ever pray:
Let my life help the other lives it passes by the way.

STRICKLAND GILLILAN

LIFE IN ABUNDANCE

THE supreme prayer of my heart is not to be learned or good, but to be radiant. I desire to radiate health, cheerfulness, sincerity, calm, courage, and good will. I wish to be simple, honest, natural, frank, clean in mind and clean in body, unaffected, ready to say "I do not know," if so it be, to meet any man on an absolute equality, and to meet every difficulty and face any obstacle unabashed and unafraid. I wish others to live their lives, too, up to their highest, fullest, and best, and to that end I pray that I may never meddle, interfere, dictate, give advice that is not wanted, nor assist when my services are not needed. If I can help others I will do so by giving them a chance to help themselves. If I can uplift or inspire, let it be by example, inference, and suggestion, rather than by dictation and injunction. That is to say, I wish to be radiant—to radiate life.

ANON.

THE MARCH OF MEN

IF you could cast away the pain,
  The sorrows and the tears,
And let the joys alone remain
  From all departed years;

If you could quite forget the sighs
   And recollect the song—
What think you: would you be as wise,
   As helpful, or as strong?

If you could lay the burden down
   That bows your head at whiles,
Shun everything that wears a frown,
   And live a life of smiles—
Be happy as a child again,
   As free from thoughts of care—
Would you appear to other men
   More noble or more fair?

Ah, no! a man should do his part
   And carry all his load,
Rejoiced to share with every heart
   The roughness of the road.
Not given to thinking overmuch
   Of pains and griefs behind,
But glad to be in fullest touch
   With all his human-kind.

CHARLES BUXTON GOING

A NARROW WINDOW

A NARROW window may let in the light,
A tiny star dispel the gloom of night,
A little deed a mighty wrong set right.

A rose, abloom, may make a desert fair,
A single cloud may darken all the air,
A spark may kindle ruin and despair.

A smile, and there may be an end to strife;
A look of love, and Hate may sheathe the knife;
A word—ah, it may be a word of life!

FLORENCE EARLE COATES

WHERE IS THY BROTHER?

Say not, "It matters not to me;
　My brother's weal is his behoof."
For in this wondrous human web
　If your life's warp, his life is woof.
Woven together are the threads,
　And you and he are in one loom;
For good or ill, for glad or sad,
　Your lives must share one common doom.

Man is dear to man: the poorest poor
　Long for some moments in a weary life,
When they can feel and know that they have been
　Themselves the fathers and the dealers-out
Of some small blessings; have been kind to such
　As needed kindness for the single cause,
That we have all of us one common heart.

WORDSWORTH

A DEED AND A WORD

A little stream had lost its way
　Amid the grass and fern;
A passing stranger scooped a well
　Where weary men might turn;
He walled it in, and hung with care
　A ladle at the brink;
He thought not of the deed he did,
　But judged that all might drink.
He passed again, and lo! the well,
　By summer never dried,
Had cooled ten thousand parching tongues,
　And saved a life beside.

A nameless man, amid a crowd
   That thronged the daily mart,
Let fall a word of hope and love,
   Unstudied, from the heart;
A whisper on the tumult thrown,
   A transitory breath—
It raised a brother from the dust,
   It saved a soul from death.
O germ! O fount! O word of love!
   O thought at random cast!
Ye were but little at the first,
   But mighty at the last.

                       CHARLES MACKAY

I SHALL NOT PASS THIS WAY AGAIN

I SHALL not pass this way again—
Although it bordered be with flowers,
Although I rest in fragrant bowers,
   And hear the singing
   Of song-birds winging
To highest heaven their gladsome flight;
Though moons are full and stars are bright,
And winds and waves are softly sighing,
While leafy trees make low replying;
Though voices clear in joyous strain
Repeat a jubilant refrain;
Though rising suns their radiance throw
On summer's green and winter's snow,
In such rare splendor that my heart
Would ache from scenes like these to part;
   Though beauties heighten,
   And life-lights brighten,
And joys proceed from every pain,—
I shall not pass this way again.

Then let me pluck the flowers that blow,
And let me listen as I go
    To music rare
    That fills the air;
    And let hereafter
    Songs and laughter
Fill every pause along the way;
And to my spirit let me say:
"O soul, be happy, soon 'tis trod,
The path made thus for thee by God.
Be happy, thou, and bless His name
By whom such marvellous beauty came."
And let no chance by me be lost
To kindness show at any cost.
I shall not pass this way again;
Then let me now relieve some pain,
Remove some barrier from the road,
Or brighten some one's heavy load;
A helping hand to this one lend,
Then turn some other to befriend.

    O God, forgive
    That now I live
As if I might, some time, return
To bless the weary ones that yearn
For help and comfort every day,—
For there be such along the way.
O God, forgive that I have seen
The beauty only, have not been
Awake to sorrow such as this;
That I have drunk the cup of bliss
Remembering not that those there be
Who drink the dregs of misery.

I love the beauty of the scene,
Would roam again o'er fields so green;
But since I may not, let me spend

My strength for others to the end,—
For those who tread on rock and stone,
And bear their burdens all alone,
Who loiter not in leafy bowers,
Nor hear the birds nor pluck the flowers.
A larger kindness give to me,
A deeper love and sympathy;
    Then, Oh, one day
    May some one say—
Remembering a lessened pain—
"Would she could pass this way again!"

EVA ROSE YORK

THE REWARD

If I can lead a man who has been blind
To see the beauty in a blade of grass;
If I can aid my fellow men to find
The friendliness of trees they daily pass;

If I can stir a soul to view the dawn
With seeing eyes and hold the vision clear
So he may drink the rapture when 'tis gone,
To purify some sordid atmosphere;

If I can help the human ear to hear
The gladness in the waterfall's refrain;
The tenderness of robin's piping clear;
The healing in the sound of falling rain;

If I can rouse but one to that rebirth
Which sees God mirrored in each flower and tree—
To feel his oneness with the whole of earth—
Why, that will be priceless joy to me!

GRACE G. BOSTWICK

STRETCH OUT YOUR HAND

STRETCH out your hand and take the world's wide gift
Of joy and beauty. Open wide your soul
Down to its utmost depths, and bare the whole
To Earth's prophetic dower of clouds that lift
Their clinging shadows from the sunlight's rift,—
The sapphire symphony of seas that roll
Full-breasted auguries from deep to shoal,
Borne from dim caverns on the salt spray's drift.
Open the windows of your wondering heart
To God's supreme Creation; make it yours,
And give to other hearts your ample store;
For when the whole of you is but a part
Of joyous beauty such as e'er endures,
Only by giving can you gain the more!

CORINNE ROOSEVELT ROBINSON

FORGIVE

FORGIVE, O Lord, our severing ways,
The rival altars that we raise,
The wrangling tongues that mar thy praise!

Thy grace impart! In time to be
Shall one great temple rise to thee,—
Thy Church our broad humanity.

White flowers of love its walls shall climb,
Soft bells of peace shall ring its chime,
Its days shall all be holy time.

A sweeter song shall then be heard,
Confessing, in a world's accord,
The inward Christ, the living Word.

That song shall swell from shore to shore.
One hope, one faith, one love restore
The seamless robe that Jesus wore.

WHITTIER

THE CHANT SUBLIME

I HEARD the bells on Christmas day
Their old familiar carols play,
And wild and sweet the words repeat
Of peace on earth, good will to men.

I thought how, as the day had come,
The belfries of all Christendom
Had rolled along the unbroken song
Of peace on earth, good will to men,—

And in despair I bowed my head:
'There is no peace on earth,' I said,
'For hate is strong, and mocks the song
Of peace on earth, good will to men.'

Then pealed the bells more loud and deep:
'God is not dead, nor doth he sleep;
The Wrong shall fail, the Right prevail,
With peace on earth, good will to men':

Till, ringing, singing on its way,
The world revolved from night to day,
A voice, a chime, a chant sublime,
Of peace on earth, good will to men!

LONGFELLOW

FOR A' THAT AND A' THAT

Is there, for honest poverty,
    That hangs his head, and a' that?

The coward-slave, we pass him by,
   We dare be poor, for a' that;
For a' that, and a' that,
   Our toil's obscure, and a' that,
The rank is but the guinea's stamp,
   The man's the gowd for a' that.

What though on hamely fare we dine,
   Wear hoddin gray, and a' that?
Gi'e fools their silks, and knaves their wine,
   A man's a man for a' that;
For a' that, and a' that,
   Their tinsel show, and a' that;
The honest man, though e'er sae poor,
   Is king o' men for a' that.

Ye see yon birkie, ca'd a lord,
   Who struts, and stares, and a' that;
Though hundreds worship at his feet,
   He's but a coof for a' that;
For a' that, and a' that,
   His ribbon, star, and a' that,
The man of independent mind,
   He looks and laughs at a' that.

A prince can make a belted knight,
   A marquis, duke, and a' that;
But an honest man's aboon his might
   Guid faith he mauna fa' that.
For a' that, and a' that,
   Their dignities, and a' that,
The pith o' sense and pride o' worth
   Are higher ranks than a' that.

Then let us pray that come it may,
   As come it will for a' that,
That sense and worth, o'er a' the earth,

> May bear the gree, and a' that.
> For a' that, and a' that,
>   It's coming yet, for a' that,
> That man to man, the warld o'er,
>   Shall brothers be for a' that.
>
> BURNS

A NEW BIRTH OF FREEDOM

FOURSCORE and seven years ago our fathers brought forth on this continent a new nation, conceived in liberty, and dedicated to the proposition that all men are created equal.

Now we are engaged in a great civil war, testing whether that nation, or any nation so conceived and so dedicated, can long endure.

We are met on a great battlefield of that war. We have come to dedicate a portion of that field as a final resting place for those who here gave their lives that that nation might live. It is altogether fitting and proper that we should do this. But, in a larger sense we cannot dedicate—we cannot consecrate—we cannot hallow—this ground. The brave men, living and dead, who struggled here, have consecrated it far above our poor power to add or detract. The world will little note nor long remember what we say here, but it can never forget what they did here. It is for us, the living, rather, to be dedicated here to the unfinished work which they who fought here have thus far so nobly advanced. It is rather for us to be here dedicated to the great task remaining before us—that from these honored dead we take increased devotion to that cause for which they gave the last full measure of devotion; that we here highly resolve that these dead shall not have died in vain; that this nation, under God, shall have a new birth of freedom; and that government of the people, by the people, and for the people, shall not perish from the earth.

ABRAHAM LINCOLN

Gettysburg, November 19, 1863.

AMERICA THE BEAUTIFUL

O BEAUTIFUL for spacious skies,
  For amber waves of grain,
For purple mountain majesties
  Above the fruited plain!
    America! America!
  God shed His grace on thee
And crown thy good with brotherhood
  From sea to shining sea!

O beautiful for pilgrim feet,
  Whose stern, impassioned stress
A thoroughfare for freedom beat
  Across the wilderness!
    America! America!
  God mend thine every flaw,
Confirm thy soul in self-control,
  Thy liberty in law!

O beautiful for heroes proved
  In liberating strife,
Who more than self their country loved,
  And mercy more than life!
    America! America!
  May God thy gold refine
Till all success be nobleness
  And every gain divine!

O beautiful for patriot dream
  That sees beyond the years
Thine alabaster cities gleam
  Undimmed by human tears!
    America! America!
  God shed His grace on thee
And crown thy good with brotherhood
  From sea to shining sea!

KATHARINE LEE BATES

A PARAPHRASE OF I CORINTHIANS, XIII

IF I create wealth beyond the dream of past ages and increase not love, my heat is the flush of fever and my success will deal death.

Though I have foresight to locate the fountains of riches, and power to pre-empt them, and skill to tap them, and have no loving vision for humanity, I am blind.

Though I give of my profits to the poor and make princely endowments for those who toil for me, if I have no human fellowship of love with them, my life is barren and doomed.

Love is just and kind. Love is not greedy and covetous. Love exploits no one; it takes no unearned gain; it gives more than it gets. Love does not break down the lives of others to make wealth for itself; it makes wealth to build the life of all. Love seeks solidarity; it tolerates no divisions; it prefers equal work-mates; it shares its efficiency. Love enriches all men, educates all men, gladdens all men.

The values created by love never fail; but whether there are class privileges, they shall fail; whether there are millions gathered, they shall be scattered; and whether there are vested rights, they shall be abolished. For in the past strong men lorded it in ruthlessness and strove for their own power and pride, but when the perfect social order comes, the strong shall serve the common good. Before the sun of Christ brought in the dawn, men competed, and forced tribute from weakness, but when the full day shall come, they will work as mates in love, each for all and all for each. For now we see in the fog of selfishness, darkly, but then with social vision; now we see our fragmentary ends, but then we shall see the destinies of the race as God sees them. But now abideth honor, justice, and love; these three; and the greatest of these is love.

WALTER RAUSCHENBUSCH

A CHURCH OF MANKIND

THE Catholic Church has her great composers in stone, artists in speech, and actors in marble; the Protestant its great composers in philosophy and literature, with their melody of thought, their harmony of ideas. One day there must be a church of mankind, whose composers of humanity shall think men and women into life, and build with living stones; their painting, their sculpture, their architecture, the manhood of the individual, the virtue of the family and community; their philosophy, their eloquence and song, the happiness of the nation, the peace and good will of all the world.

THEODORE PARKER

FROM "THE OUTLINE OF HISTORY"

. . . THE coming world state . . . will be based upon a common world religion, very much simplified and universalized and better understood. This will not be Christianity nor Islam nor Buddhism nor any such specialized form of religion, but religion itself pure and undefiled; the Eightfold Way, the Kingdom of Heaven, brotherhood, creative service, and self-forgetfulness. . . . There can be little question that the attainment of a federation of all humanity, together with a sufficient measure of social justice, to insure health, education, and a rough equality of opportunity to most of the children born into the world, would mean such a release and increase of human energy as to open a new phase in human history. . . . Life begins perpetually. Gathered together at last under the leadership of man, the student-teacher of the universe, unified, disciplined, armed with the secret powers of the atom and with knowledge as yet beyond dreaming, Life, for ever dying to be born afresh, for ever young and eager, will presently stand upon this earth as upon a footstool. and stretch out its realm amidst the stars.

H. G. WELLS

[By permission of The Macmillan Co.]

YEARS ARE COMING

YEARS are coming, years are going, creeds may change and
   pass away,
But the power of love is growing stronger, surer, day by day,
Be ye as the light of morning, like the beauteous dawn un-
   fold,
With your radiant lives adorning all the world in hues of gold.
Selfish claims will soon no longer raise their harsh, discordant
   sounds,
For the law of love will conquer, bursting hatred's narrow
   bounds;
Human love will spread a glory filling men with gladsome
   mirth,
Songs of joy proclaim the story of a fair, transfigured earth.

ANON.

THE VISION OF PEACE

O, BEAUTIFUL Vision of Peace,
   Beam bright in the eyes of Man!
The host of the meek shall increase,
   The Prophets are leading the van.
Have courage: we see the Morn!
   Never fear, tho' the Now be dark!
Out of Night the Day is born;
   The Fire shall live from the spark.
It may take a thousand years
   Ere the Era of Peace hold sway,
Look back and the Progress cheers
   And a thousand years are a day!
The World grows—yet not by chance;
   It follows some marvellous plan;
Tho' slow to our wish the advance,
   God rules the training of Man.

NATHAN HASKELL DOLE

GOD'S DREAMS

DREAMS are they—but they are God's dreams!
Shall we decry them and scorn them?
That men shall love one another,
That white shall call black man brother,
That greed shall pass from the market-place,
That lust shall yield to love for the race,
That man shall meet with God face to face—
Dreams are they all,
   But shall we despise them—
     God's dreams!

Dreams are they—to become man's dreams!
Can we say nay as they claim us?
That men shall cease from their hating,
That war shall soon be abating,
That the glory of kings and lords shall pale,
That the pride of dominion and power shall fail,
That the love of humanity shall prevail—
Dreams are they all,
   But shall we despise them—
     God's dreams!

THOMAS CURTIS CLARK

WORLD–BROTHERHOOD

My country is the world;
My flag with stars impearled,
   Fills all the skies,
All the round earth I claim,
Peoples of every name;
And all inspiring fame,
   My heart would prize.

Mine are all lands and seas,
All flowers, shrubs and trees,

All life's design,
My heart within me thrills
For all uplifted hills,
And for all streams and rills;
The world is mine.

And all men are my kin,
Since every man has been,
Blood of my blood,
I glory in the grace
And strength of every race
And joy in every trace
Of brotherhood.

The days of pack and clan,
Shall yield to love of man,
When war-flags are furled,
We shall be done with hate,
And strife of state with state,
When man with man shall mate,
O'er all the world.

ANON.

FROM "LOCKSLEY HALL"

MEN, my brothers, men the workers, ever reaping something
new:
That which they have done but earnest of the things that
they shall do:
For I dipt into the future, far as human eye could see,
Saw the Vision of the world, and all the wonder that would
be;
Saw the heavens fill with commerce, argosies of magic sails,
Pilots of the purple twilight, dropping down with costly
bales;
Heard the heavens fill with shouting, and there rain'd a
ghastly dew

From the nations' airy navies grappling in the central blue;
Far along the world-wide whisper of the south-wind rushing
    warm,
With the standards of the peoples plunging thro' the thunder-
    storm;
Till the war-drum throbb'd no longer, and the battle-flags
    were furl'd
In the Parliament of man, the Federation of the world.
There the common sense of most shall hold a fretful realm in
    awe,
And the kindly earth shall slumber, lapt in universal law.

TENNYSON

[By permission of The Macmillan Co.]

A LOFTIER RACE

THESE things shall be! a loftier race
    Than ere the world hath known shall rise
With flame of freedom in their souls,
    And light of knowledge in their eyes.

They shall be gentle, brave, and strong
    To spill no drop of blood, but dare
All that may plant man's lordship firm
    On earth, and fire, and sea, and air.

Nation with nation, land with land,
    Inarmed shall live as comrades free:
In every heart and brain shall throb
    The pulse of one fraternity.

New arts shall bloom of loftier mould
    And mightier music fill the skies,
And every life shall be a song,
    When all the earth is paradise.

JOHN ADDINGTON SYMONDS

FROM "THE SERVANT IN THE HOUSE"

Bishop. They say it's an enormous concern!

Manson. So it is.

Bishop. Well, what would such an establishment as that represent? In round numbers, now?

Manson [*calmly*]. Numberless millions.

Bishop. Numberless mil . . . ! [*He drops his fork.*] My dear sir, absurd! . . . Why, the place must be a palace—fit for a king!

Manson. It is! . . . You must understand, this is no dead pile of stones and unmeaning timber. *It is a living thing.* . . .

When you enter it you hear a sound—a sound as of some mighty poem chanted. Listen long enough, and you will learn that it is made up of the beating of human hearts, of the nameless music of men's souls—that is, if you have ears. If you have eyes, you will presently see the church itself—a looming mystery of many shapes and shadows, leaping sheer from floor to dome. The work of no ordinary builder! . . .

The pillars of it go up like the brawny trunks of heroes: the sweet human flesh of men and women is moulded about its bulwarks, strong, impregnable: the faces of little children laugh out from every corner-stone: the terrible spans and arches of it are the joined hands of comrades; and up in the heights and spaces there are inscribed the numberless musings of all the dreamers of the world. It is yet building—building and built upon. Sometimes the work goes forward in deep darkness: sometimes in blinding light: now beneath the burden of unutterable anguish: now to the tune of a great laughter and heroic shoutings like the cry of thunder. [*Softer.*] Sometimes, in the silence of the night-time, one may hear the tiny hammerings of the comrades at work up in the dome—the comrades that have climbed ahead.

CHARLES RANN KENNEDY

THE CALL OF BROTHERHOOD

HAVE you heard it, the dominant call
Of the city's great cry, and the thrall
And the throb and the pulse of its life,
And the touch and the stir of its strife,
As, amid the dread dust and the din
It wages its battle of sin?
Have you felt in the crowds of the street
The echo of mutinous feet
As they march to their final release,
As they struggle and strive without peace?
Marching why, marching where, and to what!
Oh! by all that there is, or is not,
We must march too and shoulder to shoulder.
If a frail sister slip, we must hold her,
If a brother be lost in the strain
Of the infinite pitfalls of pain,
We must love him and lift him again.
For we are the Guarded, the Shielded,
And yet we have wavered and yielded
To the sins that we could not resist.
By the right of the joys we have missed,
By the right of the deeds left undone,
By the right of our victories won,
Perchance we their burdens may bear
As brothers, with right to our share.
The baby who pulls at the breast
With its pitiful purpose to wrest
The milk that has dried in the vein,
That is sapped by life's fever and drain—
The turbulent prisoners of toil,
Whose faces are black with the soil
And scarred with the sins of the soul,
Who are paying the terrible toll
Of the way they have chosen to tread,

As they march on in truculent dread,—
And the Old, and the Weary, who fall—
Oh! let us be one with them all!
By the infinite fear of our fears,
By the passionate pain of our tears,
Let us hold out our impotent hands,
Made strong by Jehovah's commands,
The God of the militant poor,
Who are stronger than we to endure,
Let us march in the front of the van
Of the Brotherhood valiant of Man!

CORINNE ROOSEVELT ROBINSON

FROM "TOWARDS DEMOCRACY"

IN the deep caves of the heart, far down, running under the outward shows of the world and of people, running under continents, under the fields and the roots of the grasses and trees, under the little thoughts and dreams of men, and the history of races, I see, I feel and hear wondrous and divine things. I seem to see the strands of affection and love, so tender, so true and lifelong, holding together the present and past generation. . . . I dream that these are the fibres and nerves of a body . . . a network, an innumerable vast interlocked ramification, slowly being built up; all dear lovers and friends, all families and groups, all peoples, nations, all times, all worlds perhaps, members of a body, archetypal, eterne, glorious, the centre and perfection of life, the organic growth of God himself in time.

EDWARD CARPENTER

A NOBLER ORDER

A NOBLER order yet shall be than any that the world hath known, when men obey and yet are free, are loved and yet can stand alone.

For still the new transcends the old, in signs and tokens manifold; slaves rise up men, the olive waves with roots deep set in battle graves.

True word, kind deed, sweet song shall vibrate still in rings that wander through celestial air;

And human will shall build for human will fair basement to a palace yet more fair.

The end lies hid in future victory, won by the faithfulness of man to man.

Presentiment of better things on earth sweeps in with every force that stirs our souls to admiration, self-renouncing love.

Or thoughts, like light, that bind the world in one.

From out the throng and stress of lies, from out the painful noise of sighs, one voice of comfort seems to rise; "It is the meaner part that dies."

Truer church shall be than in old times, lordlier government shall bless the nations, sweeter lips shall murmur sweeter rhymes, life shall give us holier revelations.

Then shall all shackles fall; the stormy clangor of wild war music o'er the earth shall cease;

Love shall tread out the baleful fire of anger, and in its ashes plant the tree of peace.

Then shall the devout rejoice, and the profane shall mourn.

Then shall he more rejoice that hath beat down his own flesh, than he that hath abounded in all pleasure and delight.

Then shall the poor attire shine gloriously, and the precious robes seem vile and contemptible.

Then shall be more commended the poor cottage than the gilded palace.

Then shall a good and clear conscience more rejoice a man than the learning of philosophy.

Then shall the contempt of riches weigh more than all the worldling's treasure.

Then will good works avail more than many goodly words.

· · · · · · · · · ·

Out of the dark the circling sphere is rounding onward to the light; we see not yet the full day here, but we do see the paling night.

I follow, follow, sure to meet the sun, and confident that what the future yields, will be the right, unless myself be wrong.

ARR. BY STANTON COIT

SOUND OVER ALL WATERS

Sound over all waters, reach out from all lands, the chorus of voices, the clasping of hands;

Sing hymns that were sung by the stars of the morn; sing songs of the angels when Jesus was born!

With glad jubilations bring hope to the nations!

The dark night is ending and dawn has begun; rise, hope of the ages, arise like the sun.

All speech flow to music, all hearts beat as one!

Sing the bridal of nations! with chorals of love; sing out the war vultures and sing in the dove.

Till the hearts of the peoples keep time in accord, and the voice of the world is the voice of the Lord!

Clasp hands of the nations in strong gratulations;

The dark night is ending and dawn has begun;

Rise, hope of the ages, arise like the sun, all speech flow to music, all hearts beat as one!

Blow, bugle of battle, the marches of peace; east, west, north and south, let the long quarrel cease;

Sing the song of great joy that the angels began, sing of glory to God and of good-will to man!

Hark! joining in chorus the heavens bend o'er us!

The dark night is ending and dawn has begun;

Rise, hope of the ages, arise like the sun, all speech flow to music, all hearts beat as one.

STANTON COIT

NOTE XVI

THE last generation has witnessed an awakening of human interest and a desire for intelligent co-operation—man with man, and nation with nation—never before paralleled in the history of the race. An abundant literature has burst into being as a result of this great passion, and the poet, the dramatist, the essayist, and the novelist have vied with each other in giving a modern setting to the most beloved ideal of mankind.

Fellow feeling (say our authors) is an unassuageable passion which surprises one in a moment of fleeting sorrow or terror; when loss of faith threatens to leave one overwhelmed and alone in life's unequal struggle. In one's own dire need, the sorrows of a world stand appallingly revealed, and the whole bent of the life is changed from selfishness to understanding and helpfulness. Jesus' career of service is the classic example for all men. In carrying on with His spirit one finds his utmost ambition for life fulfilled; the all-satisfying Holy Grail is hard at hand to find. This brotherly spirit is the heart of worship and the only certain guarantee of world-peace and the unity of all mankind.

The shame of not being brotherly, and the happiness which men find through service; the obligation of nations as well as individuals, the duty of overcoming even the most appalling obstacles in order to realize the call of human destiny —these are the alluring themes in the minds of our writers.

Finally is sounded "the diapason closing full"—an outburst of hope and love and complete world-harmony as great men realize that what rises so full and unbidden in their own natures must some day spell the destiny of the united peoples of earth. Shall time, or bitter experience, or Religion and God—the will to live truly and naturally— bring all this to pass? Yet it is a Dream which presses on to utter fulfilment, and nothing shall be allowed to stay its course. The call to help sounds in every man's ears. God and man are partners in a Fate too great for words. God is doing his full part now. When man rises, as he can do, to the full measure of his power for achieving the nobler order which must yet be, then will real Heaven be realized upon earth, for Love and Peace shall rule the world and bring to pass the great ends toward which the race has so long been pressing.

VII

CO–OPERATION WITH GOD

XVII

NOBILITY

TRUE worth is in *being*, not *seeming*,—
  In doing, each day that goes by,
Some little good—not in dreaming
  Of great things to do by and by.
For whatever men say in their blindness,
  And spite of the fancies of youth,
There's nothing so kingly as kindness,
  And nothing so royal as truth.

We get back our mete as we measure—
  We cannot do wrong and feel right,
Nor can we give pain and gain pleasure,
  For justice avenges each slight.
The air for the wing of the sparrow,
  The bush for the robin and wren,
But alway the path that is narrow
  And straight, for the children of men.

'Tis not in the pages of story
  The heart of its ills to beguile,
Though he who makes courtship to glory
  Gives all that he hath for her smile.
For when from her heights he has won her,
  Alas! it is only to prove
That nothing's so sacred as honor,
  And nothing so loyal as love!

We cannot make bargains for blisses,
  Nor catch them like fishes in nets;

And sometimes the thing our life misses
   Helps more than the thing which it gets.
For good lieth not in pursuing,
   Nor gaining of great nor of small,
But just in the doing, and doing
   As we would be done by, is all.

Through envy, through malice, through hating,
   Against the world, early and late,
No jot of our courage abating—
   Our part is to work and to wait.
And slight is the sting of his trouble
   Whose winnings are less than his worth;
For he who is honest is noble,
   Whatever his fortunes or birth.

ALICE CARY

SONNET

WHEN we can all so excellently give
The measure of love's wisdom with a blow,—
Why can we not in turn receive it so,
And end this murmur for the life we live?
And when we do so frantically strive
To win strange faith, why do we shun to know
That in love's elemental overglow
God's wholeness gleams with light superlative?

Oh, brother men, if you have eyes at all,
Look at a branch, a bird, a child, a rose,
Or anything God ever made that grows,—
Nor let the smallest vision of it slip,
Till you may read, as on Belshazzar's wall,
The glory of eternal partnership.

EDWIN ARLINGTON ROBINSON

GOD PRAYS

THESE things shall be, these things shall be,
Nor help shall come from the scarlet skies
Till the people rise!
Till the people rise my arm is weak;
I cannot speak till the people speak;
When men are dumb, my voice is dumb—
I cannot come till my people come.

.   .   .   .

They are my mouth, my breath, my soul!
I wait their summons to make me whole.

ANGELA MORGAN

ABOU BEN ADHEM AND THE ANGEL

ABOU BEN ADHEM (may his tribe increase)
Awoke one night from a deep dream of peace,
And saw within the moonlight in his room,
Making it rich, and like a lily in bloom,
An angel writing in a book of gold:—
Exceeding peace had made Ben Adhem bold,
And to the Presence in the room he said,
"What writest thou?"—The vision raised its head
And, with a look made of all sweet accord,
Answered, "The names of those who love the Lord."
"And is mine one?" said Abou. "Nay, not so,"
Replied the Angel. Abou spoke more low,
But cheerly still; and said, "I pray thee, then,
Write me as one that loves his fellow-men."

The Angel wrote and vanished. The next night
It came again with a great wakening light,
And showed the names whom love of God had blessed,
And lo! Ben Adhem's name led all the rest.

LEIGH HUNT

I'VE TRAVELLED FAR IN MANY LANDS

I'VE travelled far in many lands,
  The open road I've trod;
And through the devious ways of men
  I've searched with them for God.

The Ancients found Him in their groves,
  The Wise Men saw the Star.
God comes to some in paths of peace,
  To some in flaming war.

Before the Buddha some men bow;
  Some love the Nazarene.
The mystic feels a presence near,
  Although no form is seen.

On desert sands the vision comes,
  As men turn toward the East,
And while some fasting see His face,
  Some find Him at the feast.

In temple, mosque, cathedral dim,
  Through vigil, chant, and prayer,
Wherever man cries out to God
  The living God is there.

Wherever man has fought for right,
  Where man for man has died;
Beside him stands, could we but see,
  One that was crucified.

Alone I have communed with Him
  Beneath a starlit sky,
And I have touched His garment hem
  Where crowds go thronging by.

And this is clear in all my search,
  As clear as noonday sun;
The name and form are nought to God,
  To Him all shrines are one.

HINTON WHITE

LABORERS TOGETHER WITH GOD

O PAINTER of the fruits and flowers,
We thank thee for thy wise design
Whereby these human hands of ours
In Nature's garden work with thine.

And he who blesses most is blest;
For God and man shall own his worth
Who toils to leave as his bequest
An added beauty to the earth.

Or soon, or late, to all that sow
The time of harvest shall be given;
The flower shall bloom, the fruit shall grow,
If not on earth, at last in heaven.

ARR. FROM WHITTIER

MAKE ROOM FOR LIFE

"MAKE room for life!" the cry goes forth—
"Make room for life!" O'er all the earth
Forever, Life has right of way—
Death shall not challenge, nor delay.
. . . The eye of Faith
Sees only Life where once was Death—
Sees only Light where once was Gloom:
"Make room for Life! For Life make room!"

TAYLOR

GOD MOVES IN A MYSTERIOUS WAY

GOD moves in a mysterious way
　　His wonders to perform:
He plants his footsteps in the sea,
　　And rides upon the storm.

Ye fearful souls, fresh courage take!
　　The clouds ye so much dread
Are big with mercy, and shall break
　　In blessings on your head.

Judge not the Lord by feeble sense,
　　But trust him for his grace:
Behind a frowning providence
　　He hides a smiling face.

His purposes will ripen fast,
　　Unfolding every hour:
The bud may have a bitter taste,
　　But sweet will be the flower.

Blind unbelief is sure to err,
　　And scan his work in vain:
God is his own interpreter,
　　And he will make it plain.

COWPER

YOU AND TO-DAY

WITH every rising of the sun,
　　Think of your life as just begun.
The past has shrived and buried deep
　　All yesterdays; there let them sleep.
Concern yourself with but to-day,
　　Woo it, and teach it to obey
Your will and wish. Since time began
　　To-day has been the friend of man;

But in his blindness and his sorrow,
  He looks to yesterday and to-morrow.
You, and to-day! a soul sublime,
  And the great pregnant hour of time,
With God himself to bind the twain!
  Go forth, I say—attain, attain!
With God himself to bind the twain!

ELLA WHEELER WILCOX

I HAVE A RENDEZVOUS WITH DEATH

I HAVE a rendezvous with Death
At some disputed barricade,
When Spring comes back with rustling shade
And apple-blossoms fill the air—
I have a rendezvous with Death
When Spring brings back blue days and fair.

It may be he shall take my hand
And lead me into his dark land
And close my eyes and quench my breath—
It may be I shall pass him still.
I have a rendezvous with Death
On some scarred slope of battered hill,
When Spring comes round again this year
And the first meadow-flowers appear.

God knows 't were better to be deep
Pillowed in silk and scented down,
Where love throbs out in blissful sleep,
Pulse nigh to pulse, and breath to breath,
Where hushed awakenings are dear . . .
But I've a rendezvous with Death
At midnight in some flaming town,
When Spring trips north again this year,
And I to my pledged word am true,
I shall not fail that rendezvous.

ALAN SEEGER

THE PATH TO HOME

It is faith that bridges the land of breath
    To the realms of the souls departed,
That comforts the living in days of death,
    And strengthens the heavy-hearted.
It is faith in his dreams that keeps a man
    Face front to the odds about him,
And he shall conquer who thinks he can,
    In spite of the throngs who doubt him.

Each must stand in the court of life
    And pass through the hour of trial;
He shall tested be by the rules of strife,
    And tried for his self-denial.
Time shall bruise his soul by the loss of friends,
    And frighten him with disaster,
But he shall find when the anguish ends
    That of all things faith is master.

So keep your faith in the God above,
    And faith in the righteous truth,
It shall bring you back to the absent love,
    And the joys of a vanished youth.
You shall smile once more when your tears are dried,
    Meet trouble and swiftly rout it,
For faith is the strength of the soul inside,
    And lost is the man without it.
                    EDGAR GUEST

UNDER THE LEAVES

Oft have I walked the woodland paths
    In sadness, not foreknowing
That underneath the withered leaves
    The fairest flowers were growing.

To-day the south-wind sweeps away
   Those wrecks of autumn splendor,
And lo, the starry hosts of Spring
   Unfolding sweet and tender!

O prophet-flowers with lips of bloom,
   Whose speech of silent beauty
Fills all the woodland aisles with song,
   Ye teach me faith and duty!

Walk life's dark ways, ye seem to say,
   In love and hope foreknowing
That, where man sees but withered leaves,
   God sees the fair flowers growing.

ALBERT LAIGHTON

THANKFUL FOR ALL

An easy thing, O Power Divine,
To thank Thee for these gifts of Thine!
For summer's sunshine, winter's snow,
For hearts that kindle, thoughts that glow.
But when shall I attain to this:—
To thank Thee for the things I miss?

For all young Fancy's early gleams,
The dreamed-of joys that still are dreams,
Hopes unfulfilled, and pleasures known
Through others' fortunes, not my own,
And blessings seen that are not given,
And never will be, this side of heaven.

Had I too, shared the joys I see,
Would there have been a heaven for me?
Could I have felt Thy presence near?
Had I possessed what I held dear?
My deepest fortune, highest bliss,
Have grown perchance from things I miss.

Sometimes there comes an hour of calm;
Grief turns to blessing, pain to balm;
A Power that works above my will
Still leads me onward, upward still;
And then my heart attains to this:—
To thank Thee for the things I miss.

THOMAS WENTWORTH HIGGINSON

WORK

A SONG OF TRIUMPH

WORK!
Thank God for the might of it,
The ardor, the urge, the delight of it—
Work that springs from the heart's desire,
Setting the brain and the soul on fire—
Oh, what is so good as the heat of it,
And what is so glad as the beat of it,
And what is so kind as the stern command,
Challenging brain and heart and hand?

Work!
Thank God for the pride of it,
For the beautiful, conquering tide of it,
Sweeping the life in its furious flood,
Thrilling the arteries, cleansing the blood,
Mastering stupor and dull despair,
Moving the dreamer to do and dare.
Oh, what is so good as the urge of it,
And what is so glad as the surge of it,
And what is so strong as the summons deep,
Rousing the torpid soul from sleep?

Work!
Thank God for the pace of it,
For the terrible, keen, swift race of it;
Fiery steeds in full control,

Nostrils a-quiver to greet the goal.
Work, the Power that drives behind,
Guiding the purposes, taming the mind,
Holding the runaway wishes back,
Reining the will to one steady track,
Speeding the energies faster. faster,
Triumphing over disaster.
Oh, what is so good as the pain of it,
And what is so great as the gain of it?
And what is so kind as the cruel goad,
Forcing us on through the rugged road?

Work!
Thank God for the swing of it,
For the clamoring, hammering ring of it,
Passion of labor daily hurled
On the mighty anvils of the world.
Oh, what is so fierce as the flame of it?
And what is so huge as the aim of it?
Thundering on through dearth and doubt,
Calling the plan of the Maker out.
Work, the Titan; Work, the friend,
Shaping the earth to a glorious end,
Draining the swamps and blasting the hills,
Doing whatever the Spirit wills—
Rending a continent apart,
To answer the dream of the Master heart.
Thank God for a world where none may shirk—
Thank God for the splendor of work!

                                    ANGELA MORGAN

QUIET WORK

ONE lesson, Nature, let me learn of thee,
One lesson which in every wind is blown,
One lesson of two duties kept at one
Though the loud world proclaim their enmity,—

Of toil unsevered from tranquillity;
Of labor, that in lasting fruit outgrows
Far noisier schemes, accomplished in repose,
Too great for haste, too high for rivalry.

Yes, while on earth a thousand discords ring,
Man's senseless uproar mingling with his toil,
Still do thy quiet ministers move on,

Their glorious tasks in silence perfecting;
Still working, blaming still our vain turmoil,
Laborers that shall not fail, when man is gone.

MATTHEW ARNOLD

[From Matthew Arnold's Poems: The Macmillan Co.]

THE NAMELESS SAINTS

WHAT was his name? I do not know his name.
I only know he heard God's voice and came,
  Brought all he had across the sea
  To live and work for God and me;
    Felled the ungracious oak;
      Dragged from the soil
      With horrid toil
  The thrice gnarled roots and stubborn rock;
With plenty piled the haggard mountain-side;
And at the end, without memorial, died.
No blaring trumpet sounded out his fame,
He lived,—he died,—I do not know his name.

No form of bronze and no memorial stones
Show me the place where lie his mouldering bones,
  Only a cheerful city stands
  Builded by his hardened hands
    Only ten thousand homes
      Where every day
      The cheerful play

Of love and hope and courage comes.
These are his monuments, and these alone.
There is no form of bronze and no memorial stone.

And I?
Is there some desert or some pathless sea
Where Thou, good God of angels, wilt send me?
  Some oak too for me to rend; some sod,
    Some rock for me to break;
    Some handful of His corn to take
    And scatter far afield,
    Till it, in turn, shall yield
      Its hundredfold
      Of grains of gold
  To feed the waiting children of my God?
Show me the desert, Father, or the sea.
Is it Thine enterprise? Great God, send me.
And though this body lie where ocean rolls,
Count me among all Faithful Souls.

                              EDWARD EVERETT HALE

GOD SEND US MEN

God send us men whose aim will be,
  Not to defend some worn-out creed,
But to live out the laws of Christ
  In every thought, and word and deed.

God send us men alert and quick
  His lofty precepts to translate,
Until the laws of Christ become
  The laws and habits of the State.

God send us men! God send us men!
  Patient, courageous, strong and true,
With vision clear and mind equipped,
  His will to learn, His work to do.

God send us men with hearts ablaze,
    All truth to love, all wrong to hate;
These are the patriots nations need,
    These are the bulwarks of the State.

F. J. GILLMAN

FROM "THE UNDYING FIRE"

THERE burns an undying fire in the hearts of men. By that fire I live. By that I know the God of my Salvation. His will is Truth, his will is Service. He urges me to conflict, without consolations, without rewards. . . . He suffers— perhaps to triumph, and we must suffer and find our hope of triumph in Him. He will not let me shut my eyes to sorrow, failure, or perplexity. Though the universe torment and slay me, yet will I trust in Him. And if he also must die— Nevertheless I can do no more; I must serve Him. . . .

I don't submit. I rebel—not in my own strength nor by my own impulse. I rebel by the spirit of God in me. I rebel not merely to make weak gestures of defiance against the black disorder and cruelties of space and time, but for mastery. I am a rebel of pride—I am full of the pride of God in my heart. I am the servant of a rebellious and adventurous God who may yet bring order into this cruel and frightful chaos in which we seem to be driven hither and thither like leaves before the wind, a God who in spite of all appearances, may yet rule over it at last and mould it to his will. . . .

The end and substance of all real education is to teach men and women of the Battle of God, . . . and to draw all men together out of themselves into one common life and effort with God.

So long as your courage endures you will conquer. . . . On the courage in your heart all things depend. . . . If that courage fail, if that sacred fire go out, then all things fail and all things go out, all things—good and evil, space and time.

H. G. WELLS

THE BATTLE–FIELD

ONCE this soft turf, this rivulet's sands,
  Were trampled by a hurrying crowd,
And fiery hearts and armed bands
  Encountered in the battle-cloud.

Ah! never shall the land forget
  How gushed the life-blood of her brave—
Gushed, warm with hope and courage yet,
  Upon the soil they fought to save.

Now all is calm, and fresh, and still;
  Alone the chirp of flitting bird,
And talk of children on the hill,
  And bell of wandering kine, are heard.

No solemn host goes trailing by,
  The black-mouthed gun and staggering wain;
Men start not at the battle-cry,
  Oh, be it never heard again!

Soon rested those who fought; but thou
  Who minglest in the harder strife
For truths which men receive not now,
  Thy warfare only ends with life.

A friendless warfare! lingering long
  Through weary day and weary year,
A wild and many-weaponed throng
  Hang on thy front, and flank, and rear.

Yet nerve thy spirit to the proof,
  And blench not at thy chosen lot.
The timid good may stand aloof,
  The sage may frown—yet faint thou not.

Nor heed the shaft too surely cast,
  The foul and hissing bolt of scorn;

For with thy side shall dwell, at last,
 The victory of endurance born.

Truth, crushed to earth, shall rise again,
 Th' eternal years of God are hers;
But Error, wounded, writhes in pain,
 And dies among his worshippers.

Yea, though thou lie upon the dust,
 When they who helped thee flee in fear,
Die full of hope and manly trust,
 Like those who fell in battle here.

Another hand thy sword shall wield,
 Another hand the standard wave,
Till from the trumpet's mouth is pealed
 The blast of triumph o'er thy grave.

WILLIAM CULLEN BRYANT

A PRAYER

O GOD, our Father, if we had but truth!
 Lost truth—which thou perchance
Didst let man lose, lest all his wayward youth
 He waste in song and dance;
That he might gain, in searching, mightier powers
For manlier use in those foreshadowed hours.

If, blindly groping, he shall oft mistake
 And follow twinkling motes
Thinking them stars, and the one voice forsake
 Of Wisdom for the notes
Which mocking Beauty utters here and there,
Thou surely wilt forgive him, and forbear!

Oh, love us, for we love thee, Maker—God!
 And would creep near thy hand,

And call thee "Father, Father," from the sod
  Where by our graves we stand,
And pray to touch, fearless of scorn or blame,
Thy garment's hem, which Truth and God we name.

                              EDWARD ROWLAND SILL

FROM "THE SAINT"

You believe your souls will be saved by the great number
of your prayers, and you do not even know how to pray.
You do not reflect that the Master (God) cares little for
many words. He desires rather that you serve Him faithfully in silence, your mind fixed always on His will. . . .

For he who gives the hungry to eat and clothes the naked
is serving God, even though he neither knows it nor wishes
it. The love of one's neighbor will, in fact, compensate for
the failure to love God.

Man may deny the existence of God without really being
an Atheist or deserving eternal death, if that God, whose
existence he denies, be placed before him in a shape repug-
nant to his intellect, and if he love Truth, Virtue, and his
fellow man, and by his life give proof of his love. . . . Religion is, above all things, action and life. . . . "The spirit
of Christ . . . is simply the spirit of love."

                                       FOGAZZARO

REQUIREMENT

WE live by Faith; but Faith is not the slave
  Of text and legend. Reason's voice and God's,
  Nature's and Duty's, never are at odds.
What asks our Father of His children, save
Justice and mercy and humility,
  A reasonable service of good deeds,
  Pure living, tenderness to human needs,

Reverence and trust, and prayer for light to see
The Master's footprints in our daily ways?
  No knotted scourge nor sacrificial knife,
  But the calm beauty of an ordered life
Whose very breathing is unworded praise!—
A life that stands as all true lives have stood,
Firm-rooted in the faith that God is Good.

WHITTIER

RELIANCE

Not to the swift, the race;
  Not to the strong, the fight;
Not to the righteous, perfect grace;
  Not to the wise, the light.

But often faltering feet
  Come surest to the goal;
And they who walk in darkness meet
  The sunrise of the soul.

A thousand times by night
  The Syrian hosts have died;
A thousand times the vanquished right
  Hath risen glorified.

The truth the wise men sought
  Was spoken by a child;
The alabaster box was brought
  In trembling hands defiled.

Not from my torch, the gleam,
  But from the stars above;
Not from my heart life's crystal stream,
  But from the depths of love.

ANON.

THE GREATEST BATTLE THAT EVER WAS FOUGHT

THE greatest battle that ever was fought—
  Shall I tell you where and when?
On the maps of the world you will find it not:
  It was fought by the Mothers of Men.

Not with cannon or battle shot,
  With sword or nobler pen;
Not with eloquent word or thought
  From the wonderful minds of men;

But deep in a walled up woman's heart;
  A woman that would not yield;
But bravely and patiently bore her part;
  Lo! there is that battlefield.

No marshalling troops, no bivouac song,
  No banner to gleam and wave;
But Oh these battles they last so long—
  From babyhood to the grave!

But faithful still as a bridge of stars
  She fights in her walled up town;
Fights on, and on, in the endless wars;
  Then silent, unseen goes down!

Ho! ye with banners and battle shot,
  With soldiers to shout and praise,
I tell you the kingliest victories fought
  Are fought in these silent ways.

                              JOAQUIN MILLER

CHALLENGE

THE quiet and courageous night,
  The keen vibration of the stars,
Call me, from morbid peace, to fight
  The world's forlorn and desperate wars.

The air throbs like a rolling drum—
　　The brave hills and the singing sea,
Unrest and people's faces come
　　Like battle-trumpets, rousing me.

And while Life's lusty banner flies,
　　I shall assail, with raging mirth,
The scornful and untroubled skies,
　　The cold complacency of earth.

LOUIS UNTERMEYER

YOU MAY COUNT THAT DAY

IF you sit down at set of sun
And count the acts that you have done,
　　And, counting find
One self-denying deed, one word
That eased the heart of him who heard;
　　One glance most kind,
That fell like sunshine where it went—
Then you may count that day well spent.

But if, through all the livelong day,
You've cheered no heart, by yea or nay—
　　If, through it all
You've nothing done that you can trace
That brought the sunshine to one face—
　　No act most small
That helped some soul and nothing cost—
Then count that day as worse than lost.

GEORGE ELIOT

ONE SHIP DRIVES EAST

ONE ship drives east, another drives west
　　While the selfsame breezes blow;

'Tis the set of the sail and not the gale
  That bids them where to go.

Like the winds of the sea are the ways of fate
  As we journey along through life;
'Tis the set of the soul that decides the goal
  And not the calm or the strife.

ANON.

BE STRONG

Be strong!
We are not here to play, to dream, to drift;
We have hard work to do, and loads to lift;
Shun not the struggle—face it; 'tis God's gift.

Be strong!
Say not, "The days are evil. Who's to blame?"
And fold the hands and acquiesce—oh shame!
Stand up, speak out, and bravely, in God's name.

Be strong!
It matters not how deep intrenched the wrong,
How hard the battle goes, the day how long;
Faint not—fight on! To-morrow comes the song.

MALTBIE DAVENPORT BABCOCK

WITHIN OUR LIVES

Unto the calmly gathered thought
The innermost of truth is taught—
The mystery dimly understood,
That love of God is love of Good;

That to be saved is only this—
Salvation from our selfishness;
From sin itself and not the pain
That warns us of its chafing chain;

That worship's deeper meaning lies
In mercy, and not sacrifice—
Not proud humilities of sense,
But love's unforced obedience;

But here amid the poor and blind,
The bound and suffering of our kind,
In works we do, in prayers we pray,
Within our lives he lives to-day.

WHITTIER

MY CREED

I WOULD be true, for there are those who trust me;
I would be pure, for there are those who care;
I would be strong, for there is much to suffer;
I would be brave, for there is much to dare.

I would be friend of all,—the foe, the friendless;
I would be giving, and forget the gift;
I would be humble, for I know my weakness;
I would look up—and laugh—and love—and lift.

HOWARD ARNOLD WALTER

UTOPIA

A DAY will come, in not undreamed of years
Where men shall wake with singing in their lips.
Their toil will bloom with hope uncursed by fears;
They will not labor to the tune of whips;
They will not close their days as battered ships!
Then all shall be as gods, Olympus-born,
And joy shall grace each heart. As beauty drips
From Summer downs, so from the fields of corn
Shall gladness be set forth on all the sons of morn.

Then lust will die, and gold will lose its lure.
No soul will gloat, while others starve for bread.
The lure of love will prove the ample cure
From all earth's ills, now meetly harvested.
Each man a king in pride shall lift his head,
And every child still bright with heaven's gleams,
Shall play in Eden gardens, tenanted
By fays and elves. By softly flowing streams
We men of earth shall find again our long-lost dreams.

THOMAS CURTIS CLARK

WORK

LET me but do my work from day to day,
  In field or forest, at the desk or loom,
  In roaring market-place or tranquil room;
Let me but find it in my heart to say,
When vagrant wishes beckon me astray,
  "This is my work; my blessing, not my doom;
  Of all who live, I am the one by whom
This work can best be done in the right way."

Then shall I see it not too great, nor small,
  To suit my spirit and to prove my powers;
  Then shall I cheerful greet the labouring hours,
And cheerful turn, when the long shadows fall
At eventide, to play and love and rest,
Because I know for me my work is best.

HENRY VAN DYKE

THEY WHO TREAD THE PATH OF LABOUR

THEY who tread the path of labour follow where My feet
    have trod;
They who work without complaining, do the holy will of God;

Nevermore thou needest seek me; I am with thee everywhere;
Raise the stone, and thou shalt find Me, cleave the wood and
    I am there.

Where the many toil together, there am I among My own;
Where the tired workman sleepeth, there am I with him alone:
I, the Peace that passeth knowledge, dwell amid the daily
    strife;
I, the Bread of heav'n, am broken in the sacrament of life.

Every task, however simple, sets the soul that does it free;
Every deed of love and mercy, done to man is done to Me.
Nevermore thou needest seek me; I am with thee every-
    where;
Raise the stone, and thou shalt find Me; cleave the wood,
    and I am there.

                    HENRY VAN DYKE

THOU MUST BE TRUE

THOU must be true thyself,
    If thou the truth wouldst teach!
Thy soul must overflow, if thou
    Another's soul wouldst reach;
It needs the overflow of heart
    To give the lips full speech.

Think truly, and thy thoughts
    Shall the world's famine feed;
Speak truly, and each word of thine
    Shall be a fruitful seed;
Live truly, and thy life shall be
    A great and noble creed.

                    HORATIO BONAR

THIS IS THE GOSPEL OF LABOUR

THIS is the gospel of labour, ring it, ye bells of the kirk!
The Lord of Love came down from above, to live with the
men who work.
This is the rose that He planted, here in the thorn-curst soil:
Heaven is blest with perfect rest, but the blessing of Earth
is toil.

HENRY VAN DYKE

A PSALM OF LIFE

TELL me not, in mournful numbers,
Life is but an empty dream!—
For the soul is dead that slumbers,
And things are not what they seem.

Life is real! Life is earnest!
And the grave is not its goal;
Dust thou art, to dust returnest,
Was not spoken of the soul.

Not enjoyment, and not sorrow,
Is our destined end or way;
But to act, that each to-morrow
Finds us farther than to-day.

Art is long, and Time is fleeting,
And our hearts, though stout and brave,
Still, like muffled drums, are beating
Funeral marches to the grave.

In the world's broad field of battle,
In the bivouac of Life,
Be not like dumb, driven cattle!
Be a hero in the strife!

Trust no Future, howe'er pleasant!
    Let the dead Past bury its dead!
Act,—act in the living Present!
    Heart within, and God o'erhead!

Lives of great men all remind us
    We can make our lives sublime,
And, departing, leave behind us
    Footprints on the sands of time;

Footprints, that perhaps another,
    Sailing o'er life's solemn main,
A forlorn and shipwrecked brother,
    Seeing, shall take heart again.

Let us then be up and doing,
    With a heart for any fate;
Still achieving, still pursuing,
    Learn to labor and to wait.

                  LONGFELLOW

EASTER, 1922

From all these things, let us arise and go;
From our mean bitterness, and foolish strife,
From feeble will that lures to easier life
Down in the valleys, while the peaks of snow,
Haughty and inaccessible, reflect the glow
Of an old hope fast fading, another sun
Sinks, like our dying faith, in the low West,
Our weak hands folded, with the work half done,
As gleams too soon the lotus-land of rest—
Dear Lord, from these let us arise and go!
But let us safely keep the dear old things
That made us, with the child's own wisdom wise;
All that did ever give the spirit wings—
With Thee uplifted, Lord, Oh, let us rise.

                  JOHN A. BELLOWS

GOMER

THROUGH all the mystery of my years,
There runs a purpose which forbids of the wail
Of passionate despair. I have not lived
At random, as a soul whom God forsakes;
But evermore his spirit led me on,
Prompted each purpose, taught my lips to speak,
Stirred up within me that deep love, and now
Reveals the inner secret.

DEAN PLUMPTRE

MY TASK

To love someone more dearly every day,
To help a wandering child to find his way,
To ponder o'er a noble thought, and pray
And smile, when evening falls,
    This is my task.

To follow truth as blind men long for light,
To do my best from dawn of day till night,
To keep my heart fit for His holy sight,
And answer when He calls,
    This is my task.

MAUDE LOUISE RAY

THE FIRES OF GOD

I

TIME gathers to my name;
Along the ways wheredown my feet have passed
I see the years with little triumph crowned,
Exulting not for perils dared, downcast
And weary-eyed and desolate for shame
Of having been unstirred of all the sound

Of the deep music of the men that move
Through the world's days in suffering and love.

Poor barren years that brooded over-much
On your own burden, pale and stricken years—
Go down to your oblivion, we part
With no reproach or ceremonial tears.
Henceforth my hands are lifted to the touch
Of hands that labour with me, and my heart
Hereafter to the world's heart shall be set
And its own pain forget.
Time gathers to my name—
Days dead are dark; the days to be, a flame
Of wonder and of promise, and great cries
Of travelling people reach me—I must rise.

II

Was I not man? Could I not rise alone
Above the shifting of the things that be,
Rise to the crest of all the stars and see
The ways of all the world as from a throne?
Was I not man, with proud imperial will
To cancel all the secrets of high heaven?
Should not my sole unbridled purpose fill
All hidden paths with light when once was riven
God's veil by my indomitable will?

So dreamt I, little man of little vision,
Great only in unconsecrated pride;
Man's pity grew from pity to derision,
And still I thought, "Albeit they deride,
Yet is it mine uncharted ways to dare
Unknown to these,
And they shall stumble darkly, unaware
Of solemn mysteries
Whereof the key is mine alone to bear."

So I forgot my God, and I forgot
The holy sweet communion of men,
And moved in desolate places, where are not
Meek hands held out with patient healing when
The hours are heavy with uncharitable pain;
No company but vain
And arrogant thoughts were with me at my side.
And ever to myself I lied,
Saying, "Apart from all men thus I go
To know the things that they may never know."

. . . .

III

. . . .

O fool, O only great
In pride unhallowed, O most blind of heart!
Confusion but more dark confusion bred,
Grief nurtured grief, I cried aloud and said,
"Through trackless ways the soul of man is hurled,
No sign upon the forehead of the skies,
No beacon, and no chart
Are given to him, and the inscrutable world
But mocks his scars and fills his mouth with dust."

. . . .

IV

. . . .

I no longer was aware
Of any will to heal the world's unrest,
I suffered as it suffered, and I grew
Troubled in all my daily trafficking,
Not with the large heroic trouble known
By proud adventurous men who would atone
With their own passionate pity for the sting
And anguish of a world of peril and snares,

It was the trouble of a soul in thrall
To mean despairs,
Driven about a waste where neither fall
Of words from lips of love, nor consolation
Of grave eyes comforting, nor ministration
Of hand or heart could pierce the deadly wall
Of self—of self,—I was a living shame—
A broken purpose. I had stood apart
With pride rebellious and defiant heart,
And now my pride had perished in the flame.
I cried for succour as a little child
Might supplicate whose days are undefiled,—
For tutored pride and innocence are one.

. . . .

VI

'Twas given me to hear. As I beheld—
With a new wisdom, tranquil, asking not
For mystic revelation—this glory long forgot,
This rediscovered triumph of the earth
In high creative will and beauty's pride
Establishèd beyond the assaulting years,
It came to me, a music that compelled
Surrender of all tributary fears,
Full-throated, fierce, and rhythmic with the wide
Beat of the pilgrim winds and labouring seas,
Sent up from all the harbouring ways of earth
Wherein the travelling feet of men have trod,
Mounting the firmamental silences
And challenging the golden gates of God.

. . . .

VII

O blessed voices, O compassionate hands,
Calling and healing, O great-hearted brothers,

I come to you. Ring out across the lands
Your benediction, and I too will sing
With you, and haply kindle in another s
Dark desolate hour the flame you stirred in me.
O bountiful earth, in adoration meet
I bow to you; O glory of years to be,
I too will labour to your fashioning.
Go down, go down, unweariable feet,
Together we will march towards the ways
Wherein the marshalled hosts of morning wait
In sleepless watch, with banners wide unfurled
Across the skies in ceremonial state,
To greet the men who lived triumphant days,
And stormed the secret beauty of the world.

JOHN DRINKWATER

SONGS OUT OF SORROW

I

SPIRIT'S HOUSE

FROM naked stones of agony
I will build a house for me;
As a mason all alone
I will raise it, stone by stone,
And every stone where I have bled
Will show a sign of dusky red.
I have not gone the way in vain,
For I have good of all my pain;
My spirit's quiet house will be
Built of naked stones I trod
On roads where I lost sight of God.

.   .   .   .

IV

WISDOM

When I have ceased to break my wings
Against the faultiness of things,
And learned that compromises wait
Behind each hardly opened gate,
When I can look Life in the eyes,
Grow calm and very coldly wise,
Life will have given me the Truth,
And taken in exchange—my youth.

.   .   .   .

VI

WOOD SONG

I heard a wood thrush in the dusk
   Twirl three notes and make a star—
My heart that walked with bitterness
   Came back from very far.

Three shining notes were all he had,
   And yet they made a starry call—
I caught life back against my breast
   And kissed it, scars and all.

VII

REFUGE

From my spirit's gray defeat,
From my pulse's flagging beat,
From my hopes that turned to sand
Sifting through my close-clenched hand,
From my own fault's slavery,
If I can sing, I still am free.

For with my singing I can make
A refuge for my spirit's sake,
A house of shining words, to be
My fragile immortality.

SARA TEASDALE

[From "Songs Out of Sorrow," The Macmillan Co.]

NOTE XVII

RECENT poetry has paid a surprising amount of attention to the subjects of God and the meaning of life, especially that phase of life which represents man's response to his world and his cosmic environment. These writers generally assume that the varied impulses arising naturally within one are the calls of God for human development and self-realization. The present group of poems attempts to show how one may best co-operate with the sacred powers of Life; how man may realize true partnership with God.

The unanimous answer is that when men cultivate the homely virtues of daily kindness and honesty, fair dealing and self-forgetting interest in others; when they bear their burdens bravely and accept their joys gratefully, keeping close touch with the Supreme Partner and hence undeterred by the failure of the many to keep faith even with the best in themselves; and when they rise to the Battle glorious for Truth and Honor and a chance for every one to live, then the love and the abiding passion for hard service and the sheer joy of living to help others will be the highest possible expression of the will to work with the Divine. And God, in his turn, will so understand man's practical devotion, and be glad. For is he not the Father of all, and is not character worth more to him than all else?

VIII

THE SPIRIT OF TRUE WORSHIP

XVIII

PRAYER

PRAYER is the soul's sincere desire,
Uttered or unexpressed,
The motion of a hidden fire,
That trembles in the breast.

Prayer is the burden of a sigh,
The falling of a tear,
The upward glancing of an eye,
When none but God is near.

Prayer is the simplest form of speech
That infant lips can try,
Prayer the sublimest strains that reach
The Majesty on high.

O thou by whom we come to God,—
The life, the truth, the way,—
The path of prayer thyself hast trod,
Lord, teach us how to pray!

JAMES MONTGOMERY

ONE SHORT HOUR

LORD, what a change within us one short hour
Spent in thy presence will prevail to make!
What heavy burdens from our bosoms take,
What parched grounds refresh as with a shower!
We kneel, and all around us seems to lower;
We rise, and all, the distant and the near,
Stands forth in sunny outline brave and clear;
We kneel, how weak; we rise, how full of power!
Why, therefore, should we do ourselves this wrong,

Or others, that we are not always strong,
That we are ever overborne with care,
That we should ever weak or heartless be,
Anxious or troubled, when with us is prayer,
And joy and strength and courage are with thee?

ARCHBISHOP TRENCH

MY CHURCH

My church has but one temple,
Wide as the world is wide,
Set with a million altars,
Where a million hearts abide.

My church has no creed to bar
A single brother man,
But says, "Come thou and worship'
To every one who can.

My church has no roof nor walk
Nor floor, save the beautiful sod,
For fear I would seem to limit
The love of the illimitable God.

E. O. G.

SONG OF HONOR

I heard the universal prayer,
The sons of light exalt their Sire
With universal song.
Earth's loveliest and loudest notes,
Her million times ten million throats
Exalt him loud and long.
And lips and lungs and tongues of grace,
From every heart and every place,
Within the shining of his face,
The universal song.

RALPH HODGSON

O MASTER, LET ME WALK WITH THEE

O MASTER, let me walk with thee
In lowly paths of service free;
Tell me thy secret; help me bear
The strain of toil, the fret of care.

Help me the slow of heart to move
By some clear, winning word of love;
Teach me the wayward feet to stay,
And guide them in the homeward way.

Teach me thy patience; still with thee
In closer, dearer company,
In work that keeps faith sweet and strong,
In trust that triumphs over wrong;

In hope that sends a shining ray
Far down the future's broadening way;
In peace that only thou canst give,—
With thee, O Master, let me live!

WASHINGTON GLADDEN

PSALM

THEY have burned to Thee many tapers in many temples:
I burn to Thee the taper of my heart.

They have sought Thee at many altars, they have carried
lights to find Thee:
I find Thee in the white fire of my heart.

They have gone forth restlessly, forging many shapes,
images where they seek Thee, idols of deed and thought:
Thou art the fire of my deeds; Thou art the white flame of
my dreams.

.   .   .   .

So little, so wholly given to its human quest,
And yet of Thee, wholly of Thee, Thou Unspeakable,
All the colors of life in a burning white mist
Pure and intense as Thou, O Heart of life!

Frail is my taper, it flickers in the storm,
It is blown out in the great wind of the world:
Yet when the world is dead and the seas are a crust of salt,
When the sun is dark in heaven and the stars have changed
 their courses,
Forever somewhere with Thee, on the altar of life
Shall still burn the white fire of my heart.

JESSIE E. SAMPTER

A NEW SONG

I KNOW not the song of thy praises,
 Till Thou teach it, my God, to me;
Till I hear the still voice of Thy Spirit,
 Who speaketh for ever of Thee;
Till I hear the celestial singing,
 And learn the new song of thy grace;
And then I shall tell forth the marvels
 I learnt in thy secret place.
Thy marvels, not mine, far surpassing
 All thoughts of my heart they must be;
I can but declare the glad tidings,
 As Thou hast declared them to me.

RICHARD ROLLE

TO THE SUPREME BEING

THE prayers I make will then be sweet indeed
If Thou the spirit give by which I pray:
My unassisted heart is barren clay,
That of its native self can nothing feed:

Of good and pious works thou art the seed,
That quickens only where thou say'st it may:
Unless Thou show to us thine own true way
No man can find it: Father! Thou must lead.
Do Thou, then, breathe those thoughts into my mind
By which such virtue may in me be bred
That in thy holy footsteps I may tread;
The fetters of my tongue do Thou unbind,
That I may have the power to sing of thee,
And sound thy praises everlastingly.

WORDSWORTH

SUMMER

IN JUNE

I THINK to-day is like that seventh day
  Of rest, when, the great marvels of creation done,
He paused to take His ease in a deep wood,
  Where the gray clouds hid the too brilliant sun
And the green beech leaves fluttered in that light
  Which is not night or day, but both in one.

Far in the forest depths a little wind
  Whispered its song of love and all the air
Was filled with leafy murmur. The great trees
  Chanted together softly. Everywhere
The world awakened and the silver rain
  Sang through the quivering twigs like a low prayer.

BERTHA TEN EYCK JAMES

THANKSGIVING

Now gracious plenty rules the board,
  And in the purse is gold;
By multitudes, in glad accord,

Thy giving is extolled.
Ah, suffer me to thank Thee, Lord,
For what Thou dost withhold!

I thank Thee that howe'er we climb
There yet is something higher;
That though through all our reach of time
We to the stars aspire,
Still, still, beyond us burns sublime
The pure sidereal fire!

I thank Thee for the unexplained,
The hope that lies before,
The victory that is not gained—
O Father, more and more
I thank Thee for the unattained—
The good we hunger for!

I thank Thee for the voice that sings
To inner depths of being;
For all the upward spread of wings,
From earthly bondage freeing;
For mystery—the dream of things
Beyond our power of seeing!

FLORENCE EARLE COATES

THE LORD IS MY LIGHT

Lord of all being, throned afar,
Thy glory flames from sun and star;
Center and soul of every sphere,
Yet to each loving heart how near!

Sun of our life, thy quickening ray
Sheds on our path the glow of day:
Star of our hope, thy softened light
Cheers the long watches of the night.

Our midnight is thy smile withdrawn;
Our noontide is thy gracious dawn;
Our rainbow arch, thy mercy's sign:
All, save the clouds of sin, are thine.

Lord of all life, below, above,
Whose light is truth, whose warmth is love,
Before thy ever-blazing throne
We ask no luster of our own.

Grant us thy truth to make us free,
And kindling hearts that burn for thee,
Till all thy living altars claim
One holy light, one heavenly flame.

OLIVER WENDELL HOLMES

WHEN·I AWAKE, I AM STILL WITH THEE

STILL, still with thee, when purple morning breaketh,
    When the bird waketh and the shadows flee;
Fairer than morning, lovelier than the daylight,
    Dawns the sweet consciousness, I am with thee.

Alone with thee, amid the mystic shadows,
    The solemn hush of nature newly born;
Alone with thee in breathless adoration,
    In the calm dew and freshness of the morn.

Still, still with thee; as to each new-born morning
    A fresh and solemn splendor still is given,
So doth this blessed consciousness, awaking,
    Breathe, each day, nearness unto thee and heaven.

When sinks the soul, subdued by toil, to slumber,
    Its closing eye looks up to thee in prayer;
Sweet the repose beneath thy wings o'ershading,
    But sweeter still to wake and find thee there.

So shall it be at last, in that bright morning,
When the soul waketh, and life's shadows flee:
O in that hour, fairer than daylight dawning,
Shall rise the glorious thought, I am with thee.

HARRIET BEECHER STOWE

NOW THE DAY IS OVER

Now the day is over,
Night is drawing nigh;
Shadows of the evening
Steal across the sky.

Now the darkness gathers,
Stars begin to peep;
Birds and beasts and flowers
Soon will be asleep.

Father, give the weary
Calm and sweet repose;
With thy tenderest blessing
May our eyelids close.

Grant to little children
Visions bright of thee;
Guard the sailors tossing
On the deep, blue sea.

Comfort every sufferer,
Watching late in pain;
Those who plan some evil
From their sin restrain.

Through the long night-watches
May thine angels spread
Their white wings above me,
Watching round my bed.

When the morning wakens,
   Then may I arise
Pure, and fresh, and sinless
   In thy holy eyes.

SABINE BARING-GOULD

IN THE MANTLE OF GOD

I PRAY to a God with a woman's face.
   (My mother's face is wondrous fair!)
The wide world is an altar-place,
   And love-in-life the only prayer.

I work for a God with a woman's hands.
   (My mother's hands are cool and strong!)
I sing for a God who understands
   The worker's work and the singer's song.

I live for a God with a woman's eyes.
   (My mother's eyes have made me whole!)
The very walls of paradise
   Are compassed in a single soul!

HAROLD TROWBRIDGE PULSIFER

CYNTHIA

O CYNTHIA! Fair Empress of the night!
How glorious 'tis to see thee sailing forth,
In splendor dight, from banks of ebon clouds,
To draw aside the curtains of the dark
And flood with mellow light the vaulted sky—
Erstwhile fast held in gyves of sable gloom—
And pour afar th' unstinted friendly beam
On pilgrim lone, benighted, hopeless lost.
New-heart'ning him along his toilsome way.

Upon thy nimbic throne with canopy
Of deep cerulean sitt'st thou serene,
Attended by thy myriad starry nymphs,
Unutterably bright in their allotted place
And marshaled by Orion, royal Prince
Of all the constellations of the skies.
At the Divine behest earth's rolling tides,
Obedient to thy undisputed sway.
At gentlest waving of thy sceptred staff
Or ebb, or flow.

In the deep hush of night
Benign thou broodest o'er the slumbering world
And scatt'rest gifts in showers of silver light.
And as earth's crystal waters—river, lake
Or bounding ocean—in their bosom catch
Thy glorious image, the enraptured waves
Show burnished silver in each lustrous fold.

When thou, sole Regent of the midnight hour,
Advancest stately o'er the azure fields
Exulting in the splendor of thy course,
The trembling stars, awe-struck at thy approach,
Their faces veil, eclipsed till thou hast passed;
While Philomela, tuneful bird of night,
With thy admiring praise the welkin fills.

Hast thou perchance forgot that, æons since,
Thy Maker called thee from abysmal naught
And, robing thee in regal robes of light
And placing in thy hand a shining wand,
Gave thee to rule the night till time's swift stream
Be blent for aye with life's eternal sea?
Ah! no, fair Cynthia! thy heart sends up
Without surcease sweet anthems to thy God.

Then teach thou me, and every man that views
Thy glory here, to lift aloft the soul

'Bove all things vain and sordid and terrene
To Him the great Creator of us all—
The shoreless sea of beauty and of truth,
Of wisdom, power, majesty and love—
And join with thee and all thy twinkling stars
And all creation vast, beyond our ken,
In adoration humble and profound
And soulful canticles of grateful praise.

JOHN D. WALSHE

MIDNIGHT

Now in the still
Shadow and glamour of the departed sun
Beauty's immortal ritual is done,
    The divine word and will.

Now, lost in lone
Worship and breathless adoration, lies
The loving at the belovèd breast and cries
    His prayer up to her throne.

Now thrills the dim
Heart of compassionate and conquering love
With solemn pride, and from her throne above
    Listens, and leans to him.

No sound is here.
Mysteriously the many are made one.—
O peace, now the eternal will is done,
    And God's own heart how near!

JOHN HALL WHEELOCK

THE EVERLASTING GOD

O GOD, the Rock of Ages,
    Who evermore hast been,
What time the tempest rages,
    Our dwelling-place serene:
Before thy first creations,
    O Lord, the same as now,
To endless generations
    The everlasting Thou!

Our years are like the shadows
    On sunny hills that lie,
Or grasses in the meadows
    That blossom but to die;
A sleep, a dream, a story,
    By strangers quickly told,
An unremaining glory
    Of things that soon are old.

O Thou, who canst not slumber,
    Whose light grows never pale,
Teach us aright to number
    Our years before they fail.
On us thy mercy lighten,
    On us thy goodness rest;
And let thy spirit brighten
    The hearts thyself hath blessed.

EDWARD HENRY BICKERSTETH

LEAD, KINDLY LIGHT

LEAD, kindly Light, amid the encircling gloom.
    Lead thou me on.
The night is dark, and I am far from home,—
    Lead thou me on.

Keep thou my feet; I do not ask to see
The distant scene,—one step enough for me.

I was not ever thus, nor prayed that thou
      Shouldst lead me on;
I loved to choose and see my path; but now
      Lead thou me on.
I loved the garish day, and, spite of fears,
Pride ruled my will; remember not past years.

So long thy power hath blest me, sure it still
      Will lead me on,
O'er moor and fen, o'er crag and torrent, till
      The night is gone;
And with the morn those angel faces smile
Which I have loved long since, and lost awhile.

                      JOHN HENRY NEWMAN

ABIDE WITH ME

ABIDE with me! fast falls the eventide;
The darkness deepens: Lord, with me abide!
When other helpers fail, and comforts flee,
Help of the helpless, O abide with me!

Swift to its close ebbs out life's little day;
Earth's joys grow dim, its glories pass away;
Change and decay in all around I see:
O thou who changest not, abide with me!

I need thy presence every passing hour:
What but thy grace can foil the tempter's power?
Who like thyself my guide and stay can be?
Through cloud and sunshine, O abide with me!

I fear no foe, with thee at hand to bless:
Ills have no weight, and tears no bitterness:
Where is death's sting? where, grave, thy victory?
I triumph still, if thou abide with me!

HENRY FRANCIS LYTE

O WORSHIP THE KING

O worship the King, all glorious above!
O gratefully sing his power and his love!
Our Shield and Defender, the Ancient of Days,
Pavilioned in splendor, and girded with praise.

O tell of his might, O sing of his grace,
Whose robe is the light, whose canopy space!
His chariots of wrath the deep thunderclouds form.
And dark is his path on the wings of the storm.

The earth, with its store of wonders untold,
Almighty, thy power hath founded of old;
Hath 'stablished it fast by a changeless decree,
And round it hath cast, like a mantle, the sea.

Thy bountiful care what tongue can recite?
It breathes in the air, it shines in the light,
It streams from the hills, it descends to the plain,
And sweetly distils in the dew and the rain.

Frail children of dust, and feeble as frail,
In thee do we trust, nor find thee to fail;
Thy mercies how tender, how firm to the end,
Our Maker, Defender, Redeemer, and Friend!

ROBERT GRANT

HARVEST THANKSGIVING

To-day, O God, amidst our flowers
  And fruits, we come to own again
The blessings of the summer hours,
  The early and the latter rain.

Once more the liberal year laughs out
  O'er richer stores than gems or gold;
Once more with harvest-song and shout
  Is Nature's bloodless triumph told.

O favors every year made new,
  O gifts with rain and sunshine sent!
The bounty overruns our due,
  The fullness shames our discontent.

We shut our eyes, the flowers bloom on;
  We murmur, but the corn-ears fill;
We choose the shadow, but the sun
  That casts it shines behind us still.

Now let these altars, wreathed with flowers
  And piled with fruits, awake again
Thanksgiving for the golden hours,
  The early and the latter rain !

WHITTIER

ANOTHER YEAR

Another year of setting suns,
  Of stars by night revealed;
Of springing grass and opening buds,
  By Winter's snow concealed.

Another year of Summer's glow,
  Of Autumn's gold and brown,

Of waving fields, and ruddy fruit
The branches weighing down.

Another year of happy work,
That better is than play;
Of simple cares, and love that grows
More sweet from day to day.

Another year of children's mirth;
Of friends, the tried and true;
Of thinker's thought, and poet's dream,
And prophet's vision new.

Another year at beauty's feast,
With every moment spread;
Of silent hours when grow distinct
The voices of the dead.

Another year to follow hard
Where better souls have trod;
Another year of life's delight,—
Another year of God!

JOHN W. CHADWICK

MARTYRS OF HUMANITY

WE praise thee, Almighty God, for thine elect, the prophets and martyrs of humanity, who gave their thoughts and
prayers and agonies for the truth of God and the freedom of
the people. We praise thee that amid loneliness and the
contempt of men, in poverty and imprisonment, when they
were condemned by the laws of the mighty and buffeted on
the scaffold, thou didst uphold them by thy spirit in loyalty
to thy holy cause.

Our hearts burn within us as we follow the bleeding feet
of thy Christ down the centuries, and count the mounts of
anguish on which he was crucified anew in his prophets and

the true apostles of his spirit. Help us to forgive those who
did it, for some truly thought they were serving thee when
they suppressed thy light, but oh, save us from the same
mistake! Grant us an unerring instinct for what is right
and true, and a swift sympathy to divine those who truly
love and serve the people. Suffer us not by thoughtless con-
demnation or selfish opposition to weaken the arm and
chill the spirit of those who strive for the redemption of
mankind. May we never bring upon us the blood of all the
righteous by renewing the spirit of those who persecuted
them in the past. Grant us rather that we, too, may be
counted in the chosen band of those who have given their
life as a ransom for the many. Send us forth with the path-
finders of humanity to lead thy people another day's march
toward the land of promise.

And if we, too, must suffer loss, and drink of the bitter
pool of misunderstanding and scorn, uphold us by thy
spirit in steadfastness and joy because we are found worthy
to share in the work and the reward of Jesus and all the
saints.

WALTER RAUSCHENBUSCH

THE INNOCENT ONES WHO COME AFTER

O GOD, we pray thee for those who come after us, for our
children, and the children of our friends, and for all the
young lives that are marching up from the gates of birth,
pure and eager, with the morning sunshine on their faces.
We remember with a pang that these will live in the world
we are making for them. We are wasting the resources of
the earth in our headlong greed, and they will suffer want.
We are building sunless houses and joyless cities for our
profit, and they must dwell therein. We are making the
burden heavy and the pace of work pitiless, and they will
fall wan and sobbing by the wayside. We are poisoning the

air of our land by our lies and our uncleanness, and they will breathe it.

O God, thou knowest how we have cried out in agony when the sins of our fathers have been visited upon us, and how we have struggled vainly against the inexorable fate that coursed in our blood or bound us in a prison-house of life. Save us from maiming the innocent ones who come after us by the added cruelty of our sins. Help us to break the ancient force of evil by a holy and steadfast will and to endow our children with purer blood and nobler thoughts. Grant us grace to leave the earth fairer than we found it; to build upon it cities of God in which the cry of needless pain shall cease; and to put the yoke of Christ upon our business life that it may serve and not destroy. Lift the veil of the future and show us the generation to come as it will be if blighted by our guilt, that our lust may be cooled and we may walk in the fear of the Eternal. Grant us a vision of the far-off years as they may be if redeemed by the sons of God, that we may take heart and do battle for thy children and ours.

WALTER RAUSCHENBUSCH

THY HIGHER CONTENTMENT

O God, we beseech thee to save us this day from the distractions of vanity and the false lure of inordinate desires. Grant us the grace of a quiet and humble mind, and may we learn of Jesus to be meek and lowly of heart. May we not join the throng of those who seek after things that never satisfy and who draw others after them in the fever of covetousness. Save us from adding our influence to the drag of temptation. If the fierce tide of greed beats against the breakwaters of our soul, may we rest at peace in thy higher contentment. In the press of life may we pass from duty to duty in tranquillity of heart and spread thy quietness to all who come near.

WALTER RAUSCHENBUSCH

THANKSGIVING

THE roar of the world is in my ears.
  Thank God for the roar of the world!
Thank God for the mighty tide of fears
  Against me always hurled!
Thank God for the bitter and ceaseless strife,
  And the sting of his chastening rod!
Thank God for the stress and pain of life,
  And oh, thank God for God!

JOYCE KILMER

AT FIRST I PRAYED FOR LIGHT

AT first I prayed for Light:—
  Could I but see the way,
How gladly, swiftly would I walk
  To everlasting day!

And next I prayed for Strength:—
  That I might tread the road
With firm unfaltering feet, and win
  The heaven's serene abode.

And then I asked for Faith:—
  Could I but trust my God,
I'd live enfolded in his peace,
  Though foes were all abroad.

But now I pray for Love;
  Deep love to God and man;
A living love that will not fail,
  However dark his plan;—

And Light and Strength and Faith
  Are opening everywhere!
God only waited for me till
  I prayed the larger prayer.

MRS. E. D. CHENEY

FELLOWSHIP WITH ALL

O GOD, we thank thee for this universe, our great home; for its vastness and its riches, and for the manifoldness of the life which teems upon it and of which we are part. We praise thee for the arching sky and the blessed winds, for the driving clouds and the constellations on high. We praise thee for the salt sea and the running water, for the everlasting hills, for the trees, and for the grass under our feet. We thank thee for our senses by which we can see the splendor of the morning, and hear the jubilant songs of love, and smell the breath of the springtime. Grant us, we pray thee, a heart wide open to all this joy and beauty, and save our souls from being so steeped in care or so darkened by passion that we pass heedless and unseeing when even the thornbush by the wayside is aflame with the glory of God.

Enlarge within us the sense of fellowship with all the living things, our little brothers, to whom thou hast given this earth as their home in common with us. We remember with shame that in the past we have exercised the high dominion of man with ruthless cruelty, so that the voice of the Earth, which should have gone up to thee in song, has been a groan of travail. May we realize that they live, not for us alone, but for themselves and for thee, and that they love the sweetness of life even as we, and serve thee in their place better than we in ours.

When our use of this world is over and we make room for others, may we not leave anything ravished by our greed or spoiled by our ignorance, but may we hand on our common heritage fairer and sweeter through our use of it, undiminished in fertility and joy, that so our bodies may return in peace to the great mother who nourished them and our spirits may round the circle of a perfect life in thee.

WALTER RAUSCHENBUSCH

THE ETERNAL PASSION

O THOU great Father of us all, we rejoice that at last we know thee. All our soul within us is glad because we need no longer cringe before thee as slaves of holy fear, seeking to appease thine anger by sacrifice and self-inflicted pain, but may come like little children, trustful and happy, to the God of love. Thou art the only true Father, and all the tender beauty of our human loves is the reflected radiance of thy lovingkindness, like the moonlight from the sunlight, and testifies to the eternal passion that kindled it.

Grant us growth of spiritual vision, that with the passing years we may enter into the fulness of this our faith. Since thou art our Father, may we not hide our sins from thee, but overcome them by the stern comfort of thy presence. By this knowledge uphold us in our sorrows and make us patient even amid the unsolved mysteries of the years. Reveal to us the larger goodness and love that speak through the unbending laws of thy world. Through this faith make us the willing equals of all thy other children.

As thou art ever pouring out thy life in sacrificial father-love, may we accept the eternal law of the cross and give ourselves to thee and to all men. We praise thee for Jesus Christ, whose life has revealed to us this faith and law, and we rejoice that he has become the first-born among many brethren. Grant that in us, too, the faith in thy fatherhood may shine through all our life with such persuasive beauty that some who still creep in the dusk of fear may stand erect as free sons of God, and that others who now through unbelief are living as orphans in an empty world may stretch out their hands to the great Father of their spirits and find thee near.

WALTER RAUSCHENBUSCH

THE LOVE THAT LEADS TO WIDER LIFE

O GOD, who comest to us disguised in lowliness to seek
Thy dwelling with the humble, may false expectations not
deceive us, nor pride shut Thee from our hearts.

If Thou comest dressed as Duty, plain, drab and unde-
sired, grant that we may not turn from Thy commands.
Often the homely figure has called in vain, and only when it
passed we saw its glory, all too late. As neglected duties
come now to mind, help us to go back and faithfully dis-
charge them, lest we stand at last condemned before Thee,
life beyond recall, with no joy of having done Thy will upon
the earth to make a heaven about us.

If Thou comest robed as Truth, white, relentless and aus-
tere, may we not fear to take Thee as our guide. We have
often been afraid that truth would strip us naked to the
blast. We could not bear the gaze that seemed to burn into
our souls. We knew not that truth would only set us free
and fearless, glad to be what we were in Thy sight, and
nothing more. Help us then to welcome all the truth
however painful and humiliating, lest when we come to gaze
upon Thy glory our eyes have lost the power to see.

If Thou comest to us as Love, clothed in flame and crowned
with sacrifice, may we not reject the offer of Thyself for
dread of fire or fear of suffering, lest we refuse that which
alone can cleanse us. and reject the love that leads to wider
life.

Let us know Thy Name, we pray Thee, lest we be left
lamed and lonely to face the light and life of the eternal
world. Amen.

W. E. ORCHARD

ETERNAL FATHER, QUEST OF AGES

ETERNAL Father, Quest of ages, long sought, oft doubted
or forsook; can it be that Thou art known to us, the Law
within our minds, the Life of every breath we draw, the Love

that yearneth in our hearts? Art Thou the Spirit who oft hast striven with us, and whom we greatly feared, lest yielding to His strong embrace we should become more than we dared to be?

An impulse toward forgiveness has sometimes stirred within us, we have felt moved to show mercy, the sacrificial life has touched our aspiration; but we were unprepared to pay the price. Was this Thyself, and have we turned from Thee? Something like this we must have done, so barren, joyless and so dead has life become. Canst Thou not visit us again?

We hush our thoughts to silence, we school our spirits in sincerity, and here we wait. O may we not feel once more the light upon our straining eyes, the tides of life rise again within our waiting hearts?

We never looked to meet Thee in the stress of thought, the toil of life, or in the call of duty; we only knew that somehow life had lost for us all meaning, dignity and beauty. How then shall we turn back again and see with eyes that fear has filmed? How can we be born again, now grown so old in fatal habit?

If we could see this life of ours lived out in Thee, its common days exalted, its circumstances made a throne, its bitterness, disappointment and failure all redeemed, then our hearts might stir again, and these trembling hands lay hold on life for evermore. Amen.

W. E. ORCHARD

THYSELF ART THE GOAL

O THOU, whose love passeth knowledge, and whose peace passeth understanding, it was Thy thought which conceived us, Thy love which bare us. We are of yesterday and know nothing, and yet we partake of Thine infinite nature; the truth we cannot attain shines ever before us, so that we know how far short of Thy glory we fall. Our hearts are restless in their search for rest, and even though we find nothing to satisfy our desire, this but witnesses that Thou Thyself art the goal of all our strivings; it is Thyself who hast made us to long for Thine infinite perfection, Thy eternal nature, Thy holy and omnipotent love.

We thank Thee for the unquenchable impulse towards Thee Thou hast planted within. We are pained by its passion, disturbed by its desire, and there have been times when we have sought to destroy its power; but we thank Thee we cannot.

We bless Thee for Him who gave full utterance to Thy Spirit, whose joy was to do Thy will, who clothed the inborn word with flesh, that all might come to know themselves and Thee. We see Thy purpose for our life on earth displayed in Christ, and we would yield our spirits to Him; but Thy purpose for our life to come is lost in unimaginable glory and light.

Set us in the light of eternity once again to-day. Reveal what we are. Make us able to bear Thy revelation, brave enough to do Thy will. Enable us to see the path that leads to Thee, in the things around us; to respond to Thy call to holy, helpful service. O give us to express something of Thee before we go hence and on our life's brief day the night comes down. Amen.

W. E. ORCHARD

BOUNDLESS LOVE

O Thou whose boundless love bestows
    The joy of life, the hope of Heaven;
Thou whose unchartered mercy flows
    O'er all the blessings Thou hast given;
Thou by whose light alone we see;
Thou by whose truth our souls set free
    Are made imperishably strong;
Hear Thou the solemn music of our song.

Grant us the knowledge that we need
   To solve the questions of the mind;
Light Thou our candle while we read,
   And keep our hearts from going blind;
Enlarge our vision to behold
The wonders Thou hast wrought of old;
    Reveal thyself in every law,
    And gild the towers of truth with holy awe.

Be Thou our strength when war's wild gust
   Rages around us, loud and fierce;
Confirm our souls, and let our trust
   Be like a wall that none can pierce;
Give us the courage that prevails,
The steady faith that never fails,
    Help us to stand in every fight
    Firm as a fortress to defend the right.

O God, make of us what Thou wilt;
   Guide Thou the labor of our hand;
Let all our work be surely built
   As Thou, the architect, hast planned;
But whatsoe'er thy power shall make
Of these frail lives, do not forsake
    Thy dwelling.   Let thy presence rest
    Forever in the temple of our breast.

HENRY VAN DYKE

WE FORGET THE GOAL

THE way is long, our Father, and sometimes very weary. We crowd and bruise one another in passing, and often we forget the goal in the heat and hurry of the pilgrimage. Start us forth, we pray, each day with fresh courage, and whisper in our hearts a little song to gladden our steps as we take up our burdens anew. Grant that the lightest of

these may ever be our conscience, and that we may never
be too laden with personal troubles to carry the balm of
sympathy for friend and foe. Above all, grant us the gift
of clear vision, that we may pierce the doubts and fears of
the passing moment, and dwell with unfaltering confidence
upon the ultimate fact of Thy love. Amen.

ALICE HEGAN RICE

A PRAYER

DEAR God, the light is come, our outgrown creeds
Drop from us as a garment, and our sight
Grows clear to see ourselves and Thee aright;
We trust our love to meet our utmost needs,
And know Thy hand sustains us. The foul breeds
Of nameless doubts and fears that thronged the night
Like phantoms disappear in Truth's clear light;
Self only, now our upward way impedes:
For Thou hast given new bottles for Truth's wine:—
Hast given a larger faith to help us live
A larger life; new knowledge that will give
A lamp to lead us on to the divine:
And though our feet may falter in the way,
Yet shall our eyes behold Love's Perfect Day.

ANON.

THREE DOORS

THREE doors there are in the temple
    Where men go up to pray,
And they that wait at the outer gate
    May enter by either way.
There are some that pray by asking;
    They lie on the Master's breast,
And shunning the strife of the lower life,

They utter their cry for rest.
There are some that pray by seeking;
  They doubt where their reason fails;
But their mind's despair is the ancient prayer
  To touch the print of the nails.
There are some that pray by knocking;
  They put their strength to the wheel,
For they have no time for thoughts sublime;
  They can only act what they feel.
Father, give each his answer,
  Each in his kindred way;
Adapt thy light to his form of night,
  And grant him his needed day.

WILLIAM WATSON

THESE ARE THE GIFTS I ASK

THESE are the gifts I ask
  Of thee, Spirit serene:
Strength for the daily task,
  Courage to face the road,
Good cheer to help me bear the traveller's load,
And, for the hours of rest that come between,
An inward joy in all things heard and seen.

These are the sins I fain
  Would have thee take away:
Malice and cold disdain,
  Hot anger, sullen hate,
Scorn of the lowly, envy of the great,
And discontent that casts a shadow gray
On all the brightness of the common day.

HENRY VAN DYKE

THE MASTER'S TOUCH

In the still air the music lies unheard;
In the rough marble beauty hides unseen;
To make the music and the beauty needs
The Master's touch, the sculptor's chisel keen.

Great Master, touch us with thy skillful hand;
Let not the music that is in us die!
Great Sculptor, hew and polish us; nor let,
Hidden and lost, thy form within us lie!
Spare not the stroke. Do with us as thou wilt.
Let there be naught unfinished, broken, marred.
Complete thy purpose, that we may become
Thy perfect image, thou our God and Lord.

HORATIO BONAR

CENTRAL CALM

My soul soars up the atmosphere
And sings aloud where God can hear,
And all my being leans intent
To mark His smiling wonderment.
O gracious dream, and gracious time,
And gracious theme, and gracious rime—
When buds of spring begin to blow
In blossoms that we used to know
And lure us back along the ways
Of time's all-golden yesterdays!

JAMES WHITCOMB RILEY

THE LEGEND GLORIFIED

Though awful tempests thunder overhead,
I deem that God is not disquieted—

The faith that trembles somewhat yet is sure
Through storm and darkness of a way secure.

Bleak winters, when the naked spirit hears
The break of hearts, through stinging sleet of tears,
I deem that God is not disquieted;
Against all stresses am I clothed and fed.

Nay, even with fixed eyes and broken breath,
My feet dip down into the tides of death,
Nor any friend be left, nor prayers be said,
I deem that God is not disquieted.

JAMES WHITCOMB RILEY

INVOCATION

O Thou whose equal purpose runs
In drops of rain or streams of suns,
And with a soft compulsion rolls
The green earth on her snowy poles;
O Thou who keepest in thy ken
The times of flowers, the dooms of men,
Stretch out a mighty wing above—
Be tender to the land we love!

If all the huddlers from the storm
Have found her hearthstone wide and warm;
If she has made men free and glad,
Sharing, with all, the good she had;
If she has blown the very dust
From her bright balance to be just,
Oh, spread a mighty wing above—
Be tender to the land we love!

When in the dark eternal tower
The star-clock strikes her trial hour,

And for her help no more avail
Her sea-blue shield, her mountain-mail,
But sweeping wide, from gulf to lakes,
The battle on her forehead breaks,
Throw Thou a thunderous wing above—
Be lightning for the land we love!

WENDELL PHILLIPS STAFFORD

AMERICA

My Country, 'tis of thee,
Sweet land of Liberty,
    Of thee I sing:
Land where my fathers died,
Land of the Pilgrims' pride,
From every mountain side
    Let Freedom ring!

My native Country, thee,
Land of the noble free,
    Thy name I love:
I love thy rocks and rills,
Thy woods and templed hills;
My heart with rapture thrills,
    Like that above.

Our fathers' God, to thee,
Author of Liberty,
    To thee we sing:
Long may our land be bright
With Freedom's holy light;
Protect us by thy might,
    Great God, our King!

SAMUEL F. SMITH

A PRAYER

LORD, not for light in darkness do we pray,
Not that the veil be lifted from our eyes,
Nor that the slow ascension of our day
    Be otherwise.

Not for a clearer vision of the things
Whereof the fashioning shall make us great,
Not for remission of the peril and stings
    Of time and fate.

Not for a fuller knowledge of the end
Whereto we travel, bruised yet unafraid,
Nor that the little healing that we lend
    Shall be repaid.

Not these, O Lord. We would not break the bars
Thy wisdom sets about us; we shall climb
Unfettered to the secrets of the stars
    In Thy good time.

We do not crave the high perception swift
When to refrain were well, and when fulfil,
Nor yet the understanding strong to sift
    The good from ill.

Not these, O Lord. For these Thou hast revealed,
We know the golden season when to reap
The heavy-fruited treasure of the field,
    The hour to sleep.

Not these. We know the hemlock from the rose,
The pure from stained, the noble from the base
The tranquil holy light of truth that glows
    On Pity's face.

We know the paths wherein our feet should press,
Across our hearts are written Thy decrees,

Yet now, O Lord, be merciful to bless
With more than these.

Grant us the will to fashion as we feel,
Grant us the strength to labour as we know,
Grant us the purpose, ribbed and edged with steel,
To strike the blow.

Knowledge we ask not—knowledge Thou hast lent,
But, Lord, the will—there lies our bitter need,
Give us to build above the deep intent
The deed, the deed.

JOHN DRINKWATER

DEAR LORD AND FATHER OF MANKIND!

DEAR Lord and Father of mankind!
Forgive our foolish ways!
Reclothe us in our rightful mind,
In purer lives thy service find,
In deeper reverence, praise.

In simple trust like theirs who heard,
Beside the Syrian sea,
The gracious calling of the Lord,
Let us, like them, without a word,
Rise up and follow thee.

O Sabbath rest by Galilee!
O calm of hills above,
Where Jesus knelt to share with thee
The silence of eternity
Interpreted by love!

With that deep hush subduing all
Our words and works that drown
The tender whisper of thy call,

As noiseless let thy blessing fall
  As fell thy manna down.

Drop thy still dews of quietness,
  Till all our strivings cease;
Take from our souls the strain and stress,
And let our ordered lives confess
  The beauty of thy peace.

WHITTIER

NOTE XVIII

WHAT has modern poetry to say upon the most difficult question of *sincere worship*—man's sense of appreciation for all the opportunities and blessings which he enjoys, the human outreach for greater being, and more and more intimate knowledge of, and oneness with, the Life Eternal from which all else seems to pour forth? Can a poet be as practical as a priest, and pack his philosophy into a deathless proverb, the text for a thousand sermons on "How to keep life sweet and strong"?

The real poet, trusting to the inspiration of his own conviction, gives fearless answer, where many a theologian and preacher has feared to tread:

1. Real worship is found in the reverential and aspiring bent of the whole life, the consuming ambition to leave a heritage of wholesome happiness in the world.

2. It is laying hold of eternal reservoirs of purpose and putting them to use in sunny, courageous living.

3. One may worship anywhere, everywhere; for all human beings yearn for some Ideal, and all Nature is one vast temple of the Spirit.

4. It is in quiet, Christ-like deeds of encouragement to the unfortunate and the needy, oftentimes, that the highest expression of worth-whileness is given; or, again, in throwing oneself into great social movements for the improvement of certain groups whose cause requires a public hearing.

5. It is in the sheer physical-spiritual joy of living, of breathing Nature's beauty and power, of having friends, of being a vitally conscious part of the life of God, that many find their most intense delight.

6. Now it is through the protective medium of fatherhood, now of gentle and rapturous motherhood, that one's thoughts rise to the point of adoration and ecstasy.

7. One's sense of daily protection, of inner guidance, of unbroken fellowship (even in the hour of death), calls out the song of gratitude and triumph.

8. Search for Truth, in any of its phases, and pursuit of Duty in any of its humble or more public forms, are also a following of the will of God.

9. Measuring ourselves and our accomplishments by the almost infinite capacities which we sometimes feel rising up, prophetic, within us—this humbling and transforming exercise is also counted sincerest worship.

10. Going the long, lonesome road of misunderstanding or of ill health—with none, not even God, to share the experience—and yet keeping on, confident (Job-like) of one's own integrity, this, too, is worship.

11. Appreciation of national blessings, with warm love of Country and her growing ideals, serves as another great outlet of life's pent-up feelings.

12. And not a few feel that the very act of aspiration, one's longings, one's very will to be more worthy, are God himself acting in the human self; so that worship seems to be the Divine in us, seeking human expression.

IX

THE ETERNAL VALUE AND CONTINUITY OF LIFE

XIX

GAUDEAMUS

BEAUTIFUL earth of stars and streams,
  Why should men fear what man can do?
He cannot rob us of our dreams,
  Born, as the rose is born, of you,
That even in the darkest hours
  Feeds with soft fire and secret dew
The tender lives of hidden flowers.

Strange fount of unexhausted joy,
  Strange hills of strength wherein abides
Faith that no sorrow can destroy,
  Beauty that ever gleams and glides,
With whispered cabalistic words,
  The huge omnipotence of tides,
The happy confidence of birds.

Brave messages of meadows green,
  And gospels of unfathomed blue;
But to have heard, but to have seen—
  I ask no more, kind earth, of you;
Enough for faith that I was born,
  And lived the magic seasons through,
And watched the marvel of the morn.

The hallowed rising of the moon
  Once to behold, to have known the sea—
That benediction and that boon
  Earth wonderfully gave to me.
O cup of brimming miracle!
  How golden it has been—to be!
Yea! and earth gave me Love as well.

RICHARD LE GALLIENNE

LORD OF MY HEART'S ELATION

LORD of my heart's elation,
Spirit of things unseen,
Be thou my aspiration
Consuming and serene!

Bear up, bear out, bear onward,
This mortal soul alone,
To selfhood or oblivion,
Incredibly thine own,—

As the foamheads are loosened
And blown along the sea,
Or sink and merge forever
In that which bids them be.

I, too, must climb in wonder,
Uplift at thy command,—
Be one with my frail fellows
Beneath the wind's strong hand.

A fleet and shadowy column
Of dust or mountain rain,
To walk the earth a moment
And be dissolved again.

Be thou my exaltation
Or fortitude of mien,
Lord of the world's elation,
Thou breath of things unseen!

BLISS CARMAN

THOUGHT FOR THE DAY

OUT of the dark the circling sphere
Is rounding onward to the light;

We see not yet the full day here,
　But we do see the paling night:

And hope, that lights her fadeless fires,
　And faith, that shines as spotless will,
And love, that courage re-inspires,—
　These stars have been above us still.

Look backward, how much has been won!
　Look round, how much is yet to win!
The watches of the night are done:
　The watches of the day begin.

SAMUEL LONGFELLOW

THE HARVEST OF TIME

TIME winnows beauty with a fiery wind,
Driving the dead chaff from the living grain.
Some day there will be golden sheaves to bind;
There will be wonder in the world again.
There will be lonely phrases born to power,
There will be words immortal and profound;
Though no man knows the coming of the hour,
And no man knows the sower or the ground.

It may be even now the ranging earth
Lifting to glory some forgotten land
Feels there deep beauty quickening to birth,
Sprung from the sowing of a hidden hand.
Beauty endures though towering empires die.
O, speed the blown chaff down the smoking sky!

HAROLD TROWBRIDGE PULSIFER

'TIS BUT THE NIGHT

MEN change, flags change, and border lines
　Move north or south, and east or west;

But still the great unaltered pines
    In centuries of green are dressed;
In warmer lands the quiet palm
Still wears its calm.

Truth stands, God reigns, Christ walks today,
    Love lives within the hearts of men;
The things that seem to pass away
    A little while, return again.
A little while the shadows fall,
And that is all.

The night comes down, and mountain peaks
    Are lost to view, the grassy slope;
Yet, at the darkest, memory speaks
    The lovely prophecy of hope;
No peaks at midnight we discern,
But they return.

The rising sun again will gild
    The summit that is lost to sight.
When darkness shuts around you, build—
    Yes, keep on building in the night,
Still undiscouraged, since you know
These things are so.

The great unalterable things
    Will never change. Though for a time
To other lands the bird takes wings,
    Though summer seeks some other clime,
Though for a time injustice hides
The mountain sides—

Doubt not, fear not; work on, and wait;
    As sure as dawn shall conquer dark
So love will triumph over hate,
    And spring will bring again the lark.

Yes, if for truth you labor here,
You need not fear.

The night comes down, but labor on;
    Despair not, yield not, neither change;
Tomorrow morn again the dawn
    Will light the unalterable range
Of God's high hills with truth's great light.
'Tis but the night.
DOUGLAS MALLOCH

THE CHOIR INVISIBLE

OH, may I join the choir invisible
Of those immortal dead who live again
In minds made better by their presence; live
In pulses stirred to generosity,
In deeds of daring rectitude, in scorn
For miserable aims that end with self,
In thoughts sublime that pierce the night like stars,
And with their mild persistence urge men's search
To vaster issues.   So to live is heaven:
To make undying music in the world,
Breathing a beauteous order that controls
With growing sway the growing life of man.
So we inherit that sweet purity
For which we struggled, failed, and agonized
With widening retrospect that bred despair.
Rebellious flesh that would not be subdued,
A vicious parent shaming still its child,
Poor anxious penitence, is quick dissolved;
Its discords, quenched by meeting harmonies,
Die in the large and charitable air.
And all our rarer, better, truer self,
That sobbed religiously in yearning song,
That watched to ease the burden of the world,

Laboriously tracing what must be,
And what may yet be better,—saw within
A worthier image for the sanctuary,
And shaped it forth before the multitude,
Divinely human, raising worship so
To higher reverence more mixed with love,—
That better self shall live till human Time
Shall fold its eyelids, and the human sky
Be gathered like a scroll within the tomb
Unread forever. This is life to come,—
Which martyred men have made more glorious
For us who strive to follow. May I reach
That purest heaven,—be to other souls
The cup of strength in some great agony,
Enkindle generous ardor, feed pure love,
Beget the smiles that have no cruelty,
Be the sweet presence of a good diffused,
And in diffusion ever more intense!
So shall I join the choir invisible
Whose music is the gladness of the world.

GEORGE ELIOT

THANATOPSIS

To him who in the love of Nature holds
Communion with her visible forms, she speaks
A various language; for his gayer hours
She has a voice of gladness, and a smile
And eloquence of beauty, and she glides
Into his darker musings, with a mild
And healing sympathy, that steals away
Their sharpness, ere he is aware. When thoughts
Of the last bitter hour come like a blight
Over thy spirit, and sad images
Of the stern agony, and shroud, and pall,
And breathless darkness, and the narrow house,

Make thee to shudder, and grow sick at heart;—
Go forth, under the open sky, and list
To Nature's teachings, while from all around—
Earth and her waters, and the depths of air—
Comes a still voice—Yet a few days, and thee
The all-beholding sun shall see no more
In all his course; nor yet in the cold ground,
Where thy pale form was laid, with many tears,
Nor in the embrace of ocean, shall exist
Thy image.   Earth, that nourished thee, shall claim
Thy growth, to be resolved to earth again,
And, lost each human trace, surrendering up
Thine individual being, shalt thou go
To mix forever with the elements,
To be a brother to the insensible rock
And to the sluggish clod, which the rude swain
Turns with his share, and treads upon. The oak
Shall send his roots abroad, and pierce thy mould.

Yet not to thine eternal resting-place
Shalt thou retire alone, nor couldst thou wish
Couch more magnificent. Thou shalt lie down
With patriarchs of the infant world—with kings,
The powerful of the earth—the wise, the good,
Fair forms, and hoary seers of ages past,
All in one mighty sepulchre. The hills
Rock-ribbed and ancient as the sun,—the vales
Stretching in pensive quietness between;
The venerable woods—rivers that move
In majesty, and the complaining brooks
That make the meadows green; and, poured round all,
Old Ocean's gray and melancholy waste,—
Are but the solemn decorations all
Of the great tomb of man. The golden sun,
The planets, all the infinite host of heaven,
Are shining on the sad abodes of death,

Through the still lapse of ages. All that tread
The globe are but a handful to the tribes
That slumber in its bosom.—Take the wings
Of morning, pierce the Barcan wilderness,
Or lose thyself in the continuous woods
Where rolls the Oregon, and hears no sound,
Save his own dashings—yet the dead are there:
And millions in those solitudes, since first
The flight of years began, have laid them down
In their last sleep—the dead reign there alone.
So shalt thou rest, and what if thou withdraw
In silence from the living, and no friend
Take note of thy departure? All that breathe
Will share thy destiny. The gay will laugh
When thou art gone; the solemn brood of care
Plod on, and each one as before will chase
His favorite phantom; yet all these shall leave
Their mirth and their employments, and shall come
And make their bed with thee. As the long train
Of ages glide away, the sons of men,
The youth in life's green spring, and he who goes
In the full strength of years, matron and maid,
The speechless babe, and the gray-headed man—
Shall one by one be gathered to thy side,
By those, who in their turn shall follow them.

So live, that when thy summons comes to join
The innumerable caravan, which moves
To that mysterious realm, where each shall take
His chamber in the silent halls of death,
Thou go not, like the quarry-slave at night,
Scourged to his dungeon, but, sustained and soothed
By an unfaltering trust, approach thy grave,
Like one who wraps the drapery of his couch
About him, and lies down to pleasant dreams.

WILLIAM CULLEN BRYANT

THE DEBT

Because the years are few, I must be glad;
Because the silence is so near, I sing;
'Twere ill to quit an inn where I have had
Such bounteous fare, nor pay my reckoning.
I would not, from some gleaming parapet
Of Sirius or Vega, bend my gaze
On a remembered sparkle and regret
That from it thanklessly I went my ways
Up through the starry colonnades, nor found
Violets in any Paradise more blue
Than those that blossomed on my own waste ground,
Nor vespers sweeter than the robins knew.

Though Earth be but an outpost of delight,
Heaven's wild frontier by tragedy beset,
Only a Shakespeare may her gifts requite,
Only a happy Raphael pay his debt.
Yet I—to whom even as to those are given
Cascading foam, emblazoned butterflies,
The moon's pearl chariot through the massed clouds driven,
And the divinity of loving eyes—
Would make my peace now with mine hostess Earth,
Give and take pardon for all brief annoy,
And toss her, far beneath my lodging's worth,
Poor that I am, a coin of golden joy.

KATHARINE LEE BATES

"IF WINTER COMES"

Eternal question with its answering aye,
    Expectant query with recurrent nod,
The *yes* that thirsty souls seek after when they cry,
    "Is life worth living?" and "Is there a God?"

The yearning heart asks in insistent tone,
  And ceaseless questions, too, the human mind;
Kind Nature answers, "Trust the unknown for the known;
  'If winter comes, can spring be far behind?'"

LAURA BELL EVERETT

FAITH

MEN buy and sell by faith; the forges burn,
The drays are laden, countless mill-wheels turn,
Great ships are chartered, trains run to and fro;
Though faith directs them all, they scarcely know
This spirit of the life of every day.
Will she desert them when they seek to pray?

A day—a single day—if faith were dead,
No field were sown, no oven fired for bread.
Faith is the hand-maid in a toiler's guise
Of all the world of workers. To tired eyes
With solace she appears at close of day
To lift their burdens when they seek to pray.

LAURA BELL EVERETT

THE WATCHERS

WHEN the red sun goes down their day begins:
For light flows to them from a thousand suns.
Theirs is the comet that unerring runs
A course ethereal; then strangely spins
A mystery about the sun, and wins
Surcease. Flashing from out the changeless dark
Burns the great system in a timeless mark,
Throne of the starry-armored paladins.

We wait the word: "What of the longed-for goal
Where troubled soul communes in peace with soul?
Or is earth, heaven? What says the starlit deep?
How fares the traveler on the ways of light?
Does he move on in joy on the eternal flight,
Or are far spaces but for dreamless sleep?"

HENRY MEADE BLAND

AT THE SET OF THE SUN

At the set of the sun,
When our work is done,
With all its tangled web;
When the clouds drift low,
And the stream runs slow,
And life is at its ebb,

As we near the goal,
When the golden bowl
Shall be broken at its fount;
With what sweetest thought
Shall the hour be fraught,
What precious most shall we count?

Not the flame of the sword,
Nor the wealth we have stored
In perishable things of earth—
Not the way we have trod
With the intellect broad,
Though that were of precious worth.

Nor the gain we achieved
Through the hearts we have grieved,
And left unhelped by the way,
Nor the laurel of fame,
When, for worldly acclaim,
We toiled in the heat and the fray.

Ah, no! 'tis not these
Will give our hearts ease,
When life sinks low in the west;
But the passing sweet thought
Of the good we have wrought,
The saddened lives we have blest.

And the love we have won,
And the love beckoning on
From His islands far and dim;
Love out of the light,
Shining into the night,
The night which leadeth to him.

ANON.

NOT ENDLESS LIFE, BUT ENDLESS LOVE

NOT endless life, but endless love, I crave,
The gladness and the calm of holier springs,
The hope that makes men resolute and brave,
The joyful life in the great Life of Things.

W. M. W. CALL

SONG

IF love were but a little thing—
Strange love, which, more than all, is great—
One might not such devotion bring,
Early to serve and late.

If love were but a passing breath—
Wild love—which, as God knows, is sweet—
One might not make of life and death
A pillow for love's feet.

FLORENCE EARLE COATES

THE LAMP

IF I can bear your love like a lamp before me,
When I go down the long steep Road of Darkness,
I shall not fear the everlasting shadows,
    Nor cry in terror.

If I can find out God, then I shall find Him,
If none can find Him, then I shall sleep soundly,
Knowing how well on earth your love sufficed me,
    A lamp in darkness.

SARA TEASDALE

[From "Love Songs," by The Macmillan Co.]

CONFESSION

WHEN I was young I made a vow
    To keep youth in my heart as long
As there were birds upon the bough
    To gladden me with song:

To learn what lessons Life might give,
    To do my duty as I saw,
To love my friends, to laugh and live
    Not holding Death in awe.

So all my lyrics sing of joy,
    And shall until my lips are mute;
In old age happy as the boy
    To whom God gave the lute.

FRANK DEMPSTER SHERMAN

MY CREED

LET us learn to be content with what we have. Let us
learn to get rid of our false estimates, set up all the higher
ideals—a quiet home; vines of our own planting; a few books

full of the inspiration of a genius; a few friends worthy of being loved, and able to love us in turn; a hundred innocent pleasures that bring no pain or remorse; a devotion to the right that will never swerve; a simple religion empty of all bigotry, full of trust and hope and love—and to such a philosophy this world will give up all the empty joy it has.

DAVID SWING

LEAVES

ONE by one, like leaves from a tree,
All my faiths have forsaken me;
But the stars above my head
Burn in white and delicate red,
And beneath my feet the earth
Brings the sturdy grass to birth.
I who was content to be
But a silken-singing tree,
But a rustle of delight
In the wistful heart of night,
I have lost the leaves that knew
Touch of rain and weight of dew.
Blinded by a leafy crown
I looked neither up nor down—
But the leaves that fall and die
Have left me room to see the sky;
Now for the first time I know
Stars above and earth below.

SARA TEASDALE

[From "Rivers to the Sea," by The Macmillan Co.]

THE IMMORTALITY IN OUR HANDS

WE ask so often, "What is Immortality?"
This—
To know that you have received from your father and

mother, and from the fathers and mothers of their fathers and mothers before them, a foundation of body and character and personality—good, bad, or indifferent, all in one;

To take the many qualities thus passed down to you, qualities doubly precious because of their very source, and to combine them with the heritance of one who is nobler and finer and dearer to you than anyone else, passing them on, molten and welded into a greater metal, to sons and daughters of your own:

To give these sons and daughters the best that lies within your self and the self of that one whom you have chosen from all mankind—to do everything in your mortal power to develop that best in them, to nurture it, to cherish it always:

To give them, for the comfort of your pettier vanity, your likeness and that of the one you hold so dear, the likeness perhaps of the fathers and mothers who gave you theirs:

To give them of your mind and to know that you have given them as well of the mind of one so precious to you:

To give them of your experience, of the things you have learned, of your sufferings, of your joys:

To give them of your ideals:

To live before them so that when it comes your time to go you can go in happiness, secure in the thought that they will strive ever toward the standards inborn and inbred in them by you:

To give thus to the world a new generation of which you may always be infinitely proud; yours in likeness, yours in mind, yours in ideals and in spirit:

To do these things and to do them well—who of us is so small and selfish, so avariciously seeking or clutching fast to the mean identity of this little life, as to be unable to realize that here, within our ken and within our very grasp, lies that wondrous Immortality of which all humanity has so long dreamed?

It is the one Immortality unselfish enough and noble

enough and human enough to have been ordained for the finite comprehension of mortal kind by the infinite wisdom of a loving God.

Whatever other Immortality there may be or there may not be, this Immortality at least lies ever in our hands, to be shaped, as we wish to shape it, to be neglected or defiled, or to be consecrated, sanctified, enshrined.

It is the first Goal on the Way.

GERALD MYGATT

TOWARDS FIELDS OF LIGHT

For me—to have made one soul
  The better for my birth;
To have added but one flower
  To the garden of the earth;

To have struck one blow for truth
  In the daily fight with lies;
To have done one deed of right
  In the face of calumnies;

To have sown in the souls of men
  One thought that will not die—
To have been a link in the chain of life;—
  Shall be immortality.

EDWIN HATCH

LOST DAYS

The lost days of my life until today,
What were they, could I see them on the street
Lie as they fell? Would they be ears of wheat
Sown once for food but trodden into clay?
Or golden coins squandered and still to pay?
Or drops of blood dabbling the guilty feet?

Or such spilt water as in dreams must cheat
The undoing throats of Hell, athirst alway?

I do not see them here: but after death
God knows I know the faces I shall see,
Each one a murdered self, with low last breath.
"I am thyself,—what hast thou done to me?"
"And I—and I—thyself" (lo! each one saith),
"And thou thyself to all eternity!"

DANTE GABRIEL ROSSETTI

SAY NOT THE STRUGGLE NAUGHT AVAILETH

SAY not the struggle naught availeth,
   The labor and the wounds are vain,
The enemy faints not, nor faileth,
   And as things have been they remain.

If hopes were dupes, fears may be liars;
   It may be, in yon smoke concealed,
Your comrades chase e'en now the fliers,
   And, but for you, possess the field.

For while the tired waves, vainly breaking,
   Seem here no painful inch to gain,
Far back, through creeks and inlets making
   Comes silent, flooding in, the main.

And not by eastern windows only,
   When daylight comes, comes in the light;
In front, the sun climbs slow, how slowly,
   But westward, look, the land is bright.

ARTHUR HUGH CLOUGH

THE DREAMER

HE whom a dream hath possessed knoweth no more of
doubting,
   For mist and the blowing of winds and the mouthing of
words he scorns;
Not the sinuous speech of schools he hears, but a knightly
shouting,
   And never comes darkness down, yet he greeteth a million
morns.

He whom a dream hath possessed knoweth no more of
roaming;
   All roads and the flowing of waves and the speediest
flight he knows,
But wherever his feet are set, his soul is forever homing,
   And going, he comes, and coming he heareth a call and
goes.

He whom a dream hath possessed knoweth no more of
sorrow,
   At death and the dropping of leaves and the fading of
suns he smiles,
For a dream remembers no past and scorns the desire of a
morrow,
   And a dream in a sea of doom sets surely the ultimate
isles.

He whom a dream hath possessed treads the impalpable
marches,
   From the dust of the day's long road he leaps to a laughing
star,
And the ruin of worlds that fall he views from eternal arches,
   And rides God's battlefield in a flashing and golden car.

SHÆMUS O'SHEEL

SELF–DEPENDENCE

WEARY of myself, and sick of asking
What I am, and what I ought to be,
At this vessel's prow I stand, which bears me
Forwards, forwards, o'er the starlit sea.

And a look of passionate desire
O'er the sea and to the stars I send:
"Ye who from my childhood up have calmed me,
Calm me, ah, compose me to the end!

"Ah, once more," I cried, "ye stars, ye waters,
On my heart your mighty charm renew;
Still, still let me, as I gaze upon you,
Feel my soul becoming vast like you!"

From the intense, clear, star-sown vault of heaven,
Over the lit sea's unquiet way,
In the rustling night-air came the answer,—
"Wouldst thou *be* as these are? *Live* as they.

"Unaffrighted by the silence round them,
Undistracted by the sights they see,
These demand not that the things without them
Yield them love, amusement, sympathy.

"And with joy the stars perform their shining,
And the sea its long moon-silvered roll;
For self-poised they live, nor pine with noting
All the fever of some differing soul.

"Bounded by themselves, and unregardful
In what state God's other works may be,
In their own tasks all their powers pouring,
These attain the mighty life you see."

O air-born voice! long since, severely clear,
A cry like thine in mine own heart I hear,—
"Resolve to be thyself; and know, that he
Who finds himself loses his misery!"

MATTHEW ARNOLD

[From "Matthew Arnold's Poems," The Macmillan Co.]

THE SURVIVOR

WHEN the last day is ended,
  And the nights are through;
When the last sun is buried
  In its grave of blue;

When the stars are snuffed like candles,
  And the seas no longer fret;
When the winds unlearn their cunning,
  And the storms forget;

When the last lip is palsied,
  And the last prayer said;
Love shall reign immortal
  While the worlds lie dead!

FREDERIC L. KNOWLES

TWO SONNETS

I

JUST as I wonder at the twofold screen
Of twisted innocence that you would plait
For eyes that uncourageously await
The coming of a kingdom that has been,
So do I wonder what God's love can mean
To you that all so strangely estimate
The purpose and the consequent estate
Of one short shuddering step to the Unseen.

No, I have not your backward faith to shrink
Love-faring from the doorway of God's home
To find Him in the names of buried men;
Nor your ingenious recreance to think
We cherish, in the life that is to come,
The scattered features of dead friends again.

II

Never until our souls are strong enough
To plunge into the crater of the Scheme—
Triumphant in the flash there to redeem
Love's handsel and forevermore to slough,
Like cerements at a played-out masque, the rough
And reptile skins of us whereon we set
The stigma of scared years—are we to get
Where atoms and the ages are one stuff.

Nor ever shall we know the cursed waste
Of life in the beneficence divine
Of starlight and of sunlight and soul-shine
That we have squandered in sin's frail distress,
Till we have drunk, and trembled at the taste,
The mead of Thought's prophetic endlessness.

EDWIN ARLINGTON ROBINSON

THEY DO NOT LIVE

THEY do not live who choose the middle way,
Whom ecstasy and anguish have not known,
Who scale no trembling heights, nor plumb the lone
Depths of an aching darkness in bright day.
They miss the passion with the pain, the gay
High tides that sweep the spirit to its own,
The lifting surge of music, the dear tone
Of a loved voice in pleading or in play.

They miss the hurts and stumblings; surely fear
Is never theirs, nor groping in the night;
In their serene cool weather come no dread
Torrents or tempests to corrupt their sight,
Nor any rainbow; neither do they hear
The sea, nor does the thunder wake these dead.

IRWIN EDMAN

I—THE DEAD

BLOW out, you bugles, over the rich Dead!
There's none of these so lonely and poor of old,
But, dying, has made us rarer gifts than gold.
These laid the world away; poured out the red
Sweet wine of youth; gave up the years to be
Of work and joy, and that unhoped serene
That men call age; and those who would have been
Their sons, they gave, their immortality.
Blow, bugles, blow! They brought us, for our dearth,
Holiness, lacked so long, and Love, and Pain.
Honor has come back, as a king, to earth,
And paid his subjects with a royal wage;
And Nobleness walks in our ways again;
And we have come into our heritage.

II—THE DEAD

THESE hearts were woven of human joys and cares,
Washed marvellously with sorrow, swift to mirth.
The years had given them kindness. Dawn was theirs,
And sunset, and the colors of the earth.
These had seen movement, and heard music; known
Slumber and waking; loved; gone proudly friended;
Felt the quick stir of wonder; sat alone;
Touched flowers and furs and cheeks. All this is ended.
There are waters blown by changing winds to laughter

And lit by the rich skies, all day. And after,
　Frost, with a gesture, stays the waves that dance
And wandering loveliness. He leaves a white
　Unbroken glory, a gathered radiance,
A width, a shining peace, under the night.

RUPERT BROOKE

FROM "THE HUMAN FANTASY"

THE vastitude of space comes down to your own door;
Equally with the stars, the common and the street
Are part of the great Beauty that shines from shore to shore.
The universe divine lies around us at our feet—
Tangible, made of dust, and holy to the core.

Not in a world beyond lies wonder, nor above,
Nor throned among the spheres, nor set for days to be—
Over you and beneath, whether you sleep or move,
Reaches the moral Fact, the starry Eternity—
And all the hell of hate and all the heaven of love. . . .

Before your generation and you go hurrying by,
Have you no word for all, of pure and starriest breath?
O, how the common doom transfigures Destiny!
In the dear thought of all who pass through life and death,
Splendid it is to live and glorious to die

JOHN HALL WHEELOCK

THE GREAT MINIMUM

IT is something to have wept as we have wept,
It is something to have done as we have done,
It is something to have watched when all men slept,
And seen the stars which never see the sun.

It is something to have smelt the mystic rose,
Although it break and leave the thorny rods,
It is something to have hungered once as those
Must hunger who have ate the bread of gods.

To have seen you and your unforgotten face,
Brave as a blast of trumpets for the fray,
Pure as white lilies in a watery space,
It were something, though you went from me today.

To have known the things that from the weak are furled,
Perilous ancient passions, strange and high;
It is something to be wiser than the world,
It is something to be older than the sky.

In a time of sceptic moths and cynic rusts,
And fatted lives that of their sweetness tire,
In a world of flying loves and fading lusts,
It is something to be sure of a desire.

Lo, blessed are our ears for they have heard;
Yea, blessed are our eyes for they have seen:
Let thunder break on man and beast and bird
And the lightning. It is something to have been.

GILBERT KEITH CHESTERTON

DAY BY DAY

I HEARD a voice at evening softly say:
    Bear not thy yesterday into to-morrow,
    Nor load this week with last week's load of sorrow;
    Lift all thy burdens as they come, nor try
    To weight the present with the by and by.
One step, and then another, take thy way—
    Live day by day.

Live day by day.
Though the autumn leaves are withering round thy way,
Walk in the sunshine. It is all for thee.
Push straight ahead as long as thou canst see.
Dread not the winter where thou mayst go;
But when it comes, be thankful for the snow.
Onward and upward. Look and smile and pray—
Live day by day.

Live day by day.
The path before thee doth not lead astray.
Do the next duty. It must surely be
The Christ is in the one that's close to thee.
Onward, still onward, with a sunny smile,
Till step by step shall end in mile by mile.
"I'll do my best," unto my conscience say—
Live day by day.

Live day by day.
Why art thou bending toward the backward way?
One summit and another thou shalt mount.
Why stop at every round the space to count
The past mistakes if thou must still remember?
Watch not the ashes of the dying ember.
Kindle thy hope. Put all thy fears away—
Live day by day.

JULIA HARRIS MAY

THE BLESSING OF WORK

Let me do my work from day to day,
    In field or forest, at the desk or loom,
In roaring market-place or tranquil room;
    Let me but find it in my heart to say,
When vagrant wishes beckon me astray,
    "This is my work; my blessing, not my doom;

Of all who live I am the one by whom
This work can best be done in the right way."
Then shall I see it not too great, nor small,
To suit my spirit and to prove my powers.

HENRY VAN DYKE

LAST CONFESSIONAL

For all ill words that I have spoken,
For all clear moods that I have broken,
    For all despite and hasty breath,
    Forgive me, Love, forgive me, Death.

Death, master of the great assize,
Love, falling now to memories,
    You two alone I need to prove,
    Forgive me, Death, forgive me, Love.

For every tenderness undone,
For pride when holiness was none
    But only easy charity,
    O Death, be pardoner to me.

For stubborn thought that would not make
Measure of love's thought for love's sake,
    But kept a sullen difference,
    Take, Love, this laggard penitence.

For cloudy words too vainly spent
To prosper but in argument,
    When truth stood lonely at the gate,
    On your compassion, Death, I wait.

For all the beauty that escaped
This foolish brain, unsung, unshaped,
    For wonder that was slow to move,
    Forgive me, Death, forgive me, Love.

For love that kept a secret cruse
For life defeated of its dues,
  This latest word of all my breath—
  Forgive me, Love, forgive me, Death.

JOHN DRINKWATER

THE JOY OF LIVING

(*A Singer*):
  I AM the Voice of the great Musician,
  Singing and singing, to let the world know
  The joy of the life to which they are called,
  The thrill of the toil for which ages are spent.

(*Response*):
  And mine the honor of sharing this Life
  Of the Master-Creator as Time unrolls;
  In my inmost being may He be known
  In all His passionate will to live.

(*Appreciation*):
  For the sorrows of men are heavy to bear
  And the cry of the race is a cry of despair;
  But the Power I have felt gives strength to endure;
  It leads to the heights where joy is made sure.

ANON.

DIVINE RHYTHM

CLOUDS, then glory of sunset;
  Darkness, then burst of the morn;
Dearth, then the gentle shower;
  Sacrifice—Truth is born!

The earth-throe, then comes the harvest;
  Silence, and then the word;
Mist, before the full starlight;
  Discord, ere music is heard!

Erring, and then the forgiveness;
   Heart's-ease after the strife;
Passion, and then the refining—
   Death, then the wonder of life!

HENRY MEADE BLAND

IS THIS THE END?

Is this the end? I know it cannot be.
Our ships shall sail upon another sea;
New islands yet shall break upon our sight,
New continents of love and truth and might.

J. W. CHADWICK

BEYOND OUR POWER OF VISION

BEYOND our power of vision, poets say,
There is another world of forms unseen,
Yet visible to purer eyes than ours.
And if the crystal of our sight were clear,
We should behold the mountain-slopes of cloud,
The moving meadows of the untilled sea,
The groves of twilight and the dales of dawn,
And every wide and lonely field of air,
More populous than cities, crowded close
With living creatures of all shapes and hues.
But if that sight were ours, the things that now
Engage our eyes would seem but dull and dim
Beside the wonders of our new-found world,
And we should be amazed and overwhelmed
Not knowing how to use the plenitude
Of vision.

HENRY VAN DYKE

LONGING

I AM not sorry for my soul
   That it must go unsatisfied,
For it can live a thousand times,
   Eternity is deep and wide.

I am not sorry for my soul,
   But oh, my body that must go
Back to a little drift of dust
   Without the joy it longed to know.

SARA TEASDALE

IMMORTAL

So soon my body will have gone
   Beyond the sound and sight of men,
And tho' it wakes and suffers now,
   Its sleep will be unbroken then;
But oh, my frail immortal soul
   That will not sleep forever more,
A leaf borne onward by the blast,
   A wave that never finds the shore.

SARA TEASDALE

ALL SOULS ARE THINE

O LORD of Life, where e'er they be,
   Safe in thine own eternity,
Our dead are living unto thee.

All souls are thine and, here or there,
   They rest within thy sheltering care;
One providence alike they share.

F. L. HOSMER

THE ULTIMATE HARVEST

GREAT palaces they fill, the shapes that, myriad page on
page,
Hold safe for us and tangible our spirits' heritage.

But vaster far the treasuries elysian that contain
The bodiless throng of those that craved a bodily guise in
vain.

The harvest of humanity's dumb eloquence is there,
Clear-voiced achievements that on earth but voiceless
yearnings were:

The books conceived but never born, dream-writ but never
paged,
Awakened beings in no flesh of lines and letters caged;

The words that great beginners left unspoken, dying young,
That laureled elders meant to sing better than they had sung,

And those, the numberless, for which no kindred testified,
Imagined children of a hope whose wings were never
tried. . . .

O restless wights who cannot put a fruitful effort through,
O minds untrained and hands unskilled that long but cannot do,

And ye who saw your vision die because ye starved for
bread,
Or starved for strength or time or chance, have faith, be
comforted,

For daily grow the heavenly stores to meet the radiant look
Of reborn souls who suddenly find each his new-born book.

Each reads his own—and Heaven begins; then in the peace
  divine
Of endless years shall each, praise God, have time for yours
  and mine!

MRS. SCHUYLER VAN RENSSELAER

JOY, SHIPMATE, JOY!

Joy, shipmate, joy!
(Pleas'd to my soul at death I cry,)
Our life is closed, our life begins,
The long, long anchorage we leave,
The ship is clear at last, she leaps!
She swiftly courses from the shore,
Joy, shipmate, joy!

WHITMAN

ODE ON INTIMATIONS OF IMMORTALITY

.   .   .   .

OUR birth is but a sleep and a forgetting:
The Soul that rises with us, our life's Star,
    Hath had elsewhere its setting,
      And cometh from afar:
    Not in entire forgetfulness,
    And not in utter nakedness,
But trailing clouds of glory do we come
    From God, who is our home:
Heaven lies about us in our infancy!

.   .   .   .

Thou, whose exterior semblance doth belie
    Thy Soul's immensity;
Thou best Philosopher, who yet dost keep
Thy heritage, thou Eye among the blind,
That, deaf and silent, read'st the eternal deep,

Haunted forever by the eternal mind,—
  Mighty Prophet! Seer blest!
  On whom those truths do rest,
Which we are toiling all our lives to find,
In darkness lost, the darkness of the grave;
Thou, over whom thy Immortality
Broods like the Day, a Master o'er a Slave,
A Presence which is not to be put by;
Thou little Child, yet glorious in the might
Of heaven-born freedom on thy being's height,
Why with such earnest pains dost thou provoke
The years to bring the inevitable yoke,
Thus blindly with thy blessedness at strife?
Full soon thy Soul shall have her earthly freight,
And custom lie upon thee with a weight,
Heavy as frost, and deep almost as life!

  O joy! that in our embers
  Is something that doth live,
  That nature yet remembers
  What was so fugitive!
The thought of our past years in me doth breed
Perpetual benediction: not indeed
For that which is most worthy to be blest,
Delight and liberty, the simple creed
Of Childhood, whether busy or at rest,
With new-fledged hope still fluttering in his breast:—
  Nor for these I raise
  The song of thanks and praise;
  But for those obstinate questionings
  Of sense and outward things,
  Fallings from us, vanishings;
  Blank misgivings of a Creature
Moving about in worlds not realized,
High instincts before which our mortal Nature
Did tremble like a guilty Thing surprised:

But for those first affections,
Those shadowy recollections,
Which, be they what they may,
Are yet the fountain light of all our day,
Are yet a master light of all our seeing;
Uphold us, cherish, and have power to make
Our noisy years seem moments in the being
Of the eternal Silence: truths that wake,
To perish never;
Which neither listlessness, nor mad endeavor,
Nor Man nor Boy,
Nor all that is at enmity with joy,
Can utterly abolish or destroy!
Hence in a season of calm weather
Though inland far we be,
Our Souls have sight of that immortal sea
Which brought us hither,
Can in a moment travel thither,
And see the Children sport upon the shore,
And hear the mighty waters rolling evermore.

Then sing, ye Birds, sing, sing a joyous song!
And let the young Lambs bound
As to the tabor's sound!
We in thought will join your throng,
Ye that pipe and ye that play,
Ye that through your hearts to-day
Feel the gladness of the May!
What though the radiance which was once so bright
Be now forever taken from my sight,
Though nothing can bring back the hour
Of splendor in the grass, of glory in the flower;
We will grieve not, rather find
Strength in what remains behind;
In the primal sympathy
Which having been must ever be;

In the soothing thoughts that spring
Out of human suffering;
In the faith that looks through death,
In years that bring the philosophic mind.

And O, ye Fountains, Meadows, Hills, and Groves,
Forbode not any severing of our loves!
Yet in my heart of hearts I feel your might;
I only have relinquished one delight
To live beneath your more habitual sway.
I love the Brooks which down their channels fret,
Even more than when I tripped lightly as they;
The innocent brightness of a new-born Day
           Is lovely yet;
The Clouds that gather round the setting sun
Do take a sober coloring from an eye
That hath kept watch o'er man's mortality;
Another race hath been, and other palms are won.
Thanks to the human heart by which we live,
Thanks to its tenderness, its joys, and fears,
To me the meanest flower that blows can give
Thoughts that do often lie too deep for tears.

WORDSWORTH

FROM "VASTNESS"

MANY a hearth upon our dark globe sighs after many a
    vanish'd face,
Many a planet by many a sun may roll with the dust of a
    vanish'd race.

Raving politics, never at rest—as this poor earth's pale
    history runs,—
What is it all but a trouble of ants in the gleam of a million
    million of suns?

Lies upon this side, lies upon that side, truthless violence
    mourn'd by the Wise,
Thousands of voices drowning his own in a popular torrent
    of lies upon lies;

Stately purposes, valour in battle, glorious annals of army
    and fleet,
Death for the right cause, death for the wrong cause, trump-
    ets of victory, groans of defeat;

Innocence seethed in her mother's milk, and Charity set-
    ting the martyr aflame;
Thraldom who walks with the banner of Freedom, and
    recks not to ruin a realm in her name.

   .   .   .   .

Star of the morning, Hope in the sunrise; gloom of the
    evening, Life at a close;
Pleasure who flaunts on her wide down-way with her flying
    robe and her poison'd rose;

Pain, that has crawl'd from the corpse of Pleasure, a worm
    which writhes all day, and at night
Stirs up again in the heart of the sleeper, and stings him
    back to the curse of the light;

   .   .   .   .

Fame blowing out from her golden trumpet a jubilant
    challenge to Time and to Fate;
Slander, her shadow, sowing the nettle on all the laurel'd
    graves of the Great;

   .   .   .   .

He that has lived for the lust of the minute, and died in
    the doing it, flesh without mind;
He that has nail'd all flesh to the Cross, till Self died out
    in the love of his kind;

Spring and Summer and Autumn and Winter, and all these
    old revolutions of earth;
All new-old revolutions of Empire—change of the tide—
    what is all of it worth?

What the philosophies, all the sciences, poesy, varying
    voices of prayer?
All that is noblest, all that is basest, all that is filthy with
    all that is fair?

What is it all, if we all of us end but in being our own corpse-
    coffins at last,
Swallow'd in Vastness, lost in Silence, drown'd in the deeps
    of a meaningless Past?

What but a murmur of gnats in the gloom, or a moment's
    anger of bees in their hive?—

*   *   *   *

Peace, let it be! for I loved him, and love him for ever:
    the dead are not dead but alive.

TENNYSON

IMMORTALITY

FOILED by our fellow-men, depressed, outworn,
We leave the brutal world to take its way,
And, *Patience! in another life*, we say,
The world shall be thrust down, and we upborne.

And will not, then, the immortal armies scorn
The world's poor, routed leavings? or will they
Who failed under the heat of this life's day
Support the fervors of the heavenly morn?

No, no! the energy of life may be
Kept on after the grave, but not begun;
And he who flagged not in the earthly strife,

From strength to strength advancing,—only he,
His soul well-knit, and all his battles won,
Mounts, and that hardly, to eternal life.

MATTHEW ARNOLD

[From "Matthew Arnold's Poems," The Macmillan Co.]

ABT VOGLER

．　．　．　．　．　．　．　．　．　．　．

WELL, it is gone at last, the palace of music I reared;
  Gone! and the good tears start, the praises that come too
    slow;
For one is assured at first, one scarce can say that he feared,
  That he even gave it a thought, the gone thing was to go.
Never to be again! But many more of the kind
  As good, nay, better perchance: is this your comfort
    to me?
To me, who must be saved because I cling with my mind
  To the same, same self, same love, same God: ay, what
    was, shall be.

Therefore to whom turn I but to thee, the ineffable Name?
  Builder and maker, thou, of houses not made with hands!
What, have fear of change from thee who art ever the
    same?
  Doubt that thy power can fill the heart that thy power
    expands?
There shall never be one lost good! What was, shall live
    as before;
  The evil is null, is naught, is silence implying sound;
What was good shall be good, with, for evil, so much good
    more;
  On the earth the broken arcs; in the heaven a perfect round.

All we have willed or hoped or dreamed of good shall exist;
  Not its semblance, but itself; no beauty, nor good, nor
    power

Whose voice has gone forth, but each survives for the
    melodist
When eternity affirms the conception of an hour.
The high that proved too high, the heroic for earth too
    hard,
    The passion that left the ground to lose itself in the sky,
Are music sent up to God by the lover and the bard;
    Enough that he heard it once: we shall hear it by and by.

And what is our failure here but a triumph's evidence
    For the fulness of the days? Have we withered or
        agonized?
Why else was the pause prolonged but that singing might
    issue thence?
    Why rushed the discords in, but that harmony should
        be prized?
Sorrow is hard to bear, and doubt is slow to clear,
    Each sufferer says his say, his scheme of the weal and
        woe:
But God has a few of us whom he whispers in the ear;
    The rest may reason and welcome: 'tis we musicians
        know.

BROWNING

FROM "ULTIMATE CONCEPTIONS OF FAITH"

PERSONALITY, therefore, is the fundamental assurance of
immortality. In virtue of it man is real, and on account of
it he shares in the best life of the race and enters into and
lays hold of the life of God. The growth of the individual
in knowledge and in character means the increase of his
grasp upon the total achievement of mankind, the larger
reproduction in himself of the higher moods of the race, the
sympathetic ownership of the spiritual possessions of humanity. Personality is this spirit of pervasiveness and fellowship in knowledge, in duty, and in hope. Learning is pos-

sible only through personality; and on account of the same fact it is possible for man to partake of the life of God. The world of human achievement is here, and God is in it and above it; and the capacity to pervade and possess more and more widely that world, and to rise evermore into a vaster sense of the Transcendent goodness, is perhaps the deepest thing in the human soul. On account of it the soul lays hold upon the highest in history and in the universe, and in virtue of it the highest in history and the universe lays hold upon the soul. In and through this profound and serious reciprocity of spiritual being, one can hear from the Creative heart the assurance, "Because I live, ye shall live also."

> "Till Death us join,
>   O voice yet more Divine!
> That to the broken heart breathes hope sublime;
>   Through lonely hours
>   And shattered powers
> We still are one, despite of change and time.

> "Death, with his healing hand,
>   Shall once more knit the band,
> Which needs but that one link which none may sever;
>   Till through the Only Good,
>   Heard, felt, and understood,
> Our life in God shall make us one forever."

GEORGE A. GORDON

FROM "PASSAGE TO INDIA"

SAIL forth—steer for the deep waters only,
Reckless O soul, exploring, I with thee, and thou with me,
For we are bound where mariner has not yet dared to go,
And we will risk the ship, ourselves and all.

O my brave soul!
O farther farther sail!
O daring joy, but safe! are they not all the seas of God?
O farther, farther, farther sail!

WHITMAN

FROM "PRESENTIMENT OF BETTER THINGS"

WE rest in faith that man's perfection is the crowning
flower, towards which the urgent sap in life's great tree
is pressing,—seen in puny blossoms now,
But in the world's great morrows to expand with broadest
petal and with deepest glow,
The faith that life on earth is being shaped to glorious ends.
Full souls are double mirrors, making still an endless vista
of fair things before, repeating things behind.
So faith is strong only when we are strong, shrinks when
we shrink.
It comes when music stirs us, and the chords, moving on
some grand climax, shake our souls with influx new
that makes new energies.
It comes in swellings of the heart and tears that rise at
noble and at gentle deeds.
At labours of the master-artist's hand, which, trembling,
touches to a finer end, trembling before an image seen
within.
It comes in moments of heroic love, unjealous joy in joy
not made for us—in conscious triumph of the good
within, making us worship goodness that rebukes.
Even our failures are a prophecy, even our yearnings and
our bitter tears after that fair and true we cannot
grasp;
As patriots who seem to die in vain make liberty more
sacred by their pangs.
Presentiment of better things on earth sweep in with every
force that stirs our souls to admiration.

Self-renouncing love, or thoughts, like light, that bind the
    world in one:
Sweeps like the sense of vastness, when at night we hear
    the roll and dash of waves that break nearer and nearer
    with the rushing tide,
Which rises to the level of the cliff because the wide At-
    lantic rolls behind, throbbing respondent to the far-
    off orbs.

GEORGE ELIOT

A FOREST HYMN

.   .   .   .

My heart is awed within me when I think
Of the great miracle that still goes on,
In silence, round me—the perpetual work
Of thy creation, finished, yet renewed
Forever. Written on thy works I read
The lesson of thy own eternity.
Lo! all grow old and die—but see again,
How on the faltering footsteps of decay
Youth presses—ever gay and beautiful youth
In all its beautiful forms. These lofty trees
Wave not less proudly that their ancestors
Moulder beneath them. Oh, there is not lost
One of earth's charms: upon her bosom yet,
After the flight of untold centuries,
The freshness of her far beginning lies
And yet shall lie. Life mocks the idle hate
Of his arch-enemy Death—yea, seats himself
Upon the tyrant's throne—the sepulchre,
And of the triumphs of his ghastly foe
Makes his own nourishment. For he came forth
From thine own bosom, and shall have no end.

BRYANT

VISIONS

THERE are hills too steep for our feet to climb,
 There are goals too far to gain,
And in every breast there's a glorious best
 The dreamer shall never attain.
For the poet dies with his songs unsung,
 And the artist at last grows faint,
And he sinks to sleep and the grave must keep
 The pictures he'd planned to paint.

We can never finish the work of life,
 Nor live to our fullest here;
We must carry away from its house of clay
 The vision we've cherished dear.
We dream fair dreams for the years to be,
 But merchant and toiler, too,
And the soldier brave take into the grave
 Some deeds they had hoped to do.

Perhaps they sing at their sweetest now,
 Those poets of yesterday,
And have caught the themes of the golden dreams
 Which came from the far away.
Perhaps the painters on canvas true
 Now see with a clearer eye
And paint the things of the visionings
 That were theirs in the days gone by.

Oh, never we reach to our fullest height,
 And never we do our all;
We must turn away at the close of day
 When the tools from our fingers fall.
But it isn't a failure to hold a dream
 That never on earth comes true,
For the tasks of worth that we miss on earth
 Are reserved for our souls to do.

EDGAR GUEST

EPILOGUE

At the midnight in the silence of the sleep-time,
  When you set your fancies free,
Will they pass to where—by death, fools think, impris-
    oned—
Low he lies who once so loved you, whom you loved so,
              —Pity me?

Oh to love so, be so loved, yet so mistaken!
  What had I on earth to do
With the slothful, with the mawkish, the unmanly?
Like the aimless, helpless, hopeless, did I drivel
              —Being—who?

One who never turned his back but marched breast forward,
  Never doubted clouds would break,
Never dreamed, though right were worsted, wrong would
    triumph,
Held we fall to rise, are baffled to fight better,
              Sleep to wake.

No, at noonday in the bustle of man's work-time
  Greet the unseen with a cheer!
Bid him forward, breast and back as either should be,
"Strive and thrive!" cry "Speed,—fight on, fare ever
            There as here!"
                                        BROWNING

RESURGENCE

Tho he that, ever kind and true,
Kept stoutly step by step with you
Your whole long gusty lifetime through,
Be gone a while before,
Be now a moment gone before,
Yet, doubt not, soon the season shall restore
Your friend to you.

He has but turned a corner; still
He pushes on with right good will,
Through mire and marsh, by heuch and hill
The self-same arduous way,—
That self-same upland hopeful way,
That you and he through many a doubtful day
Attempted still.

He is not dead, this friend; not dead,
But, in the path we mortals tread,
Got some few trifling steps ahead,
And nearer to the end,
So that you, too, once past the bend,
Shall meet again, as face to face, this friend
You fancy dead.

Push gayly on, strong heart! The while
You travel forward mile by mile,
He loiters with a backward smile,
Till you can overtake,
And strains his eyes, to search his wake,
Or, whistling as he sees you through the brake,
Waits on a stile.

ROBERT LOUIS STEVENSON

SECOND BEST

HERE in the dark, O heart;
Alone with the enduring Earth, and Night,
And Silence, and the warm strange smell of clover;
Clear-visioned, though it break you; far apart
From the dead best, the dear and old delight;
Throw down your dreams of immortality,
O faithful, O foolish lover!
Here's peace for you, and surety; here the one
Wisdom—the truth!—"All day the good glad sun
Showers love and labour on you, wine and song;

The greenwood laughs, the wind blows, all day long
Till night.'' And night ends all things. Then shall be
No lamp relumed in heaven, no voices crying,
Or changing lights, or dreams and forms that hover!
(And, heart, for all your sighing,
That gladness and those tears are over, over. . . .)

And has the truth brought no new hope at all,
Heart, that you're weeping yet for Paradise?
Do they still whisper, the old weary cries?
" *'Mid youth and song, feasting and carnival,*
Through laughter, through the roses, as of old
Comes Death, on shadowy and relentless feet,
Death, unappeasable by prayer or gold;
Death is the end, the end!"
Proud, then, clear-eyed and laughing, go to greet
Death as a friend !

'Exile of immortality, strongly wise,
Strain through the dark with undesirous eyes
To what may lie beyond it. Sets your star,
O heart, for ever!' Yet, behind the night,
Waits for the great unborn, somewhere afar,
Some white tremendous daybreak. And the light,
Returning, shall give back the golden hours,
Ocean a windless level, Earth a lawn
Spacious and full of sunlit dancing-places,
And laughter, and music, and, among the flowers,
The gay child-hearts of men, and the child-faces
O heart, in the great dawn!

RUPERT BROOKE

A COMRADE RIDES AHEAD

(TO THE MEMORY OF EMERSON HOUGH)

TIME brings not death, it brings but changes;
    I know he rides, but rides afar,

To-day some other planet ranges
　And camps to-night upon a star
　Where all his other comrades are.

For there were those who rode before him,
　As there are these he leaves behind;
Although from us time's changes bore him,
　Out there our comrade still will find
　The kinship of the comrade mind.

Time brings us change and leaves us fretting;
　We weep when ev'ry comrade goes—
Perhaps too much, perhaps forgetting
　That over yonder there are those
　To whom he comes and whom he knows.

I would not hold our loss too lightly;
　God knows, and he, how deep the pain;
But, friends, I see still shining brightly
　The brightest link in all our chain
　That links us with a new domain.

For this I swear, because believing:
　Time breaks no circle such as this.
However hurt, however grieving,
　However much a friend we miss,
　Between the worlds is no abyss.

For friendship binds the worlds together—
　World over there, world over here.
From earth to heaven is the tether
　That brings the earth and heaven near
　And makes them both a bit more dear.

Not weaker now our chain, but stronger;
　In all our loss and all our ill
We now shall look a little longer
　At ev'ry star above the hill
　And think of him, and have him still.

Whatever vales we yet may wander,
   What sorrow come, what tempest blow,
We have a friend, a friend out yonder,
   To greet us when we have to go—
   Out yonder someone that we know.

To all eternity he binds us;
   He links the planet and the star;
He rides ahead, the trail he finds us,
   And where he is and where we are
   Will never seem again so far.

DOUGLAS MALLOCH

WITH THE TIDE

(TO THEODORE ROOSEVELT)

SOMEWHERE I read, in an old book whose name
Is gone from me, I read that when the days
Of a man are counted, and his business done,
There comes up the shore at evening, with the tide,
To the place where he sits, a boat—
And in the boat, from the place where he sits, he sees,
Dim in the dusk, dim and yet so familiar,
The faces of his friends long dead; and knows
They come for him, brought in upon the tide,
To take him where men go at set of day.
Then rising, with his hands in theirs, he goes
Between them his last steps, that are the first
Of the new life—and with the ebb they pass,
Their shaken sail grown small upon the moon.

Often I thought of this, and pictured me
How many a man who lives with throngs about him,
Yet straining through the twilight for that boat
Shall scarce make out one figure in the stern,

And that so faint its features shall perplex him
With doubtful memories—and his heart hang back.
But others, rising as they see the sail
Increase upon the sunset, hasten down,
Hands out and eyes elated; for they see
Head over head, crowding from bow to stern,
Repeopling their long loneliness with smiles,
The faces of their friends; and such go forth
Content upon the ebb tide, with safe hearts.

But never
To worker summoned when his day was done
Did mounting tide bring in such freight of friends
As stole to you up the white wintry shingle
That night while they that watched you thought you slept.
Softly they came, and beached the boat, and gathered
In the still cove under the icy stars,
Your last-born, and the dear loves of your heart,
And all men that have loved right more than ease,
And honor above honors; all who gave
Free-handed of their best for other men,
And thought their giving taking: they who knew
Man's natural state is effort, up and up—
All these were there, so great a company
Perchance you marvelled, wondering what great ship
Had brought that throng unnumbered to the cove
Where the boys used to beach their light canoe
After old happy picnics—

But these, your friends and children, to whose hands
Committed, in the silent night you rose
And took your last faint steps—
These led you down, O great American,
Down to the winter night and the white beach,
And there you saw that the huge hull that waited
Was not as are the boats of the other dead,
Frail craft for a brief passage; no, for this

Was first of a long line of towering transports,
Storm-worn and ocean-weary every one,
The ships you launched, the ships you manned, the ships
That now, returning from their sacred quest
With the thrice-sacred burden of their dead,
Lay waiting there to take you forth with them,
Out with the ebb tide, on some farther quest.

EDITH WHARTON

GRIEF

III

PERCHANCE some day when we shall see the Whole
We may rejoice that he should thus depart,
With joy incarnate in his radiant soul
And one pure love, untarnished, in his heart;
For we, who near our life's relentless goal,
With tattered banners in our listless hands,
No more, head high, can answer to the Roll:
Our feet have slipped amid the shifting sands
Of standards lowered and illusions lost.
His is eternal dawn, no setting sun,
And we, so passion-driven—tempest-tossed—
May scarce regret his short, glad battle won.
And yet this anguished thought cannot be stilled—
So young, so loving, and so unfulfilled!

CORINNE ROOSEVELT ROBINSON

THE BETTER FATE

THIS—this our life—is like the moth's who flies
  In summer evenings through the dusky light,
Threading the silhouetted shapes that rise
  Against the moon and pass into the night.

So we go groping where life's shadows wind,
  We tremble through a twilight all our day,
Some burning hour, some lambent flame to find,
  Where we may fling our winged life away.

I do not know which is the better fate,
  To go unspent through life's dim dusky street,
Or, seeing Beauty beckoning to her gate,
  Scatter our life's burnt ashes at her feet.

I only know how many I could name
Die in the dusk and never find their flame.

HUGH ROBERT ORR

LOVESIGHT

WHEN do I see thee most, beloved one?
When in the light the spirits of mine eyes
Before thy face, their altar, solemnize
The worship of that Love through thee made known?

Or when in the dusk hours (we two alone),
Close-kissed and eloquent of still replies
Thy twilight-hidden glimmering visage lies,
And my soul only sees thy soul its own?

O love, my love! if I no more should see
Thyself, nor on the earth the shadow of thee,
Nor image of thine eyes in any spring,
How then should sound upon Life's darkening slope
The ground-whirl of the perished leaves of Hope,
The wind of Death's imperishable wing?

DANTE GABRIEL ROSSETTI

TO A WATERFOWL

Whither, midst falling dew,
While glow the heavens with the last steps of day,
Far, through their rosy depths, dost thou pursue
   Thy solitary way?

Vainly the fowler's eye
Might mark thy distant flight to do thee wrong,
As, darkly seen against the crimson sky,
   Thy figure floats along.

Seek'st thou the plashy brink
Of weedy lake, or marge of river wide,
Or where the rocking billows rise and sink
   On the chafed ocean-side?

There is a Power whose care
Teaches thy way along that pathless coast—
The desert and illimitable air—
   Lone wandering, but not lost.

All day thy wings have fanned,
At that far height, the cold, thin atmosphere,
Yet stoop not, weary, to the welcome land,
   Though the dark night is near.

And soon that toil shall end;
Soon shalt thou find a summer home, and rest,
And scream among thy fellows; reeds shall bend,
   Soon, o'er thy sheltered nest.

Thou'rt gone, the abyss of heaven
Hath swallowed up thy form; yet, on my heart
Deeply has sunk the lesson thou hast given,
   And shall not soon depart.

He who, from zone to zone,
Guides through the boundless sky thy certain flight,
In the long way that I must tread alone,
Will lead my steps aright.

BRYANT

REST REMAINETH

EASTER Day breaks!
Christ rises! Mercy every way is infinite—
Earth breaks up; time drops away;
In flows heaven with its new day
Of endless life—
What is left for us save in growth
Of soul to rise up, . . .
From the gift looking to the giver,
And from the cistern to the river,
And from the finite to infinity,
And from man's dust to God's divinity.

BROWNING

DEATH'S VALLEY

*(To accompany a picture; by request. "The Valley of the Shadow
of Death," from the painting by George Inness.)*

NAY, do not dream, designer dark,
Thou hast portray'd or hit thy theme entire;
I, hoverer of late by this dark valley, by its confines, having
    glimpses of it,
Here enter lists with thee, claiming my right to make a
    symbol too.
For I have seen many wounded soldiers die,
After dread suffering—have seen their lives pass off with
    smiles;

And I have watch'd the death-hours of the old; and seen the
    infant die;
The rich, with all his nurses and his doctors;
And then the poor, in meagreness and poverty;
And I myself for long, O Death, have breath'd my every
    breath
Amid the nearness and the silent thought of thee.

And out of these and thee,
I make a scene, a song (not fear of thee,
Nor gloom's ravines, nor bleak, nor dark—for I do not fear
    thee,
Nor celebrate the struggle, or contortion, or hard-tied knot),
Of the broad blessed light and perfect air, with meadows,
    rippling tides, and trees and flowers and grass,
And the low hum of living breeze—and in the midst God's
    beautiful eternal right hand,
Thee, holiest minister of Heaven—thee, envoy, usherer,
    guide at last of all,
Rich, florid, loosener of the stricture-knot call'd life,
Sweet, peaceful, welcome Death.

WHITMAN

RABBI BEN EZRA

GROW old along with me!
The best is yet to be,
The last of life, for which the first was made:
Our times are in his hand
Who saith, "A whole I planned,
Youth shows but half; trust God: see all, nor be afraid!"

.   .   .   .

Rejoice we are anied
To that which doth provide
And not partake, effect and not receive!

A spark disturbs our clod;
Nearer we hold of God
Who gives, than of his tribes that take, I must believe.

Then, welcome each rebuff
That turns earth's smoothness rough,
Each sting that bids nor sit nor stand but go!
Be our joys three-parts pain!
Strive, and hold cheap the strain;
Learn, nor account the pang; dare, never grudge the throe!

For thence,—a paradox
Which comforts while it mocks,—
Shall life succeed in that it seems to fail:
What I aspired to be,
And was not, comforts me:
A brute I might have been, but would not sink i' the scale.

.   .   .   .

Should not the heart beat once "How good to live and
    learn"?

Not once beat "Praise be thine!
I see the whole design,
I, who saw power, see now Love perfect too:
Perfect I call thy plan:
Thanks that I was a man!
Maker, remake, complete,—I trust what thou shalt do!"

.   .   .   .

Therefore I summon age
To grant youth's heritage,
Life's struggle having so far reached its term:
Thence shall I pass, approved
A man, for aye removed
From the developed brute; a God though in the germ.

.   .   .   .

All I could never be,
All, men ignored in me,
This, I was worth to God, whose wheel the pitcher shaped.

. . . .

Fool! All that is, at all,
Lasts ever, past recall;
Earth changes, but thy soul and God stand sure:
What entered into thee,
That was, is, and shall be:
Time's wheel runs back or stops: Potter and clay endure.

. . . .

Look not thou down but up!
To uses of a cup,
The festal board, lamp's flash and trumpet's peal,
The new wine's foaming flow,
The Master's lips aglow!
Thou, heaven's consummate cup, what needst thou with
earth's wheel?

But I need, now as then,
Thee, God, who mouldest men;
And since, not even while the whirl was worst,
Did I—to the wheel of life
With shapes and colors rife,
Bound dizzily—mistake my end, to slake thy thirst:

So, take and use thy work:
Amend what flaws may lurk,
What strain o' the stuff, what warpings past the aim!
My times be in thy hand!
Perfect the cup as planned!
Let age approve of youth, and death complete the same!

BROWNING

ADONAIS

. . . .

Ah woe is me! Winter is come and gone,
But grief returns with the revolving year;
The airs and streams renew their joyous tone:
The ants, the bees, the swallows reappear;
Fresh leaves and flowers deck the dead Seasons' bier;
The amorous birds now pair in every brake,
And build their mossy homes in field and brere;
And the green lizard, and the golden snake,
Like unimprisoned flames, out of their trance awake.

Through wood and stream and field and hill and Ocean
A quickening life from the Earth's heart has burst
As it has ever done, with change and motion,
From the great morning of the world when first
God dawned on Chaos; in its stream immersed
The lamps of Heaven flash with a softer light;
All baser things pant with life's sacred thirst;
Diffuse themselves; and spend in love's delight,
The beauty and the joy of their renewed might.

. . . .

Dust to the dust! but the pure spirit shall flow
Back to the burning fountain whence it came,
A portion of the Eternal, which must glow
Through time and change, unquenchably the same,
Whilst thy cold embers choke the sordid hearth of shame.

Peace, peace! he is not dead, he doth not sleep—
He hath awakened from the dream of life—
'Tis we, who lost in stormy visions, keep
With phantoms an unprofitable strife. . . .

. . . .

He lives, he wakes—'tis Death is dead, not he;

. . . .

He is made one with Nature: there is heard
His voice in all her music, from the moan
Of thunder to the song of night's sweet bird;
He is a presence to be felt and known
In darkness and in light, from herb and stone,
Spreading itself where'er that Power may move
Which has withdrawn his being to its own;
Which wields the world with never wearied love,
Sustains it from beneath, and kindles it above.

He is a portion of the loveliness
Which once he made more lovely: he doth bear
His part, while the one Spirit's plastic stress
Sweeps through the dull dense world, compelling there
All new successions to the forms they wear;
Torturing th' unwilling dross that checks its flight
To its own likeness, as each mass may bear;
And bursting in its beauty and its might
From trees and beasts and men into the Heaven's light.

The splendors of the firmament of time
May be eclipsed, but are extinguished not;
Like stars to their appointed height they climb
And death is a low mist which cannot blot
The brightness it may veil. When lofty thought
Lifts a young heart above its mortal lair,
And love and life contend in it, for what
Shall be its earthly doom, the dead live there
And move like winds of light on dark and stormy air.

.   .   .   .

The One remains, the many change and pass;
Heaven's light forever shines, Earth's shadows fly;
Life, like a dome of many-colored glass,
Stains the white radiance of Eternity,
Until Death tramples it to fragments.—Die,

If thou wouldst be with that which thou dost seek!
Follow where all is fled! . . .

Why linger, why turn back, why shrink, my Heart?
Thy hopes are gone before: from all things here
They have departed; thou shouldst now depart! . . .

That Light whose smile kindles the Universe,
That Beauty in which all things work and move,
That Benediction which the eclipsing Curse
Of birth can quench not, that sustaining Love
Which through the web of being blindly wove
By man and beast and earth and air and sea,
Burns bright or dim, as each are mirrors of
The fire for which all thirst; now beams on me,
Consuming the last clouds of cold mortality. . . .

SHELLEY

FROM "RHYMES OF A ROLLING STONE"

THANK God! there is always a Land of Beyond
    For us who are true to the trail;
A vision to seek, a beckoning peak,
    A farness that never will fail;
A pride in our soul that mocks at a goal,
    A manhood that irks at a bond,
And try how we will, unattainable still,
    Behold it, our Land of Beyond!

ROBERT SERVICE

FROM "MAKATOOB"

WHEN to the last assault our bugles blow:
Reckless of pain and peril we shall go,
Heads high and hearts aflame and bayonets bare,
And we shall brave eternity as though

Eyes looked on us in which we would see fair—
One waited in whose presence we would wear,
Even as a lover who would be well-seen,
Our manhood faultless and our honor clean.

. . . .

Guard that, not bowed nor blanched with fear
   You enter, but serene, erect,
As you would wish most to appear
   To those you most respect.

So die, as though your funeral
   Ushered you through the doors that led
Into a stately banquet hall
   Where heroes banqueted;

And it shall all depend therein
   Whether you come as slave or lord,
If they acclaim you as their kin
   Or spurn you from their board.

                  ALAN SEEGER

EASTER GLADNESS

O DAY of light and gladness,
   Of prophecy and song,
What thoughts within us waken,
   What hallowed memories throng!
The soul's horizon widens,
   Past, present, future blend,
And rises on our vision
   The life that hath no end.

Earth feels the season's joyance;
   From mountain-range to sea
The tides of life are flowing,
   Fresh, manifold and free.

In valley and on upland,
  By forest pathways dim,
All Nature lifts in chorus
  The Resurrection hymn.

O Lord of life eternal,
  To thee our hearts upraise
The Easter song of gladness,
  The Passover of praise!
Thine are the many mansions;
  The dead die not to thee,
Who fillest from thy fullness
  Time and eternity!

FREDERICK L. HOSMER

CREDO

I CANNOT find my way: there is no star
In all the shrouded heavens anywhere;
And there is not a whisper in the air
Of any living voice but one so far
That I can hear it only as a bar
Of lost, imperial music, played when fair
And angel fingers wove, and unaware,
Dead leaves to garlands where no roses are.

No, there is not a glimmer, nor a call,
For one that welcomes, welcomes when he fears,
The black and awful chaos of the night;
For through it all—above, beyond it all—
I know the far-sent message of the years,
I feel the coming glory of the Light.

EDWIN ARLINGTON ROBINSON

OCTAVES

I

WE thrill too strangely at the master's touch;
We shrink too sadly from the larger self
Which for its own completeness agitates
And undetermines us; we do not feel—
We dare not feel it yet—the splendid shame
Of uncreated failure; we forget,
The while we groan, that God's accomplishment
Is always and unfailingly at hand.

.   .   .   .

V

There is one battle-field whereon we fall
Triumphant and unconquered; but, alas!
We are too fleshly fearful of ourselves
To fight there till our days are whirled and blurred
By sorrow, and the ministering wheels
Of anguish take us eastward, where the clouds
Of human gloom are lost against the gleam
That shines on Thought's impenetrable mail.

VI

When we shall hear no more the cradle-songs
Of ages—when the timeless hymns of Love
Defeat them and outsound them — we shall know
The rapture of that large release which all
Right science comprehends; and we shall read,
With unoppressed and unoffended eyes,
That record of All-Soul whereon God writes
In everlasting runes the truth of Him.

.   .   .   .

X

Where does a dead man go?—The dead man dies;
But the free life that would no longer feed
On fagots of outburned and shattered flesh
Wakes to a thrilled invisible advance,
Unchained (or fettered else) of memory;
And when the dead man goes it seems to me
'Twere better for us all to do away
With weeping, and be glad that he is gone.

.   .   .   .

XIV

Though the sick beast infect us, we are fraught
Forever with indissoluble Truth,
Wherein redress reveals itself divine,
Transitional, transcendent. Grief and loss,
Disease and desolation, are the dreams
Of wasted excellence; and every dream
Has in it something of an ageless fact
That flouts deformity and laughs at years.

XV

We lack the courage to be where we are:—
We love too much to travel on old roads,
To triumph on old fields; we love too much
To consecrate the magic of dead things,
And yieldingly to linger by long walls
Of ruin, where the ruinous moonlight
That sheds a lying glory on old stones
Befriends us with a wizard's enmity.

.   .   .   .

XVIII

Like a white wall whereon forever breaks
Unsatisfied the tumult of green seas,

Man's unconjectured godliness rebukes
With its imperial silence the lost waves
Of insufficient grief. This mortal surge
That beats against us now is nothing else
Than plangent ignorance. Truth neither shakes
Nor wavers; but the world shakes, and we shriek.

XIX

Nor jewelled phrase nor mere mellifluous rhyme
Reverberates aright, or ever shall,
One cadence of that infinite plain-song
Which is itself all music. Stronger notes
Than any that have ever touched the world
Must ring to tell it—ring like hammer-blows,
Right-echoed of a chime primordial,
On anvils, in the gleaming of God's forge.

.   .   .   .

XXII

Forebodings are the friends of Recreance;
The master of the moment, the clean seer
Of ages, too securely scans what is,
Ever to be appalled at what is not,
He sees beyond the groaning borough lines
Of Hell, God's highways gleaming, and he knows
That Love's complete communion is the end
Of anguish to the liberated man.

XXIII

Here by the windy docks I stand alone,
But yet companioned. There the vessel goes,
And there my friend goes with it; but the wake
That melts and ebbs between that friend and me
Love's earnest is of Life's all-purposeful

And all-triumphant sailing, when the ships
Of Wisdom loose their fretful chains and swing
Forever from the crumbled wharves of Time.

EDWIN ARLINGTON ROBINSON

BREAK, BREAK, BREAK

BREAK, break, break,
  On thy cold gray stones, O Sea!
And I would that my tongue could utter
  The thoughts that arise in me.

O well for the fisherman's boy,
  That he shouts with his sister at play!
O well for the sailor lad,
  That he sings in his boat on the bay!

And the stately ships go on
  To their haven under the hill;
But O for the touch of a vanish'd hand,
  And the sound of a voice that is still!

Break, break, break,
  At the foot of thy crags, O Sea!
But the tender grace of a day that is dead
  Will never come back to me.

TENNYSON

[From "The Works of Tennyson," The Macmillan Co.]

IN MEMORIAM A. H. H.

STRONG Son of God, immortal Love,
  Whom we, that have not seen thy face,
  By faith, and faith alone, embrace,
Believing where we cannot prove;

Thine are these orbs of light and shade;
　　Thou madest Life in man and brute;
　　Thou madest Death; and lo, thy foot
Is on the skull which thou hast made.

Thou wilt not leave us in the dust:
　　Thou madest man, he knows not why,
　　He thinks he was not made to die;
And thou hast made him: thou art just.

Thou seemest human and divine,
　　The highest, holiest manhood, thou:
　　Our wills are ours, we know not how;
Our wills are ours, to make them thine.

Our little systems have their day;
　　They have their day and cease to be:
　　They are but broken lights of thee,
And thou, O Lord, art more than they.

We have but faith: we cannot know;
　　For knowledge is of things we see;
　　And yet we trust it comes from thee,
A beam in darkness: let it grow.

Let knowledge grow from more to more,
　　But more of reverence in us dwell;
　　That mind and soul, according well,
May make one music as before,

But vaster. We are fools and slight;
　　We mock thee when we do not fear:
　　But help thy foolish ones to bear;
Help thy vain worlds to bear thy light.

Forgive what seem'd my sin in me;
　　What seem'd my worth since I began;
　　For merit lives from man to man,
And not from man, O Lord, to thee.

Forgive my grief for one removed,
   Thy creature, whom I found so fair.
   I trust he lives in thee, and there
I find him worthier to be loved.

Forgive these wild and wandering cries,
   Confusions of a wasted youth;
   Forgive them where they fail in truth,
And in thy wisdom make me wise.

.   .   .   .

Oh yet we trust that somehow good
   Will be the final goal of ill,
   To pangs of nature, sins of will,
Defects of doubt, and taints of blood;

That nothing walks with aimless feet;
   That not one life shall be destroy'd,
   Or cast as rubbish to the void,
When God hath made the pile complete;

That not a worm is cloven in vain;
   That not a moth with vain desire
   Is shrivell'd in a fruitless fire,
Or but subserves another's gain.

Behold, we know not anything;
   I can but trust that good shall fall
   At last—far off—at last, to all,
And every winter change to spring.

So runs my dream: but what am I?
   An infant crying in the night:
   An infant crying for the light:
And with no language but a cry.

The wish, that of the living whole
   No life may fail beyond the grave,

Derives it not from what we have
The likest God within the soul?

Are God and Nature then at strife,
    That Nature lends such evil dreams?
    So careful of the type she seems,
So careless of the single life;

That I, considering everywhere
    Her secret meaning in her deeds,
    And finding that of fifty seeds
She often brings but one to bear,

I falter where I firmly trod,
    And falling with my weight of cares
    Upon the great world's altar-stairs
That slope thro' darkness up to God,

I stretch lame hands of faith, and grope,
    And gather dust and chaff, and call
    To what I feel is Lord of all,
And faintly trust the larger hope.

. . . .

This truth came borne with bier and pall,
    I felt it, when I sorrow'd most,
    'Tis better to have loved and lost,
Than never to have loved at all.

. . . .

You say, but with no touch of scorn,
    Sweet-hearted, you, whose light-blue eyes
    Are tender over drowning flies,
You tell me, doubt is Devil-born.

I know not: one indeed I knew
    In many a subtle question versed,
    Who touch'd a jarring lyre at first,
But ever strove to make it true:

Perplext in faith, but pure in deeds,
At last he beat his music out.
There lives more faith in honest doubt,
Believe me, than in half the creeds.

He fought his doubts and gather'd strength,
He would not make his judgment blind,
He faced the spectres of the mind
And laid them: thus he came at length

To find a stronger faith his own;
And Power was with him in the night,
Which makes the darkness and the light,
And dwells not in the light alone. . . .

.   .   .   .

Ring out, wild bells, to the wild sky,
The flying cloud, the frosty light:
The year is dying in the night;
Ring out, wild bells, and let him die.

Ring out the old, ring in the new,
Ring, happy bells, across the snow:
The year is going, let him go;
Ring out the false, ring in the true.

Ring out the grief that saps the mind,
For those that here we see no more;
Ring out the feud of rich and poor,
Ring in redress to all mankind.

Ring out a slowly dying cause,
And ancient forms of party strife;
Ring in the nobler modes of life,
With sweeter manners, purer laws.

Ring out the want, the care, the sin,
The faithless coldness of the times;

Ring out, ring out my mournful rhymes,
But ring the fuller minstrel in.

Ring out false pride in place and blood,
  The civic slander and the spite;
  Ring in the love of truth and right,
Ring in the common love of good.

Ring out old shapes of foul disease;
  Ring out the narrowing lust of gold;
  Ring out the thousand wars of old,
Ring in the thousand years of peace.

Ring in the valiant man and free,
  The larger heart, the kindlier hand;
  Ring out the darkness of the land,
Ring in the Christ that is to be.

.   .   .   .

O living will that shalt endure
  When all that seems shall suffer shock,
  Rise in the spiritual rock,
Flow thro' our deeds and make them pure,

That we may lift from out of dust
  A voice as unto him that hears,
  A cry above the conquer'd years
To one that with us works, and trust,

With faith that comes of self-control,
  The truths that never can be proved
  Until we close with all we loved,
And all we flow from, soul in soul.

.   .   .   .

That friend of mine who lives in God,

That God, which ever lives and loves,
  One God, one law, one element,

And one far-off divine event,
To which the whole creation moves.
                                        TENNYSON

[From " The Works of Tennyson," The Macmillan Co.]

THE INVISIBLE

If there is naught but what we see,
What is the wide world worth to me?
But is there naught save what we see?
A thousand things on every hand
My sense is numb to understand. . . .

.   .   .   .

If there is naught but what we see,
The friend I loved is lost to me:
He fell asleep; who dares to say
His spirit is so far away?
Who knows what wings are round about?
These thoughts—who proves but from without
They still are whispered? Who can think
They rise from morning's food and drink!
These thoughts that stream on like the sea,
And darkly beat incessantly
The feet of some great hope, and break,
And only broken glimmers make,
Nor ever climb the shore, to lie
And calmly mirror the far sky,
And image forth in tranquil deeps
The secret that its silence keeps.

Because he never comes, and stands
And stretches out to me both hands
Because he never leans before
The gate, when I set wide the door
At morning, nor is ever found
Just at my side when I turn round,

Half thinking I shall meet his eyes,
From watching the broad moon-globe rise,—
For all this, shall I homage pay
To Death, grow cold of heart, and say,
"He perished, and has ceased to be;
Another comes, but never he"?
Nay, by our wondrous being, nay!
Although his face I never see
Through all the infinite To Be,
I know he lives and cares for me.

EDWARD ROWLAND SILL

A QUESTION

To Fausta

Joy comes and goes, hope ebbs and flows
        Like the wave;
Change doth unknit the tranquil strength of men.
        Love lends life a little grace,
        A few sad smiles; and then
        Both are laid in one cold place,—
        In the grave.

Dreams dawn and fly, friends smile and die
        Like spring flowers;
Our vaunted life is one long funeral.
        Men dig graves with bitter tears
        For their dead hopes; and all,
        Mazed with doubts and sick with fears,
        Count the hours.

We count the hours! These dreams of ours,
        False and hollow,
Do we go hence, and find they are not dead?
        Joys we dimly apprehend

Faces that smiled and fled,
Hopes born here, and born to end,
   Shall we follow?

MATTHEW ARNOLD

[From "Matthew Arnold's Poems," The Macmillan Co.]

OVERNIGHT, A ROSE

THAT overnight a rose could come
   I one time did believe,
For when the fairies live with one,
   They wilfully deceive.
But now I know this perfect thing
   Under the frozen sod
In cold and storm grew patiently
   Obedient to God.
My wonder grows, since knowledge came
   Old fancies to dismiss:
And courage comes. Was not the rose
   A winter doing this?
Nor did it know, the weary while,
   What color and perfume
With this completed loveliness
   Lay in that earthy tomb.
So maybe I, who cannot see
   What God wills not to show,
May, some day, bear a rose for Him
   It took my life to grow.

CAROLINE GILTINAN

THE BUTTERFLY

I HOLD you at last in my hand,
   Exquisite child of the air.
Can I ever understand
   How you grew to be so fair?

You came to my linden tree
  To taste its delicious sweet,
I sitting here in the shadow and shine
  Playing around its feet.

Now I hold you fast in my hand,
  You marvelous butterfly,
Till you help me to understand
  The eternal mystery.

From that creeping thing in the dust
  To this shining bliss in the blue!
God give me courage to trust
  I can break my chrysalis too!

ALICE FREEMAN PALMER

"I ACCEPT"

I SHALL go out as all men go,
Spent flickers in a night wind,
Then I shall know, as all must know,
What lies the great gray veil behind.

There may be nothing but a deep
Unutterable void without a name
Where no sun hangs, no dead stars sleep,
And there is neither night nor flame.

There may be meadows there and hills,
Mountains and plains and winds that blow,
And flowers bending over rills
Springing from an eternal snow.

There may be oceans white with foam
And great tall ships for hungry men
Who called our little salt seas home
And burn to launch their keels again.

There may be voices I have known
And fingers that have touched my hair,
There may be hearts that were my own.
Love may abide forever there.

Who knows? Who needs to understand
If there be shadows there, or more,—
To live as though a pleasant land
Lay just beyond an open door?

HAROLD TROWBRIDGE PULSIFER

FOLLOW THE GLEAM

HE lived, a slow and stupid round of life,
    Contented, but how empty and how grey!
He never saw the wondrous things that fill
    The golden glory of the world, until
It came! Out of the greyness of the greyest day.

A lovely thing! It seemed to him to be
    A glimpse of heaven, straying from a dream.
He followed it, it sailed above his head,
    To death, and yet, can he be dead
Who passes onward, following the gleam!

BERTHA TEN EYCK JAMES

ON THE VERGE

HERE begins the sea that ends not till the world's end. Where
    we stand,
Could we know the next high sea-mark set beyond these
    waves that gleam,
We should know what never man hath known, nor eye of
    man hath scanned.

. . . .

Sail on sail along the sea-line fades and flashes: here on land
Flash and fade the wheeling wings on wings of mews that
    plunge and scream.
Hour on hour along the line of life and time's evasive strand
Shines and darkens, wanes and waxes, slays and dies: and
    scarce they seem
More than motes that thronged and trembled in the brief
    noon's breath and beam.
Some with crying and wailing, some with notes like sound of
    bells that toll,
Some with sighing and laughing, some with words that
    blessed and made us whole,
Passed, and left us, and we know not what they were, nor
    what were we.
Would we know, being mortal? Never breath of answering
    whisper stole
From the shore that hath no shore beyond it set in all the
    sea.

Shadows, would we question darkness? Ere our eyes and
    brows be fanned
Round with airs of twilight, washed with dews from sleep's
    eternal stream,
Would we know sleep's guarded secret? Ere the fire con-
    sume the brand,
Would it know if yet its ashes may requicken? yet we deem
Surely man may know, or ever night unyoke her starry team,
What the dawn shall be, or if the dawn shall be not: yea, the
    scroll
Would we read of sleep's dark scripture, pledge of peace or
    doom of dole.
Ah, but here man's heart leaps, yearning toward the gloom
    with venturous glee,
Though his pilot eye behold nor bay nor harbor, rock nor
    shoal,
From the shore that hath no shore beyond it set in all the
    sea.

Friend, who knows if death indeed have life or life have
    death for goal?
Day nor night can tell us, nor may seas declare nor skies
    unroll
What has been from everlasting, or if aught shall always be.
Silence answering only strikes response reverberate on the
    soul
From the shore that hath no shore beyond it set in all the
    sea.

SWINBURNE

ON A GLOOMY EASTER

I HEAR the robins singing in the rain.
    The longed-for Spring is hushed so drearily
    That hungry lips cry often wearily,
"Oh, if the blessed sun would shine again!"

I hear the robins singing in the rain.
    The misty world lies waiting for the dawn;
    The wind sobs at my window and is gone,
And in the silence come old throbs of pain.

But still the robins sing on in the rain,
    Not waiting for the morning sun to break,
    Nor listening for the violets to wake,
Nor fearing lest the snow may fall again.

My heart sings with the robins in the rain,
    For I remember it is Easter morn,
    And life and love and peace are all new born,
And joy has triumphed over loss and pain.

Sing on, brave robins, sing on in the rain!
    You know behind the clouds the sun must shine,
    You know that death means only life divine
And all our losses turn to heavenly gain.

I lie and listen to you in the rain.
Better than Easter bells that do not cease,
Your message from the heart of God's great peace,
And to his arms I turn and sleep again.

ALICE FREEMAN PALMER

DEATH

I AM the key that parts the gates of Fame;
I am the cloak that covers cowering Shame;
I am the final goal of every race;
I am the storm-tossed spirit's resting-place:

The messenger of sure and swift relief,
Welcomed with wailings and reproachful grief;
The friend of those that have no friend but me,
I break all chains, and set all captives free.

I am the cloud that, when Earth's day is done,
An instant veils an unextinguished sun;
I am the brooding hush that follows strife,
The waking from a dream that Man calls—Life!

FLORENCE EARLE COATES

FROM "THE LAST ENIGMA"

SOUL:
I am the pure ethereal Ray,
That flutters on the breast of God;
I vitalize the vulgar clay,
That looms in man from earthen sod.

Co-eval with Man's mortal frame,
And prisoned in its crumbling walls,
My presence, like a Vestal flame,
Forestalls the Fate that Man appals.

Instinctively, as scented flower,
Seeks freedom for its perfumed breath,
I seek release from mortal power,
Ere freed by courtesy of death.

My feet, like down in dewy dusk,
Fall stealthily and soft;
My wings, like follicles of musk,
Ascend unseen the airs above.

As mist arises from the sea;
And, wind-wound, wends its moon-lit way;
Casts silver sheen athwart the lea,
And, dying, greets the new-born day;

So, float I o'er the minds of men,
And filter on their trembling hearts,
A light ne'er seen on field or fen,
That briefly lingers and departs.

Who seeks me, loses ere he finds:
As dusk with gloaming vapor reeks,
My form in tremulous folds unwinds,
Like vanishing clouds on mountain peaks.

Nor here, nor there, yet everywhere;
Though rooted in the earth yet free:
As steals a perfume through the air,
I float through space insensibly.

The flower that earns its golden crown,
Through death's decay and struggle came:
Thus I, this mortal flesh outgrown,
Shall elsewhere flaunt my wings of flame.

. . . .

I know not how my Fate is writ;
The stars my destiny may scorn:

His judgment will my deeds befit,
Who summons me to Death's dark bourne.

Perchance, like wraith of sun and sea,
Which glides awhile o'er crested wave,
Then melts in air invisibly,
I may dissolve above the grave.

Methinks, as soul of soil and seed
Is winged upon the flower's breath;
So I, from fleshly substance freed,
May, like a breath, float on through death.

HENRY FRANK

ULTIMA VERITAS

In the bitter waves of woe,
   Beaten and tossed about
By the sullen winds that blow
   From the desolate shores of doubt,—

While the anchors that faith had cast
   Are dragging in the gale,
I am quietly holding fast
   To the things that cannot fail.

I know that right is right,
   That it is not good to lie;
That love is better than spite,
   And a neighbor than a spy;

I know that passion needs
   The leash of a sober mind;
I know that generous deeds
   Some sure reward will find;

That the rulers must obey;
That the givers shall increase;
That Duty lights the way
For the beautiful feet of Peace;—

In the darkest night of the year,
When the stars have all gone out,
That courage is better than fear,
That faith is truer than doubt;

And fierce though the fiends may fight,
And long though the angels hide,
I know that Truth and Right
Have the universe on their side;

And that somewhere, beyond the stars,
Is a Love that is better than fate;
When the night unlocks her bars
I shall see Him, and I will wait.

WASHINGTON GLADDEN

HIGHER TOWERS

WIELDING the tools of being great,
Man strains to build.
And when his hands are stilled,
Do there await
Yet higher towers to try his skill again?
—A workman with still nobler fellow-men?
Is this what he shall be, or rotting ground
No more a part of color, motion, sound?

Man's swift mind swings the world around!
But like the puny flower,
Each in his hour,
Man must be buried in the ground
And from his own decay
Rise to new day;

He must be prisoned in the earth
Of grief, and after pain, find birth
Again in glory and in mirth.
  Then, truer still, may he be one
  With light and sun.
But there are graves where man must go
  Slain by remorse and for a while
Must hide from life, till he shall know
  That after pain, in God's own smile
He shall arise, his soul
Joyous and whole.
So with small griefs that slay,
So with the little deaths of every day,
And so with that old death we fear and dread.
But why, then, should we fear? The dead
Who take their place beneath the sod
Are only on their way to God.

MARY CAROLYN DAVIES

NATURE

As a fond mother, when the day is o'er,
  Leads by the hand her little child to bed,
  Half willing, half reluctant to be led,
And leave his broken playthings on the floor,
Still gazing at them through the open door,
  Nor wholly reassured and comforted
  By promises of others in their stead,
Which, though more splendid, may not please him more;
So Nature deals with us, and takes away
  Our playthings one by one, and by the hand
  Leads us to rest so gently, that we go
Scarce knowing if we wish to go or stay,
  Being too full of sleep to understand
  How far the unknown transcends the what we know.

LONGFELLOW

AUTUMN AND DEATH

They are coy, these sisters, Autumn and Death,
And they both have learnt what it is to wait.
Not a leaf is jarred by their cautious breath,
The little featherweight
Petals of climbing convolvulus
Are scarcely even tremulous.

Who hears Autumn moving down
The garden-paths? Who marks her head
Above the oat-sheaves? A leaf gone brown
On the ash, and a maple-leaf turned red—
Yet a rose that's freshly blown
Seals your eyes to the change in these,
For it's mostly green about the trees.

And Death with her silver-slippered feet,
Do you hear her walk by your garden-chair?
The cool of her hand makes a tempered heat,
That's all, and the shadow of her hair
Is curiously sweet.
Does she speak? If so, you have not heard;
The whisper of Death is without a word.

The sisters, Autumn and Death, with strange
Long silences, they bide their time,
Nor ever step beyond the range
Allotted to a pantomime.
But the soundless hours chime,
One after one, and their faces grow
To an altered likeness, slow—slow.

Grim is the face which Autumn turns
To a sky all bare of obscuring leaves,
And her hair is red as a torch where it burns
In the dry hearts of the oaten sheaves.

But Death has a face which yearns
With a gaunt desire upon its prey,
And Death's dark face hides yesterday.

Then Autumn holds her hands to touch
Death's hands, and the two kiss, cheek by cheek,
And one smiles to the other, and the smiles say much,
And neither one has need to speak.
Two gray old sisters, such
Are Autumn and Death when their tasks are done,
And their world is a world where a blackened sun
Shines like ebony over the floes
Of a shadeless ice, and no wind blows.

AMY LOWELL

CODICIL

AND when I die call in, too, if you will,
The priest. And, if he will, let him say o'er
The brave old words that I could not believe.
So many have believed them—and who knows?
And if you must, why, dig for me a grave—
Near open water, or on some high place
From which there is a vision of the world.
Is not the cold seed, buried in the dark,
Thrilled back into the miracle of life?
Yet let me go more quickly, if you may.
Give me to pass by fire into the light
That I have always loved, and let me be
At once a part of God's clean wind. But oh,
Grant me one little mercy, gentle friends.
I let you call the priest. I let you say
The "dust to dust" of those immortal words.
I shrink not from the darkness of a grave.
But if you bear this heart that beats no more
Unto the pyre, wait not to gather there

My ashes into any foolish urn,
As something sacreder than the good brown mould.
Or if you leave the speechless part of me
In the unanswering earth, oh, on my grave
Spare me the humiliation of a stone!
I could sleep softly in the marble bed
Where Alexander lay, watched round about
By proud young men and stallions and wild beasts,
In the pale beauty of his vanished world.
I could find truce of dreams in that white room
In Florence where the mighty statues muse,
Stilling all chatter in their air of stars—
Or in another chamber that I know,
Tile-tapestried and flickering with a fire
Of jewel panes, where a dead Caliph lies.
But oh, it would be ill for me 'neath a weight
Of stupid stone, carved with well-meaning words!
Why stammer to the world a few vain years
Of one whom it had never known? Why mock
Your friend with dear but ill-considered praise—
To make another generation smile,
To topple slowly into invading weeds
And keep so much of nature from the sun?
Carve me no monument. But on my grave
Plant me a young tree—chestnut, oak, or pine.
Or if shine on me last a southern sun,
A plane-tree, born to prop the sky—or best
A cirque of cypresses, that, feeling down,
May gather me into their green and leap
The higher into spires of emerald flame.
So when the air flows through their woven boughs
The voice you hear will be a little mine.
So in the later years, when you are gone
And no one knows why cypresses are there,
My fluent leaves, inspired by the stars,
Shall utter things this tongue could never say—

Hap to some bitter heart that will not rest
Until it give them immortality.
So, when young lovers seek the fairy ring
Where my slim shadows bar the moonlit grass,
I shall still have a part in this sweet world.
And so the Sculptor of the Woods shall make
Even for me a worthy sepulchre
Of laurelled bards and conquerors and kings;
The Poet of the Sky shall stoop to chant
An epitaph of wonder for my grave.

H. G. DWIGHT

THE FAR LAND

WE are sighing for you, far land—
We are praying for you, far land,
All our life long, working, waiting, night and day:
But as waves that die to reach the farther shore
Break our hearts that die to reach you evermore—
All our hearts are breaking, breaking toward that shore,
O far land, so near and far away!

．　．　．　．　．　．　．　．　．　．　．

Through the terror of the ages
We have sought it, till the ages
Have stamped our lifted faces with our love:
But long though we have wandered, where we are
The far land is not. O that land is far!
Beyond the night, beyond the morning-star
The far land grows further as we move.

In music and in story,
In song and sacred story
We yearned to it, in color and in sound:
But swifter than the soul the secret flies,
The vision pales—beyond, beyond it lies,
Beyond all songs, beyond all harmonies,
The far land that we have never found.

In the sweat of daily labor,
In the anguish of our labor
We strove to bind it fast in steel and stone:
But lo—the walls were dust, the work was naught,
And O it was not what the heart had sought!
'Twas something dearer that our blood had bought—
The far land that we have never known.

Beyond long sea-horizons,
Beyond sad sea-horizons
Our furrowing keels have wandered in that quest;
Beyond the sunset, tremulous and dear,
Glimmered that land, but as our prows drew near
Faded the dream, the far land is not here,
The far land, the home-land of the breast.

So we built ourselves a heaven,
Our God we set in heaven,
With prayer and praise we wrought them to our will:
But they could not fill the measure of our love
For the far land—O they were not great enough!
There is nothing, there is nothing great enough!
The far land is something greater still.

We are sighing for you, far land—
We are dying for you, far land,
In the trenches, in the bloody ruck and blind.
We are coming, we are coming, every breath
Is a wave that bears us nearer to you, death
Seals our cry. O might our children find ere death
The far land that we have died to find!

JOHN HALL WHEELOCK

FAITH

THE sea was breaking at my feet,
And looking out across the tide,

Where placid waves and heaven meet,
 I thought me of the Other Side.

For on the beach on which I stood
 Were wastes of sand, and wash, and roar,
Low clouds, and gloom, and solitude,
 And wrecks, and ruins—nothing more.

"O tell me if beyond the sea
 A heavenly port there is!" I cried,
And back the echoes laughingly
 "There is! there is!" replied.

JAMES WHITCOMB RILEY

A SONG OF TO-DAY

Sing pæans over the past!
We bury the dead years tenderly,
To find them again in eternity,
All safe in its circle vast.
Sing pæans over the past!

Farewell, farewell to the Old!
Beneath the arches, and one by one,
From sun to shade and from shade to sun,
We pass, and the years are told.
Farewell, farewell to the Old.

And hail, all hail to the New!
The future lies like a world new born,
All steeped in sunshine and mists of morn,
And arch'd with a cloudless blue.
All hail, all hail to the New!

All things, all things are yours!
The spoil of nations, the arts sublime
That arch the ages from eldest time,

The Word that for aye endures,—
All things, all things are yours!

Arise and conquer the land!
Not one shall fail in the march of life;
Not one shall fall in the hour of strife
Who trusts in the Lord's right hand.
Arise and conquer the land!

The Lord shall sever the sea!
And open a way in the wilderness,
To faith that follows—to feet that press
On, into the great To-Be!
The Lord shall sever the sea!

[Copyright, 1882, by J. H. Vincent.]

THE UNKNOWN DEAD

*(Stanzas in Commemoration of the Unknown American Soldier,
to be Interred at Arlington, Nov. 11, 1921, at the Convening of the
Conference on the Limitation of Armaments.)*

I AM the numberless Unknown
  Who have cast the shrouds of things that seem.
My grave is a planet's cornerstone,
  Holding the ashes of a dream
Whose sacrificial fire blazes from zone to zone.

I am the wastrel child whom War
  Hath rendered baptism, not in birth
But death, where the unseen hosts that pour
  Libation on the blood-dark earth,
Intone through my mute lips the eternal: *Nevermore!*

Yea, *Nevermore!* By that mystic name
  Youth's hallow'd blood hath christened me—
Nevermore! Ye living, let it flame
  The challenge of your destiny—
Nevermore!—to pride and pestilence and hate and shame!

War—Nevermore! O lives that pray
   For liberation, make that will
Your watchword, till the thing ye say
   Because the law your deeds fulfill;
Then I with Christ will rise in sanction from my clay.

For I am dust of a deathless spark;
   Unmastered engine self-ensnared;
The bullet-molder and his mark,
   Shattered by dazzling creeds I shared
With you—and your own blindness muffles me in dark.

But my dark shall have no need of the sun
   Neither of the moon to shine in it,
If Christ His dawning Will be done,
   And this my clay-bed shall be lit
By the stars that blanket me, if my last fight be won.

Masters of life! On your decree,
   Unknown and numberless, I wait:
From war's earth-blind captivity
   Untomb me! Let your love be fate
And crown my risen youth with timeless victory!

                                        PERCY MACKAYE

SONG OF THE MOTH

   NIGHT into the universe
      Frees us from the walls of day,
   And Death, into the starry All,
      When ourselves have passed away.

                            JOHN HALL WHEELOCK

ZENITH

Now in my breast the sole and sovereign Power
  Puts forth his strength, and through a million veins
  I feel the tidal stream of life that strains
Toward the dark sea that doth all streams devour:
This is the noontide of my spirit's hour,
  Through all my frame the imperious rhythm reigns—
  And the one self, that deep in me sustains
His being, stands fulfilled in fullest flower.

Now through my brain the blood's rich purple roars,
  Washing her cells with wine of song and dream,
And in my breast the embattled Splendor wars
  On the dark foe, and rages for extreme
Wrath and delight; and all my being pours
  Through Love and Song toward the escape supreme.

JOHN HALL WHEELOCK

EXILE FROM GOD

I DO not fear to lay my body down
  In death, to share
The life of the dark earth and lose my own,
  If God is there.

I have so loved all sense of Him, sweet might
  Of color and sound,—
His tangible loveliness and living light
  That robes me 'round.

If to His heart in the hushed grave and dim
  We sink more near,
It shall be well—living we rest in Him.
  Only I fear

Lest from my God in lonely death I lapse,
   And the dumb clod
Lose Him; for God is life, and death perhaps
   Exile from God.

JOHN HALL WHEELOCK

MEMORIES OF PRESIDENT LINCOLN

When Lilacs Last in the Dooryard Bloom'd.

. . . .

COME lovely and soothing death,
Undulate round the world, serenely arriving, arriving,
In the day, in the night, to all, to each,
Sooner or later delicate death.

Prais'd be the fathomless universe,
For life and joy, and for objects and knowledge curious,
And for love, sweet love—but praise! praise! praise!
For the sure-enwinding arms of cool-enfolding death.

Dark mother always gliding near with soft feet,
Have none chanted for thee a chant of fullest welcome?
Then I chant it for thee, I glorify thee above all,
I bring thee a song that when thou must indeed come, come
   unfalteringly.

Approach, strong deliveress,
When it is so, when thou hast taken them I joyously sing
   the dead,
Lost in the loving floating ocean of thee,
Laved in the flood of thy bliss O death.

From me to thee glad serenades,
Dances for thee I propose saluting thee, adornments and
   feastings for thee,
And the sights of the open landscape and the high-spread
   sky are fitting,
And life and the fields, and the huge and thoughtful night.

The night in silence under many a star,
The ocean shore and the husky whispering wave whose
   voice I know,
And the soul turning to thee O vast and well-veil'd death,
And the body gratefully nestling close to thee.

Over the tree-tops I float thee a song,
Over the rising and sinking waves, over the myriad fields
   and the prairies wide,
Over the dense-pack'd cities all and the teeming wharves
   and ways,
I float this carol with joy, with joy to thee O death.

WHITMAN

THERE IS A SOUL ABOVE THE SOUL

THERE is a Soul above the soul of each a mightier soul,
   which yet to each belongs:
There is a sound made of all human speech. and numerous
   as the concourse of all songs:
And in that soul lives each, in each that soul, though all the
   ages are its lifetime vast;
Each soul that dies, in its most sacred whole receiveth life
   that shall for ever last.
And thus for ever with a wider span Humanity o'erarches
   time and death;
Man can elect the universal man and live in life that ends
   not with his breath,
And gather glory that increaseth still till Time his glass with
   Death's last dust shall fill.

RICHARD WATSON DIXON

L'ENVOI

Now in a thought, now in a shadowed wood,
Now in a voice that thrills eternity,
Ever there comes an onward phrase to me

Of some transcendent music I have heard;
No piteous thing by soft hands dulcimered,
No trumpet crash of blood-sick victory,
But a glad strain of some vast harmony
That no brief mortal touch has ever stirred.

There is no music in the world like this,
No character wherewith to set it down,
No kind of instrument to make it sing.
No kind of instrument? Ah, yes, there is;
And after time and place are overthrown,
God's touch will keep its one chord quivering.

EDWIN ARLINGTON ROBINSON

ETERNAL HOPE

ETERNAL Hope! When yonder spheres, sublime,
Pealed their first notes to sound the march of Time,
Thy joyous youth began,—but not to fade.
When all the sister planets have decayed;
When, wrapped in fire, the realms of ether glow,
And Heaven's last thunder shakes the world below,
Thou, undismayed, shalt o'er the ruins smile,
And light thy torch at Nature's funeral pile.

ANON.

PROSPICE

FEAR death?—to feel the fog in my throat,
    The mist in my face,
When the snows begin, and the blasts denote
    I am nearing the place,
The power of the night, the press of the storm,
    The post of the foe;
Where he stands, the Arch Fear in a visible form,

Yet the strong man must go:
For the journey is done and the summit attained,
  And the barriers fall,
Though a battle's to fight ere the guerdon be gained,
  The reward of it all.
I was ever a fighter, so—one fight more,
  The best and the last!
I would hate that death bandaged my eyes, and forbore,
  And bade me creep past.
No! let me taste the whole of it, fare like my peers
  The heroes of old,
Bear the brunt, in a minute pay glad life's arrears
  Of pain, darkness and cold.
For sudden the worst turns the best to the brave,
  The black minute's at end,
And the elements' rage, the fiend-voices that rave,
  Shall dwindle, shall blend,
Shall change, shall become first a peace out of pain,
  Then a light, then thy breast,
O thou soul of my soul! I shall clasp thee again,
  And with God be the rest!

BROWNING

REVERIE

I know there shall dawn a day
  —Is it here on homely earth?
Is it yonder, worlds away,
  Where the strange and new have birth,
That Power comes full in play?

Is it here, with grass about,
  Under befriending trees,
When shy buds venture out,
  And the air by mild degrees
Puts winter's death past doubt?

Is it up amid whirl and roar
　Of the elemental flame
Which star-flecks heaven's dark floor,
　That, new yet still the same,
Full in play comes Power once more?

Somewhere, below, above,
　Shall a day dawn—this I know—
When Power, which vainly strove
　My weakness to o'erthrow,
Shall triumph. I breathe, I move,

I truly am, at last!
　For a veil is rent between
Me and the truth which passed
　Fitful, half-guessed, half-seen,
Grasped at—not gained, held fast.

I for my race and me
　Shall apprehend life's law:
In the legend of man shall see
　Writ large what small I saw
In my life's; tale both agree.

As the record from youth to age
　Of my own, the single soul—
So the world's wide book: one page
　Deciphered explains the whole
Of our common heritage.

　.　.　.　.　.　.　.　.

Then life is—to wake not sleep,
　Rise and not rest, but press
From earth's level where blindly creep
　Things perfected, more or less,
To the heaven's height, far and steep.

Where, amid what strifes and storms
  May wait the adventurous quest,
Power is Love—transports, transforms
  Who aspired from worst to best,
Sought the soul's world, spurned the worms'.

I have faith such end shall be:
  From the first, Power was—I knew.
Life has made clear to me
  That, strive but for closer view,
  Love were as plain to see.

When see? When there dawns a day,
  If not on the homely earth,
Then yonder, worlds away,
  Where the strange and new have birth,
And Power comes full in play.

BROWNING

AFTER SUNSET

I HAVE an understanding with the hills
At evening, when the slanted radiance fills
Their hollows, and the great winds let them be,
And they are quiet and look down at me.
Oh, then I see the patience in their eyes
Out of the centuries that made them wise.
They lend me hoarded memory, and I learn
Their thoughts of granite and their whims of fern,
And why a dream of forests must endure
Though every tree be slain; and how the pure,
Invisible beauty has a word so brief,
A flower can say it, or a shaken leaf,
But few may ever snare it in a song,
Though for the quest a life is not too long.
When the blue hills grow tender, when they pull

The twilight close with gesture beautiful,
And shadows are their garments, and the air
Deepens, and the wild veery is at prayer,
Their arms are strong around me; and I know
That somehow I shall follow when they go
To the still land beyond the evening star,
Where everlasting hills and valleys are,
And silence may not hurt us any more,
And terror shall be past, and grief and war.

GRACE HAZARD CONKLING

CROSSING THE BAR

SUNSET and evening star,
  And one clear call for me!
And may there be no moaning of the bar,
  When I put out to sea,

But such a tide as moving seems asleep,
  Too full for sound and foam,
When that which drew from out the boundless deep
  Turns again home.

Twilight and evening bell,
  And after that the dark!
And may there be no sadness of farewell,
  When I embark;

For tho' from out our bourne of Time and Place
  The flood may bear me far,
I hope to see my Pilot face to face
  When I have crost the bar.

TENNYSON

[From "The Works of Tennyson," The Macmillan Co.]

NOTE XIX

MODERN poetry rises to its greatest heights in dealing with the few major experiences common to mankind: Birth, Love; Doubt, Faith; Death and Destiny. The recent literature which deals with faith in Immortality runs almost the whole gamut of human feeling, so many-sided is this most persistent outreaching of the life within. Some men find this faith rising unbidden and unchallenged, out of an even-tempered experience. Others see the vision, for one entrancing moment, then plunge into doubt, and finally work their way, through bitter struggle, back again to a reasoned confidence in life's deeper meaning and happy goal.

Here and there, one will rise to the point of ecstasy in expressing his irrepressible joy in the larger significance of life. Another has the note of utter despair running through all his life; but in a moment of desperate faith, he casts aside all barriers and hurls himself headlong upon the very mercy of Fate—at last convinced that hope does spring eternal for the soul that dares aspire.

Persistent longing, of a calm and optimistic sort, sometimes reaches the same mature conclusion—calmly, as a rose opens to the timely rays of the sun. And, not infrequently, men grow into this faith through a very gradual and all-around experience with life, no one experience standing out especially, yet all converging to beget in them this supreme faith in the worth and continuity of Life.

1. In "Gaudeamus," "Lord of My Heart's Elation," "The Human Fantasy," "The Joy of Living," "Song of the Universal," and "Joy, Shipmate, Joy," we have ample illustration of that rather rare, and yet most blissful, mood which finds all Life one and all of it full of rapture and abounding inspiration. Artists, poets, musicians, lovers, and even some supposedly cold scientists, have this experience. One may not be able to remain long at this high level; but, Jacob-like, he usually erects his soul's altar there as a memorial of spiritual attainment; returning thither, from time to time, as if to renew the warmth and inspiration of that holy hour of mystic uplift. Some happy souls learn the secret of

remaining on the heights, and even climbing higher, sharing the vicissitudes and the adventures of the Spirit of all Life.

2. At the other pole of experience stand the many perplexed and grief-stricken folk who find faith in life and its goodness almost impossible. Poems like "If Winter Comes," "Self-Dependence," "The Dead," "Longing," and "Immortal," "Vastness," "Abt Vogler," "Second Best," "Grief," "Adonais," "Credo," "In Memoriam," "The Far Land," "The Trumpet of the Law," and "Reverie" reveal the intensity of the struggle through which so many must pass before they find courage to face life and its common ills. Hope comes to them, not as a refuge to cowards, but as the only possible solution for a problem as yet too deep for human thinking. A dead and faithless universe were unthinkable. Out of the desperation, new powers of vision are born; and the unshakable confidence born of actual life-and-death experiences always yields courage for new advances of faith.

3. Between these extremes, lie the more calm and studied types of faith, sometimes representing the unprotesting acceptance of tradition, again the philosophic mind, or a rich and active experience which generally produces balance and maturity of thought. To this group belong: "Thought for the Day," "The Harvest of Time," " 'Tis But the Night," "The Choir Invisible," "Thanatopsis," "Song," "The Lamp," "Two Sonnets," "The Great Minimum," "Ode on Intimations of Immortality," "Ultimate Conceptions of Faith," "The Better Fate," "Death's Valley," "Rabbi Ben Ezra," "Octaves," "The Last Enigma," "Higher Towers," and "Crossing the Bar."

4. There is a fourth group of poems which stands out boldly from all others on the subject of Immortality. They represent the daring and fierceness of men bent on nothing less than the conquest of Eternity. Life upon earth has been one continuous warfare for them. Only by the most strenuous measures have they arrived at a faith with solid foundations. They are not content, however, to rest upon their attainments, but feel that access to the gates of the unknown future must be made certain through a determined, daring, and even joyful entrance—an attitude which in itself shall disarm all possible opposition.

Matthew Arnold suggests this view in his "Immortality"; and *Whitman* in "Passage to India"; *Browning* in "Epilogue"; *Alan Seeger* in "Makatoob." The latter part of "Octaves" also sounds this challenging note; as do "The Unknown Dead," "Zenith," "Prospice," and "Reverie."

But whether human faith in the immortal worth and the unbroken continuity of Life develops through determined Faith or dark Despair; whether through intriguing Love or heart-breaking Loss; whether through the sudden Vision which forever clarifies the future, or toiling up the strong steeps of a hopeless and harassed life—as this greatest literature of modern times shows so clearly, the race is thus working out a prophecy of destined greatness that is the very warp and woof of all human life. We are drawn, and we are driven, by forces—by a Hand of Destiny—too great for our understanding. Nevertheless we press on, increasingly confident of the way we take, and ever more certain that we share the great venture of the Eternal whithersoever we may go.

INDEXES

INDEX OF POEMS

457

PAGE

PAGE

INDEX OF AUTHORS

NOTES OF EXPLANATION